New Testament Themes for Contemporary Man

Rosalie M. Ryan, C.S.J.

New Testament Themes for Contemporary Man

PRENTICE-HALL INTERNATIONAL, INC., *London*
PRENTICE-HALL OF AUSTRALIA, PTY. LTD., *Sydney*
PRENTICE-HALL OF CANADA, LTD., *Toronto*
PRENTICE-HALL OF INDIA PRIVATE LTD., *New Delhi*
PRENTICE-HALL OF JAPAN, INC., *Tokyo*

New Testament Themes for Contemporary Man

ROSALIE M. RYAN, C.S.J.

Professor of Theology, College of Saint Catherine

Library
Southwestern State College
Weatherford, Oklahoma

Prentice-Hall, Inc.   *Englewood Cliffs, New Jersey*

© 1969 by Prentice-Hall, Inc.
Englewood Cliffs, N.J.

All rights reserved. No part of this book
may be reproduced in any form or by any
means without permission in writing from
the publisher.

LIBRARY OF CONGRESS CATALOG CARD NO.: 69–20491
PRINTED IN THE UNITED STATES OF AMERICA
CURRENT PRINTING (LAST NUMBER):

10   9   8   7   6   5   4   3   2   1

261.8
R95m

Introduction

The second half of the twentieth century may eventually be known as the age of warring ideologies. In a world of violence, disorder, wars of national liberation, and changing social structures, the foundations of men's beliefs, especially their religious beliefs, are being shaken. Many fearful or impatient persons are taking refuge in the extremes of conservatism or revolutionary action.

For the first half of the twentieth century, there were earnest attempts to meet challenges to belief by applying various scientific disciplines to religious studies, especially Biblical studies. The contributions of archaeologists, anthropologists, cultural historians, scholars of ancient languages and literatures have been many and beneficial. We actually have more knowledge about the Biblical languages, culture, and background than we can incorporate into historical theory.

Yet for many students and teachers of theology, there is still something missing. In a world where war, devastation, and death are becoming continually more widespread and where total destruction is a distinct possibility, more is needed than just the approach offered by specialized scholarly disciplines. Father Barnabas Ahern, in a recent address to the Catholic Biblical Association, urged Biblical scholars to be more active in communicating the relevance of God's words to men. Karl Rahner, in a striking essay, "Exegesis and Dogmatic Theology" wrote:

> The ecclesiastical sciences, and above all exegesis, have more to do today than to fulfill the scientific tasks which interest scholars. They must be front-line fighters for the faith and the Church. They must make the possibility of faith clear to modern man. They must instruct, strengthen and console the intellectual. . . . He who does not admit the need of faith misunderstands the real

v

151038

problems of our times. Such a need is there and ecclesiastical sciences have not to go in for inbreeding but must think of the men of today. But if theology is to do this, it cannot by-pass difficult and dangerous questions. It must look for solutions that are novel and untested, because it is simply impossible to go on repeating the good old truths that have been tried and tested.[1]

James A. T. Robinson calls theological writing "a work of translation" and urges Biblical scholars and theologians to bring the Biblical message into contemporary terms: "The fallacy of biblicism is not its faithfulness to the Bible, but rather its retention of biblical language at the expense of biblical meaning, so that biblical formulae are recited but God's word does not resound in the hearts of the people." [2] He urges the development of a "theology of translation," a hermeneutic for the world of today:

> God is crying out to be heard in our daily lives, and it is the task of proclamation to carry through the word-event inaugurated by Jesus, by saying in human language what God has to say to us so it is heard. All too often a doctrine of the word of God leaves what God has to say on a remote pedestal of Biblical language so that one must infer God has nothing to say about life where I am actually living it.[3]

But where is this translation of the Biblical message to take place? The Biblical scholar studies text, literary form, and cultural background. The systematic theologian is concerned chiefly with matters like reason and faith, revelation, sin, and sacraments. Even pastoral theologians are intent on problems of preaching, missions, liturgy, and institutional reform. The question remains: Who is speaking to modern man about his concerns of life, death, poverty, war, and suffering?

This anthology brings together some of the essays in which contemporary theologians speak about these concerns. In order to bridge the gap between Biblical exegesis and theology, which Karl Rahner has pointed out, and to build a bridge between these disciplines and the world today, many points of view are represented: Biblical, theological, philosophical, and sociological. Prescinding

[1] "Exegesis and Dogmatic Theology" in *Dogmatic vs. Biblical Theology*, ed. Herbert Vorgrimler (Helicon, 1964), p. 57.
[2] James A. T. Robinson, "Theology as Translation," *Theology Today*, 20 (1963–64), 525.
[3] Robinson, pp. 525–26.

from the more specialized aspects of their disciplines, the writers focus on the relations of God's word to the world today.

Considerations of space have made it necessary to be selective not only in topics represented but in whole areas of concern. The point of view in these selections is "worldly." Church renewal, liturgy, and sacraments are receiving adequate attention elsewhere. These essays deal with the problems of twentieth-century man working in the world, especially the twentieth-century Christian, and aim to illuminate to some extent the present and the future.

It is my pleasure to thank a few of the many people who have helped in compiling this collection. To Sister Vera Chester who read the manuscript, to the librarians and administrators of the College of Saint Catherine for their generous cooperation, and to my two assistants, Patrice Harper and Patricia Whalen, I am very grateful.

My thanks are due also to the authors and publishers who allowed copyright materials to be reprinted. To many others who have helped and encouraged the project, I am grateful.

Rosalie M. Ryan, C.S.J.

Contents

V HOPE AND THE UNKNOWN FUTURE   183

New Testament Themes
for Contemporary Man

1 Who Is the Christian?

In the twentieth century the ready response of faith to preaching or teaching about Jesus Christ is not so frequent or stable as it was in previous generations, for the New Testament challenge to faith in Jesus Christ is today experienced in a different way. Those who accepted Christian faith as children often put it aside as adults for other demands which seem more pressing.

Modern man finds it difficult to respond with clarity and certainty to the New Testament demands: "Do you believe in the Son of Man?" (Jn 9:35) or "What do you think of the Christ? Whose son is he?" (Mt 22:43). Even the man who at one time responds affirmatively in faith, at another time is filled with questions and doubts. His society no longer supports Christian faith and somehow makes him doubt its reality.

Frequently he must ask himself: "What does it mean to be a Christian? Does it make me more or less a human being? Does Christianity force me to give up, in some way, my freedom, my concern for truth, my dedication to my fellow men?" His humanist friends rebuke him with lack of concern for the world in which he lives. And sociologists declare that regular church-goers are likely to be less interested in social and economic justice, in the relief of poverty and illiteracy, than those who are not. Are the sociologists correct? And if so, does the fault lie in the nature of Christianity or with its adherents?

Much that is relevant to Christian faith and theology is contained in questions like these. A direct confrontation of the New Testament message with the realities of twentieth-century technological society may provide some of the answers for concerned Christians. It may also serve to illustrate some directions of Biblical and theological thought as they relate to the modern world.

To be a Christian is to be a fully human person. Recent theological statements have begun to describe what it is to be a person, rather than the more abstract concept of what "man" is. To modern ears, what Thomas Aquinas said of "person" seems too abstract: "A person is an individual substance of a rational nature" (*Summa Theologica* I, 1, q. 29), for more of the human qualities which make the person unique must be included in such a definition. Rahner's description evidences a fuller awareness of the qualities of "person":

> To be a person is to possess oneself as a subject in conscious, free relation to reality as a whole and its infinite ground and source, God. The notion of person is of great importance in theology because it draws attention to those human characteristics which are the necessary condition of man's relationship to God: his spirituality (as grounded in his transcendence) and presence to himself, his permanent and inescapable orientation to being as a whole and thus to God ... his freedom of choice in relation to all that is recognized as finite, particular being, dealing with it in critical detachment.[1]

What it means to be a person is also the focus of some humanist and materialist philosophies. Rahner has protested against those humanists who think that transforming man's environment will produce the "new man" who will live happily in a materialistic utopia:

> No one will suffer want any more; there will be enough time and money to give everyone the best education possible and to offer him all the cultural goods he desires.... But one gets the impression that all this is not very much different from what is already possible and in part already normal

[1] Karl Rahner and Herbert Vorgrimler, *Theological Dictionary* (New York: Herder & Herder, n. d.), p. 351.

even today—in other words, that the new man will look hope-
lessly like the old one.[2]

In contrast to a materialist concept of man's potentiality, it
is possible to formulate the Christian concept of the person,
one who is capable not only of enjoying physical well-being
but also of a fuller development of his spiritual powers: his
consciousness, his free relation to reality, and his transcendence.
Further, his Christian orientation gives him a new dimension of
relationship to himself, to his fellow men, and to God.

The Christian dimension of man's life may be described in a
philosophical, theological, or Biblical context. Many studies are
necessary if we are to understand the Christian response to
God's revelation in Christ and relate it to the historical milieu
of the twentieth century. The three articles in this section
assess the transformation of the human being by baptism as explained by Schnackenburg, the centrality of faith and hope as
victorious over anxiety and death as explained by Stringfellow,
and the possibility and nature of freedom in the Christian life
as explained by Schlette.

Rudolf Schnackenburg, Biblical scholar, professor, and theologian, takes his point of departure for the study of the Christian today from Paul's encounter with the Christian option.
Paul, whose life parallels that of modern man to a marked degree—a man of the city, a scholar, a traveller, and a passionate
believer—looked at the world in terms of a challenge to action.
Paul saw that a new energy had emerged in the Semitic world
of Palestine and the Hellenistic world of the Roman empire, a
dynamism that was to break down barriers, bring men together, and set them to work at bringing about a new order.
Schnackenburg sees in Paul's existential experience of Christ a
genuine answer to the questions: How will man survive and
attain his salvation? Who is the Christian and what is his work?
How does he relate to the personal and social tension of his
world?

The "new man" created by God and recreated in Christ is

[2] Karl Rahner, *Theological Investigations* (Baltimore: Helicon Press,
1963), V, 146.

able to overcome in himself the negative and destructive tendencies of evil. He sees the goodness of creation even in the midst of its historical perversion and corruption. The decisive insight for Christian faith is not how and when this world will end but that in its present form it cannot be final; it cries out in suffering for a new form. The hidden reality of the Christian's new life urges him to transform his environment and offer a powerful moral challenge to his world.

William Stringfellow, lawyer, writer, and Christian revolutionary, sees the world today as the place of God's action: The Christian is the one who is able to discern God's Word (his dynamic presence) in the events of everyday life. To be a Christian is to come face to face with the power of truth. It is to know that the truth will be victorious—over suffering, anxiety, and death. But being a Christian does not allow one to escape from crisis; rather, he is confronted with the suffering which must be faced before he can claim that God is working through man in the world.

Heinz Schlette, theologian, professor, and author, studies the complexity of human and Christian freedom. He describes the freedom in which a Christian is reborn and for which he is responsible as including both eschatological freedom and secular freedom, eschatological freedom being that which is present now but only as a knowledge of one's destiny. Its present condition is one of servitude to corrupt nature, but its constant drive is toward a full revelation of freedom in the future. Our present freedom partakes of the mystery of our destiny: It is a freedom founded on love and moving toward a community of love.

The man of today who realizes that union with Christ is a beginning of that which he can become ultimately, who is willing to work in suffering and hope, who knows that freedom requires him to work toward a better human, yet transcendent community—such a man is well on his way to understanding: Who is the Christian today?

RUDOLF SCHNACKENBURG

The Christian
as a New Man

If one can make the representation of man a test for a "Weltanschauung," then the Bible's representation of man, particularly in the
New Testament, becomes the center of the Christian understanding
of the world. Holy Scripture explicitly relates the world, or "creation," to man. "For the creation was subjected to futility, not of its
own will but by the will of him who subjected it in hope; because
the creation itself will be set free from its bondage to decay and obtain in the glorious liberty of the children of God" (Rom 8:2of.).
This anthropocentric view of the world may be difficult for modern, scientifically thinking man. Therefore we do not want to begin
with the world as "creation" and to relate it to man and human
history. Rather we shall consider man as the New Testament sees
him in his Christian existence, that is, as a historical being in this
world, and ask how the world in which man lives and works represents itself as his world. After correlating man and world, we shall
attempt to formulate a Christian notion of the world. The text from
Colossians (3:9–11) offers an excellent guide:

> Do not lie to one another, seeing that you have put off the old
> man with his practices and have put on the new man who is being
> renewed in knowledge after the image of his creator. Here there
> cannot be Greek and Jew, circumcised and uncircumcised, Barbar-
> ian and Scythian, slave and free man, but Christ is all, and in all.

From *Present and Future* (Notre Dame, Ind.: University of Notre Dame
Press, 1966), pp. 81–100. Reprinted with permission of the publisher and the
author. The original article appeared as "The New Man According to Paul";
for full footnote documentation, see original publication.

Creation and Present Reality

We often draw from the New Testament a negative and pessimistic idea of the world: The world is treated as an enemy of God, an area that has become a slave to evil, filled with corrupt tendencies and lust (1 Jn 2:15ff.). It passes away and is doomed to destruction (1 Cor 7:31), so that friendship with the world is hostility toward God (Jas 4:4). Such a dualistically colored view of "this world" and "this age," which was influenced by contemporary intellectual currents of thought (Apocalyptic, Gnosis), actually dominates the language of New Testament authors.[1] One often overlooks, first, the intention of the statements, which in these texts is directed toward the moral admonition not to make oneself "conformed to this world" (Rom 12:2). In these passages the world is not judged as God's creation, but as a sphere of man's conduct. Second, one overlooks that the Bible considers the world in the temporal dimension.[2] It does not treat of its natural evolution, but of its "history" as it is made by man. This latter was the pernicious development. Third, one overlooks the historical limitations of the authors, who emphasize the dark and ominous aspects of life and are caught in the intellectual current characteristic of their time. Finally, one overlooks the eschatological mood of early Christianity, that of apprehensive expectation, which as such does not belong essentially to the Christian faith, but must be understood from the contemporary situation.

In view of the "new man" which is depicted in Colossians 3:10, our thought focuses on the original creation, reminding us that man was created according to the "image and likeness" of God (Gn 1:26f.). The priestly codex places the creation of man after the rest of creation as the final and highest act. The other creatures are, as it were, summed up in him, but at the same time man surpasses all creatures because of his likeness to God. Therefore, all of creation is elevated and drawn closer to God through man, as God conceived

---

[1] For the notion of "world" in the New Testament see R. Loewe, *Kosmos und Aion* (Gütersloh, 1935); H. Sasse, "κόσμος," *ThWNT*, III (1939) 882–96; and J. M. Robinson, "The Biblical View of the World," *Encounter*, XX (1959) 470–83.

[2] It is important that in Hebrew there is only one expression for "world" which means its temporal dimension ('olam), and a similar one for the spatial category is lacking. In order to denote the "universe" Hebrew uses the transcription "the heavens and the earth" (Gn 1:1, etc.) or "all" (Ps 8:7; Is 44:24 *et al.*).

and created him. The likeness of man with God may be difficult to describe, but one thing is clear: Man receives all creation that he might participate in God's sovereignty. Man, belonging to the world of creation, surpasses and governs it, thus bestowing upon it a splendor that is a reflection of God. Since the culmination of creation in man draws creation nearer to God and binds it more closely to him, the creation of man "according to God's image and likeness," as it is alluded to in Colossians 3:10, confirms the essential goodness of creation and its relationship with God. This knowledge of the goodness of the world created by God is never lost in the Bible, even when the New Testament speaks of "this age" and considers this present world, which we experience, as evil and filled with suffering.

Both notions of the world—positive and negative—are not separated from each other. This becomes clear if we consider man in his present state. Although he continues to be the image of God, he experiences himself as a being inclined to evil. This is expressed by the "old man." As man now finds himself in his earthly existence, he is a terrifying vision of evil inclinations and sinful desires. A whole catalog of vices can be enumerated, "Immorality, impurity, passion, evil desire and covetousness (v. 5) ... anger, wrath, malice, slander, and foul talk from your mouth (v. 8)." If the natural man consists of such evil instincts, though he is capable of good actions, the destructive tendency of his nature remains a sinister reality that justifies and makes understandable the negative evaluation of the world. Considered honestly and objectively the world as the sphere of historical action must appear to man in the same way that he experiences himself. The Bible, with its tradition of the fall of man, comprehends and preserves a primitive knowledge of man's nature, which is represented in the paradise narrative as a "myth"—a myth nevertheless that contains profound truth (Gn 2–3). Man is fallen from God and has exchanged "the glory of the incorruptible God" for the image according to corruptible men (Rom 1:23). "Therefore God gave them up in the lusts of their hearts to impurity, to the dishonoring of their bodies among themselves, because they exchanged the truth about God for a lie and worshiped and served the creature rather than the creator ..." (Rom 1:24f.).

It is a peculiar phenomenon of the Old Testament that the idea of man created in the image and likeness of God is maintained in spite of man's sinful self-idolization in subsequent history. After the fall of man the likeness to God given in creation is not lost. The "genealogy of Adam," with which the history of human generation begins, explicitly calls to mind this fact (Gn 5:1f.). God gives to Noe and his sons the blessing of creation after the flood, and he establishes again the dignity of man "according to his image" (Gn 9:1–7). Psalm 8 praises God who crowned man "with splendor and glory" (v. 6). But another passage states, "The instinct of the human heart is inclined to evil from youth" (Gn 8:21). This truth is verified throughout the history of Israel, even in the conduct of the pious and just. The two aspects of the religious notion of the world, the goodness and glory of creation and the historical perversion and corruption, cannot be more clearly and realistically expressed than in this view of man.

This primitive knowledge and this intense experience have also entered into the baptismal exhortation of the epistle to the Colossians (3). The Apostle does not directly reflect upon the creation narrative and the likeness of man to God. He does not keep directly before his eyes the entire history of mankind which is under the curse of sin, but he views man in his naked existence and historical situation. Man always bears the image of his creator, but only in the distorted reflection of his ungodlike conduct and action. Paul emphasizes this behavior of the worldly man, the "old man" (v. 9): Through his actions he is alienated from God. He no longer knows his creator and he therefore does not know himself, his dignity, or his glory. Because the Bible thinks "anthropocentrically," it is by anthropocentric thinking that we find the key to its notion of the world.

The created world was subjected to "futility" or "vanity" ($\mu\alpha\tau\alpha\iota\acute{o}\tau\eta\varsigma$ [Rom 8:20]). This is a term that sounds moral: It is a vain, ineffective striving condemned to failure, an attempt at self-existence leading directly to self-annihilation (1 Cor 3:20; Eph 4:17; Ac 14:15). It actually means the frailty and transitoriness of the creature ($\phi\theta o\rho\acute{\alpha}$ [v. 21]), but this instability appears more as a moral quality than an essential quality. It does not simply say that creation was freed from the curse, but creation was freed from the "bondage" or "slavery" of the curse (v. 21). Existence itself does not appear to have changed, but the "character" of creation—its experiential situation—has changed. According to the Apostle's understanding, we might say: Creation, through man's fall from God, has been torn away from its relation with the creator and has lost its deep significance. Therefore, it groans and sighs in the present situation, waiting impatiently and hoping impetuously for its future liberation.

Basically the Bible reveals the relation of the world to man and the effect of his moral conduct on the world. Since man through his moral guilt has turned his existential situation into evil, the rest of the world insofar as it is "his" world, his sphere of existence, has been drawn into corruption with him. The Bible in its unique way makes this clear, when it uses human speech to describe a creation that is nonrational. If the world is to find salvation, then salvation must be inaugurated by man.

Renewal of Man and of the World

Christian faith does not come to terms with the "old man" and the existing conditions of the world. The coming of a new man and of a new world belong to the central message of faith. The doctrine of the "new heaven and new earth" (Apoc 21:1–5) is frequently understood as an apocalyptic event having no relation to us because of our scientific way of thinking. The modern man looks critically and skeptically upon such religious promises. In his famous lecture, "The New Testament and Mythology," R. Bultmann says: "He who is convinced that the world which is known to us will end in the future imagines its end still as the result of a natural evolution, as a terminating in a natural catastrophe and not as the mythical event of which the New Testament speaks." The decisive insight for the Christian faith, however, is not when and how this world will end, but that it cannot in its present form be final. In its need and suffering it cries out for a new form. This idea is in some way emphasized by all human envisioning of the future. That man might endure the present world, as he experiences it with its enigma and obscurity, and in order that he might overcome the future, he conceives a vision of an idealistic end that corresponds to his "Weltanschauung." Christian faith is a genuine answer to the question engaging all men: How will the world survive in the future and how will man attain his salvation? The decisive impulse for our mentality toward the present world proceeds from our view of the future. Christian faith foresees a transfigured world created anew through the power of God. It is not a mere fantasy, for it is founded on the conviction of man's present renewal.

The text from Colossians (3:9–11) emphasizes the "new man" as opposed to the "old man." This "new man" is not a vague image in the mind of the believer—but rather a reality. The coming world of glory is revealed in this "new man" and yet the very same man conceals this revelation. The text is a baptismal exhortation, which refers to the mysterious divine event in baptism, and from this draws conclusions. The participle (ἀπεκδυσάμενοι) attached to the imperative "Do not lie to one another" can be understood in different ways. It could be a continuation of the admonition, or, since it would not appear in the past form without good reason, it probably should be interpreted as an indicative referring to the baptismal event ("seeing that you have put off"). In the final analysis both questions are irrelevant, since the paragraph in either case presupposes the statements concerning our salvation (Col 2): By circumcision performed "without hands" (that is, "the circumcision of Christ") we were buried with Christ in baptism, in which we were also raised with him (v. 12). We possess in Christ a new life, hidden with him in God (3:3), but which will appear in glory (3:4). This hidden reality, grasped only in faith, urges us to form a new external life and becomes a powerful moral challenge in this world. Both aspects—the grace-giving event that happens to us and the moral appeal arising from it—are equally emphasized. With the "old man" and his deeds we should take off and put to death the bad inclinations in us, the evil passions ruling us (3:5ff.). We have put on the "new man" who is being renewed according to the image of his creator, but it is a renewal "in knowledge," in moral trial, in a maturing relationship with God, so that the admonition unfolds: "Put on then, as God's chosen ones, holy and beloved, compassion, kindness, lowliness, meekness, and patience..." (3:12ff.).

In summing up the aspects that are standard for the "new man," and that elucidate the Christian understanding of the world, there is, first, the grace of the hidden renewal, which comes to us from God. Second, there is included in it the hope for future fulfillment. This is not an empty and unfounded expectation, but one based upon faith in the risen Christ, who is the first-born from the dead (Col 1:18). Finally, there is the moral renewal that makes possible with the help of God a new way of life, a new conduct transforming man and human society. All these aspects are inextricably bound together and overlap each other in man's world. Therefore, a new form arises for the existing world that man historically experiences. The new creation of man is more clearly described in the parallel passage (Eph 4:24): The *new man* is "created after the likeness of God in true righteousness and holiness." This is a fundamental affirmation of the order of creation. But this idea is possible through the hope of a future new creation, which will be a restoration (cf. ἀποκατάστασις [Acts 3:21]), a "new birth" (cf. παλιγγενεσία [Mt 19:28]) of the original godlike world. It will not be a destruction but rather a consummation of the first creation. Faith in the eschatological perfection bestows upon the first creation its full excellence. Just as man in the past was God's steward and the administrator of the created world, the "new man in the present should be the same for the renewal of his own humanity; he is therefore called a "new creation" in Christ (2 Cor 5:17).

The concept of "renewal" conveys the eschatological aspect of the new creation. The declaration of the "renewal," however, forces us to examine that new creation. In the end God will say, "Behold I make all things new" (καινά [Apoc 21:5]). What God gives to the Christian is a present anticipation of the future. It takes place in the fundamental act of baptism ("the washing of regeneration and renewal in the Holy Spirit" [Tit 3:5]), but retains also its effect and power (present), internally strengthening and regenerating the "new man" in daily life (2 Cor 4:16). It also works toward the renewal of our mind (Rom 12:2). In the passage quoted above, Paul formulates the idea more tersely and precisely, "If any one is in Christ, he is a new creation; the old has passed away, behold, the new has come" (2 Cor 5:17; Gal 6:15). What the entire world will experience happens to a man who in faith and in baptism is already united with God; he attains in Christ a new existence that has an eschatological nature. Life, therefore, appears in the midst of this present age, which is a future life, and it gains power over man who through and in Christ has become a "new creation."

At the same time a further element comes to light, which in the epistle to the Colossians is not so clearly expressed: The "new man" is a man formed in *Christ*. Only with difficulty can one directly apply to Christ the expression "according to the image of the creator," although in another passage he is called "the image of the invisible God" (Col 1:15; 2 Cor 4:4). Pauline theology affirms that the idea is adapted to Christ, the first-born to the life of future glory (1 Cor 15:22). Christ is the Second Adam, the "man of heaven," whose image we should bear, just as we have carried the image of the first Adam, the "man of dust" (1 Cor 15:49). God also pre-

destined us to be "conformed to the image of his Son," in which
we are united with him (Rom 8:29; Phil 3:21). Beholding the glory
of the Lord, with unveiled face, we are being changed into his
likeness from one degree of glory to another (2 Cor 3:18). The
expression "put on the new man" (Gal 3:27) becomes the other
parallel "put on Christ." That the "new man" is one elevated by
Christ, one formed in him, a man filled with his life and nature, is
evident from Colossians 3:11. Our fulfillment in Christ is established
here not individually, but collectively for all who are united through
Christ to a new community: "Christ is all and in all." The Christian
thus has a clear goal in his aspiration to be a "new man": Christ the
resurrected, clothed in his transfigured body, who has entered into
the glory of God. The whole man, "flesh" and "body," is included
in this process, which with the resurrection attains its final consummation.

This is and remains a mystery of faith, which only he who believes in the resurrection of Jesus from the dead can affirm. The
actual new creation remains hidden in the present age, and the real
"transfiguration" remains reserved for the future world. But the
immediate need of the present is moral renewal.

We will once again consider the moral aspect. Any enthusiastic
attempt to project the glory of the perfected man (and the future
world) into the present world is hindered by a severe moral imperative. It takes as its basis the previous world with its trials and
needs. The Christian must first "suffer with Christ in order that we
may also be glorified with him" (Rom 8:17). Just as the baptismal
exhortation gives the admonition "not to lie to one another," Paul
also warns us against a self-deception that might let the Christian
think himself to be above temptation and fall. "Let anyone who
thinks that he stands take heed lest he fall" (1 Cor 10:12). In Corinth
there were fanatics who thought themselves to be "already perfect"
because of their spiritual experiences (1 Cor 2:6). Paul attacked their
self-centered boasting with the description of the wretched existence of Christ's apostles: "Already you are filled! Already you
have become rich! Without us you have become kings! And would
that you did reign, so that we might share the rule with you! For
I think that God has exhibited us apostles as last of all, like men
sentenced to death . . ." (1 Cor 4:8f.). The Christian must be realistic
and open his eyes to both things, the continuing moral struggle and
the necessity of suffering. The existential situation of the Christian,

who stands in the world but endures it with the power of God, is described well in the words of the Apostle: "For though we live in the world we are not carrying on a worldly war, for the weapons of our warfare are not worldly, but have divine power to destroy strongholds" (2 Cor 10:3f.). The powers of the future world do not break out openly and perceptibly but are hidden. At most they are capable of being perceived in faith and in the moral struggle of the new man who is formed by Christ and grows in the likeness of God. For man, who is responsible for the moral decline and the historical deterioration of the world, salvation itself must begin in the old world with its needs and obscurities. Man is the starting point for the renewal of our existing world. The battle of man, the "new man," must be fought as long as this world lasts. With the transfiguration of man at the end of the world, the new creation of God, a transfigured world, will emerge.

The New Human Race

The passage with which we are concerned (Col 3:9–11) contains another statement that is important for our understanding of man and the world: With the "new man" there comes into existence also a new community, where "there cannot be Greek and Jew, circumcised, barbarian, Scythian, slave, free man, but Christ is all and in all" (v. 11). Two additional passages with similar negative enumerations (Gal 3:28; 1 Cor 12:13) confirm that baptism is the place where the previous natural differences disappear. In Galatians it also says that the sexual differences (man and woman) are abolished, because all are one in Christ. This can be easily misunderstood, so that the Christian appears to have no more sense of the fundamental sexual differences which lie in the created order itself (Gn 1:27). The Pauline idea refers only to the new order of redeemed mankind, our being "in Christ," and it is therefore a foreshadowing of the final consummation. It is not so much a recourse to the original creation as it is a preview of the new creation that is to come, which exceeds and perfects the first creation. The future world will certainly retain the features of the present, but the transfiguration will banish all sorrow, want, and pain (Apoc 21:4). Insofar as the worldly differences—national, religious, social, cultural, and sexual— lead to conflict, they will become ineffective; the previous sorrowful history of man will come to an end. The transfiguration of the body, the glory of God exalting the entire new creation and its life, will abolish all earthly conflict and involvements in our earthly life. All enmity between nations, social inequality, differences in language, and similar things will cease; all will stand in the light of God (Apoc 21:23f., 22:4f.).

The expression which is perhaps already a formula, "Christ is all and in all," makes clear that the unity of previously conflicting elements is realized in the sphere of Christ's influence and dominion. The entire new collectivity ("all") represents Christ, who appears as a corporate personality: All are "the one" in Christ Jesus (Gal 3:28). This (collective) Christ is one body, which has many members and yet is still a single body (1 Cor 12:12). It is the body of Christ (1 Cor 12:27), the body which after Christ's resurrection is constituted by the Spirit, or as we could also say, "a single body in Christ" (Rom 12:5). This is a peculiar conception: This new human community which is constituted "in Christ" cannot be considered close enough with Christ. The second part of the formula "and Christ is in all" is important for the understanding of the first part "Christ is all." In all these men who differ in their very origin and earthly type, Christ is present and operative. Insofar as they stand in the sphere of his dominion, they have become a unity, and their previous differences disappear.

Instead of pursuing these notions that raise special problems for theologians, it might be well to find what this image of the new human race in Christ signifies for the Christian understanding of the world. In his world man conceives himself in a peculiar tension, which is both individual and social. Each conception must provide a solution to the relation between individual and community: In the East the socialistic man is absorbed by the community; in the West the freely developing personality is limited as little as possible by social institutions. In both conceptions the relation is unsatisfactorily solved—one can say unsolved. According to the order of creation the Christian man is seen in personal dignity as the "image and likeness of God," and this is affirmed in the new creation. But the social relationship of man is not overlooked. In the Old Testament it appears in the unity of the individual with "natural" communities of family and clan, tribe and folk, which is understandable among Semites and Orientals. Therefore, one can speak of a "collective" way of thinking. The narrowness arising from this outlook is overcome in the New Testament by the universal inclusion of the entire human race in the redemption-event. The individual is not only placed in a free area of individual activities but is also strongly bound to and deeply rooted in this new community of the redeemed. He who "in Christ" has become a "new creation," becomes at the same time a member of a new community: "You are all one in Christ Jesus" (Gal 3:28).

A Christian cannot free himself from the obligation of Christ's community. The unity of all is nowhere more strongly expressed than in the idea of the "body of Christ." This "builds itself up in love" (Eph 4:16), and the law of love and harmony is imposed on all who are "members one of another" (Eph 4:25). It becomes explicit in the admonition to brotherly love (Col 3:12ff.). This new community of the redeemed is also "open" for the entire human race, and it is its task in the world, through the power of its faith and the witness of its love, to call and incorporate all men into the community of Christ (Eph 3:9f., 4:15 f.).

The Christian idea of a "new human race" is more fundamental and more comprehensive than the ideas of worldly ideologies. A new human race remains as the goal of the new man, which will be realized in the future, in the new world that originates from God. But the uniting force of that perfect community, namely, love, can and should even now mitigate and overcome the present tensions and struggles. Love, which has its deepest source in the one triune God, becomes an eschatological force in the midst of the present world. Hence, this passage from Colossians reveals the basic Christian view of the world reflected in the Christian image of man. It deals with man and his existence in this world. It brings the Christian closer to an understanding of himself and the community to which he belongs. Therefore, he gains an insight into the world wherein he lives and operates. The world is seen in its historical reality, but through faith it is placed in the perspective of creation and new creation. With a glimpse into the future the original creation rises in its pure divine splendor, which it has never lost but which has been tarnished by man and his deeds. The new creation, which will restore and surpass the splendor of the first creation, begins in man. Human history, which litigates against salvation, has through the coming of the Son of God become again a history of salvation. Christ, the image of the invisible God, in his role of the resurrected and transfigured, becomes the goal of the redeemed man and the head of the redeemed human race. In Christ the future is already present and effective; in him those bound to him participate in the life of the future world but remain also citizens of the historical world, which they should penetrate with the power of faith and love until God makes all things new.

WILLIAM STRINGFELLOW

The Meaning
of the Christian Life

Though the Word of God dwells in the world and is present within the common life of the world, not every man by any means knows or acknowledges that presence in history and in his own action and experience. Though the Word of God may be discerned in the passion and conflict of East Harlem gang society, for instance, that is no warrant that the very people within whose words and action the Word of God is hidden will see or hear the Word, will understand the theological meaning of their own lives, will care about the knowledge of God given to them in and through their own concrete and everyday existence. And if a man cannot see and sense the Word of God within his own history, he will not have the eyes to see or the sense to realize the presence of the Word in the larger history of the world or in the lives of other men or of nations, much less see any importance or relevance to the Church and the peculiar life of the Church in proclamation and celebration of the presence of the Word of God in the common life of the world.

The power to discern the Word of God is the mark of the Christian. It is not just one of an assortment of marks of the Christian; it is, in a sense, the unique mark essential to everything else which generally characterizes the Christian life. There can be no witness in the world to the Word of God by Christians individually or as the Church, save by the exercise of this power. There can be, of

From *A Private and a Public Faith* (Grand Rapids, Michigan: William B. Eerdmans Company, 1962), pp. 68–73. Reprinted with permission of the publisher and the author.

course, some witness to the Church, or to the churches, but neither of these is the same as the witness of Christians to the Word of God.

God witnesses to Himself in history whether or not there are Christians engaged in any witness to Him. The possibility of the witness of Christians as the Body of Christ and as members of the Body of Christ to the Word of God in the world depends upon the power given to Christians to discern the presence of the Word in the world. Further, and in the same fashion, there can be no worship, unless the power to discern the Word of God in the world is present. For how shall men worship that which they do not know? What is there to declare and present and celebrate, if the Word of God is not continually discovered and exposed in the life of the world? That which is called worship that is not consequent to the power to discern the Word of God in the world is not worship in a Biblical and Christian sense, but some superstitious practice, some foolish religiosity, some obscene idolatry.

The event of witness and the possibility of worship both originate in the power given to Christians to discern the presence of the Word of God in the world's common life.

Now if God's Word is present in common life, even though hidden except to the apprehension of faith, then the Word of God itself constitutes the essential and radical truth of common life and of every and any aspect of the world's existence at any and all times. It is in the Word of God that the secret of life is to be known. It is the Word of God that surpasses the dominion of death over the world's existence. The power, then, to discern the presence of the Word of God in the saga of the world's existence, reckoning with even the most puny human life, is a saving knowledge. The power to discern the presence of the Word of God in common life is the gift of life itself, the restoration of life, the beginning of new life. The power to discern the presence of the Word of God in the world is the knowledge of the Resurrection.

I have found that my own anxieties always contain the knowledge, the triumph and the enjoyment of God.

He descended into Hell.

That is very cheerful news.

There is nothing less than Hell unknown to Him. There is nothing that I have known this side of Hell that is unfamiliar to Him. There is nothing known to me which I am wont to call Hell which He has not already known. Nor is there anything beyond these realms which, even though unknown to me, He does not know.

Anxieties, therefore, are not unwelcome in my life or in my household, since anxieties do not end in themselves, as the psychiatrists assert.

Now, unlike the existentialists, I have no particular fondness for despair or loneliness or indifference or lust or boredom or the similar anxieties. But they beguile me no more. Nor do I any more fear them—either for the attraction and terror they own in themselves, or for that dreadful power of which they are the foretaste: *death*.

Anxieties do not end in death.

Anxieties end in God.

Anxieties are both overcome and completed in Christ. Christ is both the end and fulfillment of all anxieties.

Christ means, after all, simply that God is radically intimate with human history and experience in all its grandeur and diversity and personality. Christ has already lived my life. Christ has already died my death. Christ is risen from death for me.

And for any man at all.

The event of becoming a Christian is that event in which a man confronts and confesses the presence and power of death in his own life—in every facet and detail of his own personality, in every fact and experience of his own biography, in recollection of every word he has ever uttered and of every one he has ever known, and of every thing he has ever done while in the same event he is exposed to and beholds the power and presence of God which is greater than death. In that event he is given the power to discern God's presence in the world.

By that event in my own history I am sure—as sure as I am of my own being and biography—that no man confronts and struggles with and surrenders to any of the powers of death—any anxieties—any crisis—without beholding the power and the truth of the Resurrection: the presence of God in history which is greater than any of death's threats or temptations and more potent and which endures forever.

Now I am sure of the Resurrection.

In this way, by the demonstration of the presence of God confronted in my own dying, I become a witness to the timeliness, excitement, veracity, scope and grace of the Resurrection. It is not just some long ago event. It is at once long ago and here and now. It is no myth. It is no mere imaginative interpretation of the Truth: It is the Truth at work in my own existence. It is no abstract moral or philosophical proposition, but the disclosure of the vitality of God in this world. It is no self-induced, positive thought but involves risking death as the conclusive power in human experience and then and there being found by the grace of God in the midst of death. It may not be earned, nor sought; it is rather the drama of God proving Himself as God, showing Himself in the common affairs of men. It is no special possession or knowledge of my own, but it is the very event in which my own solidarity with every other man is constituted. It is that unequivocal assurance that I am loved by One who loves all others which enables me to love myself and frees me to love another, any other, every other.

Mind you, all this does not mean that the existence of crisis can be rationalized, or in any way minimized, or denied. Leave that to the sentimentalists and the stupid and the pietistic. Nor can crisis be easily simplified, as the mass evangelists of Protestantism suppose. Neither can crisis be ignored, nor regarded as an unfortunate embarrassment, as some ecclesiastical authorities vainly think. There is no place to hide from crisis—especially not in the Church of Christ; on the contrary, the making of a Christian anticipates the extreme and signal experience of crisis which is the exposure to death.

For what these anxieties which afflict and assail men in their ordinary lives foretell and even now represent is the concrete and profound reign of death in a man's own, immediate, actual life and circumstances and—at the same time and in the same event—the personal and decisive exposure to the presence of God which subdues death and ends death's reign once and for all.

In a sense, therefore, the existence of crisis in any man's life conceals the mystery of Christ. Crisis—if we do not hide from it or suppress it or flee it or become its victims—is the visitation of death in our lives which holds the fact that the life of God is stronger than death and embraces human life and prevails over death in the specific history of a man. Crisis—that is, the serious encounter of a man with exactly that which now threatens his own life, with that which represents, signifies and warns of his own death—is always terrible, wonderful, eventually inescapable, saving and holy.

In other words, the most notorious, plain, and victorious truth of

God is that God participates in our history—even *yours and mine.* Our history—all our anxieties—have become the scene of His presence and the matter of His care. We are safe. We are free. Wherever we turn we shall discover that God is already there. Therefore, wherever it be, fear not, be thankful, rejoice, and boast of God.

The power to discern God's presence in common life is imparted when one becomes a Christian, an event in which the power of the Word of God in one's own personal history is manifest over and over against the power of death. Then and thereafter the Christian lives in any and all events in reliance upon the presence of the Word of God. Then and thereafter the Christian lives to comfort other men, whatever their afflictions, with the news of God's care for the world. Then and thereafter the threat of his own eventual historic death holds no fear for the Christian, for there is nothing which he will on that day experience which he has not already foretasted in the event of his becoming a Christian, in the event of his surrender to the power of death and of his being saved from that power by the presence of God. Then and thereafter he is free from the most elementary and universal bondage of men: the struggle to maintain and preserve, whatever the cost, his own existence against that of all other men. Then and thereafter he is free to give his present life away, since his life is secure in the life of God.

All this has been recited and observed in the Church in the sacrament of Baptism, of course, since the earliest days of Christian life. Yet it cannot be overlooked that Baptism is a much misunderstood and, ironically, since it is the most common experience of Christians, the most neglected of sacraments. It is regarded in a very perfunctory and cavalier fashion in many of the congregations of Protestantism. The obvious sign of that is the frequency with which it is placed in a context outside the corporate worship of a congregation and is thus degraded to a ritual of family life, involving only the immediate relatives and designated sponsors of a child. To find Baptism reduced to the mere observance of the natural birth of a child or to a ceremony for naming a child or to separate it from the center of the life of a congregation is especially anomalous in the instance of infant Baptism. For while, to put it succinctly, the responsible party to Baptism in the case of an adult convert to the Christian faith who is baptized is the convert now taking his place as a member of the Church; the responsible party in the case of the infant who is baptized but who is neither instructed in the Christian faith nor converted to the faith is the congregation. Not even the natural parents of the child have as much responsibility in this event as does the congregation and as do those designated as immediate representatives of the Church to the child, the godparents. In the case of the adult convert who is baptized, his Baptism is the public announcement to the world that he has been freed in his own life from the power of death by the grace of God for him and, therefore, joins the company of all baptized people, the Church, and covenants with his fellow members of the Church to serve the world by honoring God's presence in the world. But as for the infant who is baptized, his Baptism is the public proclamation to the world by the Church, and specifically of a congregation of the Church, of the faith of the Church, and concretely of the members of that congregation, in the power of God to raise the dead and of the care of God that this child, which at his birth death claimed, be saved from death. And this is proclaimed by the congregation in the Baptism of an infant out of the confidence in God's compassion for all men, a compassion to which the congregation is witness.

HEINZ ROBERT SCHLETTE

Responsibility for Freedom

When freedom is discussed today, it can be done only when one considers those past and present realities which have nothing in common with freedom as such. Therefore we are not here concerned with giving a discourse in praise of freedom—as it were, a memorial to what men formerly called "freedom." It is only in meeting the lack of freedom that we can today significantly think, write, and speak about freedom, its nature, and its demands.

This situation, however, should not be understood as though thinking about freedom were possible only in the well-known political controversies. The real difficulty, more precisely, is to concern oneself much more positively and constructively with freedom in view of the many ghostly faces of "unfreedom." The real difficulty thus is to understand freedom not only from its opposite, the friend-enemy relationship, but from its own structure and significance. With this approach to the problem, the existential relevance of freedom becomes completely clear, and at the same time we avoid an overly narrow view. It is not easy for anyone to think and speak with detached impartiality and indifference about an issue in which he is most deeply involved. Since we are, however, convinced that the thinking of a man equipped with mind and freedom still keeps its legitimacy after such an involvement, we must adapt ourselves to the demands and ground rules of this thinking and begin with resolved objectivity.

From *The Christian and the World* (New York: P. J. Kenedy & Sons, 1965), pp. 178–205. Reprinted with permission of the author. For full documentation, see original publication.

If the methods and habits of thought have demanded our entire commitment, so also does the very topic to which we now turn: freedom, and more exactly, the responsibility which the Christian has for freedom. One must immediately ask whether man can be responsible for freedom at all. Is not freedom the kind of thing that we always "have"—such as free will, freedom of choice, and freedom of action, which traditional philosophy teaches? And is it not the kind of thing with which we have always acted? Perhaps, then, should not "responsibility for freedom" be called only "correct use of freedom"? If responsibility for freedom were concerned only with its correct usage, then our topic would be in the general field of ethics, and we would have to emphasize that the free man has to conduct himself according to moral norms.

But Western thought has for a long time now concerned itself basically with something else: On the one hand, the norms according to which freedom is to be used have been brought into question; on the other, the concept and the issue of freedom are in no way still taken for granted and uncritically assumed, as happens in the average talk about the right use of freedom. In a more penetrating consideration of freedom, therefore, responsibility for freedom undoubtedly does not mean the correct use of freedom, but freedom itself.

With this first agreement it is true that we have avoided a possible misunderstanding, but new questions arise immediately: What is the freedom for which the Christian is responsible? And what kind of responsibility is this? As with all living, concrete acts in which one has his existence, so too in the case of freedom is it a waste of time to work on a "definition of the concept." Therefore we shall immediately turn to freedom itself; we shall proceed to describe it and, insofar as it is here possible, to take up questions we meet.

The freedom for which the Christian has to assume responsibility —a responsibility which, although it has not appeared today for the first time, nevertheless is of particular concern today—has in my opinion two forms: the freedom of which the New Testament speaks—we call this *eschatological freedom*—and the freedom of every human person in the order of the State, that is, social and political freedom, the freedom of thinking, working, believing and speaking, of science and of the press; I call this second form of freedom *secular freedom*. The expression "secular" (*welthaft*) is not the best; yet I do not want to call the freedom "worldly" (*welt-*

lich), because that could suggest the idea that we are dealing with a worldly and an unworldly or spiritual freedom, or with a natural and a supernatural freedom. In what follows we will try as much as possible to avoid such distinctions, which are loaded with philosophical and theological problems.

Eschatological Freedom

Eschatological freedom signifies first of all—which might sound surprising—present freedom. It is present among us as the *basileia tou Theou*, the dominion and kingdom of God. The fullness of time has begun; the perfection of all things has become a reality. Jesus the Christ has been experienced as the first witness of the new creation by the community of those who have been called from the mass of the people and have become worthy to enter into that completely new form of existence which the New Testament calls *pistis*, faith. The faith of the New Testament, and therefore of the Christian, in its original and true meaning refers to the entrance of the *community* into union with the risen Messiah Jesus, whom every page of the New Testament calls the *Kyrios*, the Lord.

The only way man can enter this community is totally and without reserve. The old man is crucified with Christ (Rom 6:6); he is laid aside like a garment (Col 3:9; Eph 4:22). The old has gone, and a completely new creation appears, a *kaine ktisis* (2 Cor 5:17; Gal 6:15), a newness of life (2 Cor 5:17), and that means the fullness of time and existence (Gal 4:4; Eph 1:10). The new wine bursts the old skins (Mk 2:22; Mt 9:17; Lk 5:37–39); the water of the old aeon is changed into the wine of the dominion of God (Jn 2:1–10). Those who have been invited and chosen, those who have been given a share in the faith of the new existence in Christ (which signifies love and unity), celebrate the eschatological banquet with God (Lk 14:15–23). After John the Baptist had proclaimed the tidings that "the Messiah will come," the proclamation of Jesus is: "the time is fulfilled"—this by all means is the testimony of the gospels (cf. Mk 1:1–15).

The presence of the kingdom of God is again and again characterized in the New Testament by the word "new." Even the liturgy, especially that of the central eschatological feast, Easter, announces the discovery of the *novitas*, the newness of existence, in contrast to the moribund *vetustas*, the aged and senile aeon. The

newness of the existence which can be achieved in faith is both indicative and imperative. It signifies that something *has happened*
to man, that he finds his end not at the side of man but at the side
of God; at the same time it *requires* that the new existence entrusted to man be embraced by him and exercised in a life of assent,
fidelity and hope. You *are* holy, we read time and again, and then
follows the imperative: *Live* in a way that is fitting for saints and
citizens of the dominion of God.

The eschatological, new life in and from unity with Christ is
proclaimed by John and Paul in continually new ideas and pictures.
Exegesis and theology have long recognized that the experience of
the resurrection of Jesus was the central event for the primitive
community. Its members recognized this event as the initial transformation of the earth, as the basis for firm faith, and as the conquest of death and sin, the characteristics of the old aeon. The new
life was described in human terms like peace, joy, hope, truth,
fullness. It was conceived as "being in Christ" or "abiding in him."
In fact it was understood simply as freedom.

The eschatological existence comprehended and realized in faith
could be called freedom...; it could be described with the
pictures of the wine and the meal just as well as with the sign
of washing of feet. All these statements and pictures refer
to that great incomprehensible mystery which surpasses the possibilities of human language, that mystery of the kingdom of God
which has become present on earth. Freedom must be called eschatological because it is a constituent of that new—of the already
anticipated coming—form of existence which could be opened up
only by God.

All this could be explained as fanaticism or gnosticism, if it were
not for a decisively important "but." This difficulty endangers
the authenticity of what has been presented up to now, but it is
nevertheless a prime characteristic of the presence of the eschatological: the *eschata*, the last things, the dominion of God, are present, *but* only in the form of a mystery, which as such is still not
revealed and manifest. Paul sketched this situation of our epoch
in salvation-history with clear terms in the famous eighth chapter
of his letter to the Romans (18–25):

> For I reckon that the sufferings of our present time are not
> worthy to be compared with the glory to come that will be re-
> vealed in us. For the eager longing of creation awaits the revelation

of the sons of God. For creation was made subject to vanity (impermanence) ... in hope, because creation itself also will be delivered from its slavery to corruption into the freedom of the glory of the sons of God. For we know that all creation groans and travails in pain until now.

And not only it, but we ourselves also who have the first fruits of the Spirit—we ourselves groan within ourselves, waiting for the adoption as sons, the redemption of our body. For in hope were we saved. But hope that is seen is not hope. For how can a man hope for what he sees? But if we hope for what we do not see, we wait for it with patience.

Pauline and Johannine theology, indeed that of the entire New Testament, sees a striking conflict: The kingdom of God has definitively become a reality, but it can be grasped only in faith. The future things are now no longer the last things; rather, they are present, but they are hidden at the same time. Salvation has been offered to us, but we must patiently persevere and first bring forth more fruit. The elements which make up the eschatological life, namely joy, freedom, peace, love, truth, the glorification of God, are already present in the new heart into which the holy Pneuma was infused with faith (Rom 5:5), so that Paul can once more proclaim with confidence and courage in the eighth chapter of his letter to the Romans (35–39):

Who shall separate us from the love of Christ? Shall tribulation, or distress, or persecution, or hunger, or nakedness, or danger, or the sword? Even as it is written, "For thy sake we are put to death all the day long. We are regarded as sheep for the slaughter" (Ps 43:23). But in all these things we overcome because of him who has loved us. For I am sure that neither death, nor life, nor angels, nor principalities, nor things present, nor things to come, nor powers, nor height, nor depth, nor any other creature will be able to separate us from the love of God, which is in Christ Jesus our Lord.

In fact, Paul not only had an idea of this, but experienced with his own body day after day that all the glory into which man is thrown when he believes is a hidden glory. The old aeon still lingers on, and the life of the community must take place under its laws. The hiddenness of the new is not only a concealment from the eyes and ears of the unbelieving world, but it is a concealment which goes right through the heart of the Christian. Faith does not take place in such a way that a man once and for all makes a confirming act of assent and then stubbornly maintains it. Faith requires a continually renewed, vital openness without which the personal encounter to which God calls man cannot take place.

Therefore the imperative "Be what you already are!" is a part of the epoch of salvation-history in which the eschatological is simultaneously present and hidden. For the time being the fullness can be obtained only if affliction is accepted along with it (cf. Mk 10:29f.). Sin, the law, and death are those forces which still threaten the freedom of the eschatological life. There still exist defection, disobedience, and temptation. It is still possible to betray the eschatological gifts of peace and freedom which have been entrusted to us. It is still necessary to bring to God our requests which the Lord's Prayer formulates; there are basically only *two:* that through God's activity the *basileia* might come, and that we might be suitable for it.

What makes up the eschatological freedom becomes understandable through the dialectic of the present and the future, the presence and the obscurity of the eschatological salvation: *To the extent that the Christian believes,* he is in Christ and abides in him, and God has taken up his abode in him. He has entered into a new existence, in which the non-saving trinity of the law, sin, and death is overcome. In this conquest is found what the New Testament calls freedom. "Where the Spirit of the Lord is, there is freedom" (2 Cor 3:17). The Spirit of the Lord is the *Kyrios* himself who has become present in history. Ingo Hermann has presented this convincingly in his book about Pauline Christology.[1] Therefore where Christ is, there is *freedom,* namely, freedom from sin, the law and death.

But the characteristic and expression of the new life is not only this "freedom from," but also—and above all—the "freedom to." What purpose, then, does the eschatological freedom have? Paul gives us a surprising answer when he explains to the Galatians in his most enthusiastic testimony for the Christian's new freedom: "Therefore, brethren, we are not children of a slave-girl, but of the free woman—in virtue of the freedom wherewith Christ has made us free. Stand fast, and do not be caught under the yoke of slavery" (Gal 4:31–5:1).

[1] *Kyrios und Pneuma, Studien zur Christologie der Paulinischen Hauptbriefe* (Munich: Kösel-Verlag, 1961). Cf. p. 113: "The Pneuma is the medium of the encounter between God and man."

We obtain in faith, then, the freedom for freedom itself. He who has not previously become free in faith and been placed in freedom cannot exist for and in freedom. But after faith has opened the dimensions of freedom and has destroyed the old servitude to sin and death and to the law which bears witness to sin and death, then we are free for freedom; we can live according to the insight and discovery which Paul again describes in his eighth chapter to the Romans with the words: "Now we know that for those who love God all things work together unto good" (v. 28).

A "royal" freedom becomes visible here, freedom which is just as little of this world as the kingdom of which it is an expression and sign. In this eschatological freedom the distinctions of the old eon are obsolete. Here social, racial and national differences no longer have a place. Here begins the Christian equality, for with God there is "no regard for the person" (Dt 10:17; Wis 6:8; Sir 35:15; Mt 22:16; Ac 10:34; Rom 2:11; Jam 2:1–9; 1 Pet 1:17). A new fraternity and friendship are born out of the eschatological freedom, so that everyone who believes can with a free heart speak the words of Paul in the letter to the Galatians:

> But now that faith has come, we are no longer under a tutor. For you are all the children of God through faith in Christ Jesus. For all you who have been baptized into Christ, have put on Christ. There is neither "Jew nor Greek"; there is neither "slave nor free-man"; there is neither "male nor female." For you are all one in Christ Jesus. (Gal 3:25–28.)

Here, then, is the Christian's *primary responsibility* for freedom: not to betray this totally unique and unsurpassed freedom of God. "Do not be caught under the yoke of slavery"—this warning of Paul (Gal 5:1) describes the Christian obligation to preserve the freedom from sin, the law and death, to safeguard the freedom for freedom through all dangers and temptations. In fact, he is even to carry this freedom in the hope which defies all human hope, the hope of faith (Rom 4:18), which awaits and longs for the manifestation of the dominion of God. We could also say: Keep that one central commandment which alone still prevails in the new order, the commandment of love, and you will be free. Then the same mystery would be stated with a different picture, for love is the real freedom. The refusal of eschatological-Christian love means falling back into the old aeon and into the middle of its law which brings sin and death. In the first letter of John we read:

He who says that he is in the light, and hates his brother, is in the darkness still. He who loves his brother abides in the light, and for him there is no stumbling. But he who hates his brother is in the darkness, and walks in the darkness, and he does not know whither he goes; because the darkness has blinded his eyes. (1 Jn 2:9–11.)

That freedom is love and love freedom is the meaning of St. Augustine's famous words which are understandable only in the eschatological situation: *"Dilge, et quod vis fac"*—"Love, and then do what you will" (in the Letter of John to Parthos VII, 4, 8; PL 35, 2033).

There is no further need to stress that eschatological freedom does not mean moral anarchy, but that it keeps the quality of an obligation—and in such a way, in fact, that the obligatory quality is in the very freedom itself. For freedom which is not love and does not bring forth the fruit of the Spirit would not be freedom at all but only the old servitude again, which is now, of course, even worse. Eschatological freedom is itself the only law, so that St. James can speak of a "law of freedom" (Jam 1:25; 2:12). By this he means the same as Paul, who contrasts the "law of the Pneuma" to the law of sin and death (Rom 8:2). The Johannine Jesus declares the same experience of freedom, when concerning "truth" (which means the eschatological reality of the new life) he maintains that it will grant man freedom: "If you abide in my word, you shall be my disciples indeed, and you shall know the truth, and the truth shall make you free" (Jn 8:31f.).

If we look back to what the New Testament says about eschatological freedom, we still have this to add: That new freedom, based on what it is, cannot be fundamentally violated by the powers of this world. It has its foundation in Christ himself and in faith in him; this foundation cannot be destroyed from the outside but only by man himself. Force and coercion might not be able to annihilate this freedom, but it is possible—and today no one fails to recognize this any more—for the eschatological freedom to be put under such intense pressures that the supreme commitment is demanded of man. We need only think of the first three centuries of the Church. They present a situation which is not simply to be eliminated from the history of the aeon, but necessarily belongs to it at least in principle. Today we know that there are temptations—I am not referring only to those outside the Church—which do not directly affect and touch upon eschatological freedom, but endeavor slowly and steadily to take away from it its foundation, namely faith.

With this we are already approaching the second form of freedom to be discussed. But first there is one more problem which deserves our attention and which may not be overlooked when Christian freedom is discussed. The eschatological freedom—as we have seen—is indeed present; however, it is not of this world and is therefore hidden and not in the realm of psychological experience. For that reason it must be stated and maintained that this freedom is in no way to be related to that problem which we can call "freedom in the Church."

For the eschatological kingdom of God, of which we have been speaking, does not quite coincide with the visible, hierarchical-juridical Church to which we belong. It is true that the Church as the community of the elect is and should be the place where the eschatological freedom can be met in the midst of this depraved and perverse generation (cf. Phil 2:15). And even if, in the sense of Karl Rahner, one must speak of the Church as the tangible sacrament of the Pneuma (which is the freedom of our freedom),[2] nevertheless and for this very reason one may *not* approach the Church with the expectation that he will certainly find in her the fullness of that freedom.

For in this "meanwhile" the Church is subject to the laws of history and thus of the old aeon. Nevertheless, the manner in which the Church as the *Universitas fidelium* ("totality of the faithful") exerts herself in the cause of freedom—for the new freedom of course is not individualistic, but (as love) is directly related to the community—and the manner in which the Church bears witness to the eschatological freedom all throughout history could and must be perceptible to the world. It is quite obvious that here lies the responsibility of every individual and of the Church as a community, as the body of Christ, and here especially lies the responsibility of the hierarchy.

Insofar as the Church is inserted into the laws of the already antiquated and obsolete aeon, the eschatological freedom is also bound up in the form of the old. But it is not for this reason to be interpreted as lawless and capricious freedom, and certainly not as a

---

[2] "Freedom in the Church," in *Theological Investigations II* (Baltimore: Helicon, 1963), p. 96.

license for evil (cf. 1 Pet 2:16). It is also worth stressing that, precisely *because* the Church must bear and tolerate the contours of the old, freedom would be essentially better executed in her if she would achieve secular freedom within her walls. Granted this belongs to the old aeon, yet it belongs there in such a way that it preserves and presents the inalienable inheritance of God's creative act. Eschatological freedom can be active even in the midst of the secular unfreedom; this is also completely true of its fate even within the Church herself.

Yet the testimony to eschatological freedom which the Church is called to give in this world would be much more plausible if from the great richness of that freedom the entire fullness and depth of creaturely and secular freedom would find its place in the Church. This is especially true since the *full* revelation of the new spiritual freedom must remain reserved for the coming aeon. The more easily the eschatological freedom of the Christian forms itself and finds a place in the secular freedom of the Church, the more acceptable will be not only the testimony in faith of God's freedom, but also the testimony of faith itself.

Only when one sees in theological reflection, i.e., through an insight in and from faith, that all juridical-legal order and dogmatic teaching have their "meta-canonical" and "meta-dogmatic" domain within the Church can the law in the Church be properly understood. Law in the Church no longer means the same thing as the law in the Old Covenant; much more than that, it indicates the New Covenant, the covenant written in the heart, the *analogia legis*: all law is to be considered only in the analogical sense. It has as its function the task of leading the Church as an earthly, visible community within the old aeon, and of preserving the eschatological freedom. A justification on the grounds of the law itself, i.e., merely for the fulfilment of the law, does not exist. Of sole importance is confidence in God, who entered into history and, bringing salvation, became present in the man Jesus. It is this attitude of confidence which the New Testament calls faith.

Freedom within the Church succumbs to the dialectic which is caused by the presence of the eschatological in world history. This means that misunderstandings and incorrect notions of freedom are always possible in the Church. Concerning this unfortunate situation, Karl Rahner writes:

Since the Church is always also a Church made up of sinful men, even as far as the holders of her authority are concerned, she can also in her individual actions offend against her own principles and against the freedom of the individual both within and without. This has happened often enough in the course of history. It can happen even today. And this is what the Church must guard against, for today more than ever she must be the champion of true freedom. But even by such individual offenses she does not become a totalitarian system. For she acts in these cases against her own proclaimed and practiced principles, whereas a really totalitarian system does not recognize such principles of freedom and dignity of the individual either expressly or tacitly, but on the contrary idolizes the collectivity and degrades the individual. But the Church must reckon with the real danger of giving scandal of an apparent totalitarianism.[3]

We know only too well today that the Church appears suspect to many of our contemporaries in the matter of freedom. It is unfortunate that Christians often find themselves in the position of having to assert that freedom and Christian (or more exactly Catholic) faith are completely compatible. People refer us to the 2414 canons of the Church's lawbook, to the Church's hesitant-to-opportunistic stand toward democracy (one thinks of the Maurras case), and to her tendency to sympathize with authoritarian governments if they seem to feel sympathetic toward her and if they seem ready to compromise. They refer to the Church's authority over the individual conscience (perhaps in connection with a political election), to the use of force in the medieval Church and in not a few missions in which they think it is possible to recognize the pure and distinguishing expression of the Catholic. They also refer us to the censure and supervision of scientific investigation, such as exegesis (but naturally not only exegesis), and to innumerable similar examples.

Here we cannot go into particulars to show that since the end of the Middle Ages the word "freedom" has become more and more the slogan of rationalistic and dechristianized modern thinking, and no longer sounds convincing in the mouth of the Church. The case of Galileo, which Bert Brecht took up, is symptomatic of the fate of freedom and of the free man within a Christianity which considers a particular historical form absolute. The attitude of the offi-

[3] *Ibid.*, pp. 99–100.

cial Church toward the rising natural sciences finds a striking, no less unpleasant parallel in the relationship of the Church toward democratic and liberal ideas and aspirations, especially in the nineteenth and early twentieth centuries. It would be a disregard for the truth if we wished to ignore the undeniable fact concisely formulated by Karl Rahner: "St. Paul spoke of the freedom of the Christian. After that, this particular topic was no longer mentioned very much." [4]

The primary responsibility of the Christian for freedom demands that he live in the midst of the eschatological freedom according to the original source, namely the spirituality of the New Testament, and that he think and speak about it. It demands that in his free existence he give freedom a continually greater guarantee; it demands that freedom become almost second nature to him. In any case, says Rahner, freedom must be spoken of today, and he gives several reasons:

> For in times when there is no freedom, we search anxiously for it in whatever place we still hope to find it; and today people are listening more thoughtfully once again to the message of the Faith, especially such as it issued originally from the pages of the New Testament. We must speak of this subject nowadays, because one has become sensitive and delicate about transgressions against the holy spirit of freedom in the Church, since one does not at any cost wish to confuse the Church with a totalitarian collectivity.[5]

Secular Freedom

Now we shall turn to the consideration of secular freedom. This refers to what we feel and think when we speak of a "free world," of freedom in the political-social sphere and therefore in the terrestrial order. To approach the problem as such correctly, we must first put aside the theological aspect and proceed phenomenologically. This methodological observation is not merely an incidental pre-consideration. Rather the correct approach to the question is crucial for understanding the topic itself. The methodological abstinence from theology is not easy to observe, especially when one comes from the biblical-theological considerations we have sketched. Nevertheless it will prove useful just to accept and bear with this distinction of formal points of view here in the beginning.

[4] *Ibid.*, p. 89.
[5] *Ibid.*, p. 90.

World—an extremely ambiguous concept—is here understood as the totality of men insofar as they are present on the earth and constitute the open and communal quality of being-with-one-another (*Mitsein*). Man who makes up this world wants simply this one thing: He would like to live. He does not want to vegetate, but to live as a human primarily wants to live according to his nature and in a basically meaningful way. He wants to live, therefore, without fear and without want and sickness. Positively stated: Man wants to live in a state of peace and happiness as imperturbably as possible, in a state of order—as a "necessary evil" which is not to be overlooked —and finally also in freedom (which is presumed and included in all the others).

These assertions are not exactly original; they sound like simple little idylls or simply like slogans. Nevertheless, just as soon as we ask only a few questions to examine the suppositions behind these statements, we find ourselves in almost insoluble difficulties, and the importance of the problem becomes only too clear.

Secular freedom, which we usually assume every man basically strives for and claims, obviously presupposes personal freedom. Secular freedom cannot be considered except as that state in which the individual man attains a maximum of his own being because and insofar as he possesses a unique, irreplaceable combination of specific characteristics which no one can take away, a unit in which the dignity of his person can be seen. And certainly this dignity of the person is exactly that which on the one hand today and always is questioned and even not recognized by threatening forces, and which on the other therefore must be convincingly proven to human thought to be legitimate so that it can receive some historical value.

Here we stand before an almost insurmountable difficulty. It concerns giving a foundation for the dignity of man. This is not to be done through some favorite solution, but rather on a basis which is as broad as possible, which is in principle open to all men, and which each man—disregarding the manifold differences which separate men—finds acceptable. This approach may not be understood as though human dignity could or should be once and for all guaranteed, explained, and where possible also recovered through a particular theory, philosophy, ideology or religion. Indeed one can never say that one must rationally define and understand the nature of freedom and human dignity before he is in a position to know what secular freedom is and how man achieves it.

With respect to the problem of time, Augustine in his *Confessions* wrote these famous lines (xi, 14):

> What is time? Who can easily and briefly explain this? Who can comprehend this even in thought, so as to express it in a word? Yet what do we discuss more familiarly and knowingly in conversation than time? Surely we understand it when we talk about it, and also understand it when we hear others talk about it. What, then, is time? If no one asks me, I know; if I want to explain it to someone who asks me, I do not know.[6]

What Augustine refers to here seems to be true for the problem of freedom also: Thinking about freedom and speaking about it already presume a still unreflected, sketchy, but elementary knowledge of freedom. We call this "pre-understanding." The pre-understanding comprises very simple things; yet this simplicity plainly seems to be—and it is in this that its trans-historical actuality lies—what man continually strives after and longs for before all reflection only because of what he is and what he encounters.

The pre-understanding of freedom, the straightforward comprehension of what freedom means, in its most general form obviously refers to this: that every individual as such can perform or omit what he wants—the Greeks speak of *autopraxia*, the ability to work by one's self, to decide on one's own actions. It means that the individual can strive after happiness and peace, and work and drive himself for it as he considers right and necessary. It means, finally, that this being-free, which presents itself to the pre-understanding already as a primary and pre-given *right*, in any case finds its limit where there are another or many other persons who are likewise free and have a claim to freedom in the same way that he does.

From these theoretical considerations it can be said: A community, whether it be a group, a nation, or the global "family of man," can realize secular freedom to the degree that each individual achieves his own freedom while preserving the other individuals' title to it. In fact, we can go a step further: The individual (not a complete unit, a personality isolated within himself, but a being made for society) achieves his true freedom only in the community, in the encounter with others.

Opposed to this true freedom, the alleged freedom of individualism appears to be silly isolation and servile dependence on the "I."

[6] *The Confessions of St. Augustine*, tr. John K. Ryan (Garden City, N.Y.: Doubleday & Company, Inc., 1962), p. 287.

Here need not be mentioned that at the very basis of the suggested principles differences of opinion, disputes, hardness and injustices might arise. To overcome such problems and to develop the principles of freedom in the most favorable proportion according to the situation is the function of politics. It is definite, meanwhile, from the viewpoint of the philosophy of history, of political philosophy and of anthropology, that the principle of freedom as such is considered completely guaranteed.

What this central problem involves is where we find the biggest obstacle: that the pre-understanding of freedom, which we attributed to every man who experiences and understands himself as an individual (or, we can say, as a person), on one side is too general and vague for a worldwide society to be built on it; and on the other side what it wants to be and requires seems to be continually questionable.

Can we really trust the human pre-understanding of freedom? Can we rest assured that what man wants and strives after in a basic and primitive way, such as freedom, is "right" for him and the world; that it is true and good not only for the individual but for all? Does not an affirmative answer to these questions mean that we are of the opinion that men in themselves are always good, and that "nature," primitiveness, is all good and salvation for men? And finally there would be the question: Is it really so, that men are primitively directed toward freedom? Is not the goal basically sought by men much more "salvation" in some sort of transcendental or religious understanding of this concept, so that the personal and secular freedom takes second or third place in relation to this end?

For all those who have not come into contact with the personal-dialogue understanding of man which is common in biblical thought or for those who have rejected it and hold something else, does not the last and highest end consist in being absorbed into the totality of the clan, the nation, the collectivity, or else in becoming one with the All or with the Transcendence? When we consider the spirituality of India, China, Africa, and even Greek philosophy, the existential claims of the proposed questions become clearly acceptable.

Since it is here impossible to go into the numberless difficult problems individually, much less to find an objective, practical solution, I would like to indicate just a few ways in which one could approach the problem of secular freedom with at least a little meaning.

Above all, it evidently seems possible to admit that the pre-understanding of freedom cannot establish an order of secular freedom. In no way are there agreeing views on what one can perhaps call the "natural man." Neither Christianity, nor Buddhism, nor Marxism-Leninism (certainly not the latter) is of the opinion that the individual is the way he discovers himself: always on the road of goodness and order, on a road which, so to speak, inevitably leads to freedom as long as he only stay on it. The optimism about nature of a Locke or Rousseau and the rationalism of the Enlightenment not only become shipwrecked in the realm of the absurd and of the demoniac in the world and in the heart of each individual; they also are incapable of conveying any generally essential information about the nature of man, since they presume to see clarities which do not exist; on the other hand they are not capable of preserving all of the dimensions of reality and of human experience, such as the holy and the beautiful.

When one considers the variety of philosophies and philosophers who are often struggling passionately with one another, and the variety of flagrantly divergent world outlooks, ideologies, and religions, then one may certainly say that de facto there is no *one* "truth" and with it no *one* foundation for freedom which would be recognizable for the whole world and thus binding on all. One certainly would observe that we are concerned here with the problem of the *binding force*. It naturally is far beyond me to dispute or bring into doubt the sense of philosophy and religion or their seriousness and necessity.

But it may also not be overlooked that philosophy itself, whether it be that of Socrates, Kant, or Wittgenstein, knows more or less explicitly how far it can go and where the area begins in which it can impart no more *definite* information, and where, therefore, it must remain silent. It cannot be overlooked that religions rest on freedom and assent, not on mathematically positive certainty which everyone can examine and follow.

Christianity itself, finally, stands or falls with the mystery of salvation-history, namely the mystery of election and vicarious redemption, and thus of faith also. Concerning this mystery, and in reference to philosophy since the days of Paul, Christianity explicitly explains that the wisdom of this world is "foolishness" (1 Cor 1:20–25). In the language of St. Augustine and of the Middle Ages, philosophy, in spite of all its efforts and with all due respect to the ability of human reason, cannot attain the fundamentals of reality, the true *sapientia Dei*, since this can be received only from the hand of the God who reveals himself in history.

With the question of the foundation and the nature of secular freedom, we find ourselves facing a fundamental problem of human knowledge. Even when someone, such as the Christian, knows what the order of creation and the law of human creatures are and what they comprise, there still remains with respect to knowledge and its development the already stated problem: Within the order of knowledge it is never possible, according to the testimony of philosophy, religion, and Christian faith also, to arrive at a general agreement among men concerning the ultimate principles, concerning being and its orders, and also, therefore, concerning a philosophical-metaphysical explanation of secular freedom.

Although a closer and more intensive agreement may be possible within wider cultures because of the history of these cultures (such as within the culture of Europe), in global dimensions agreement in the metaphysical-fundamental explanation of the meaning of human existence as well as of history and the world is neither to be found nor expected. Although this assertion is basically in no way surprising, it seemed advisable to present it here in this manner so as to draw the conclusions more clearly.

Since secular freedom cannot be postponed until men have agreed on what the principles of true human freedom are, there is only *one* answer, that is, to come to the best practical arrangement possible. Secular freedom can be achieved only through this, if at all: through an agreement on it and its essential requirements right in the midst of the great differences in principles.

But now we find ourselves in a vicious circle; for the necessity of an arrangement on secular freedom only raises anew the question of a comprehensive and binding knowledge, or at least a pre-understanding, of freedom, i.e., of man. If one wants to bring up the question of and search for a "minimal anthropology" here, then the the chain of thoughts begins again at the same spot where we found ourselves earlier. But perhaps the posing of the question, or at least the situation in which the question is posed, has received a different nuance: It has left the phenomenological and philosophical basis, and now stands on the level of bare existence. Anyone who has lived without freedom experiences and knows directly what freedom on this level means, whether his experience has been that of his own body or in the mental confrontation with terror and fright which have caused our century to become a century of horror.

It becomes apparent that on the level of thinking (even with an appeal to the existential experience of freedom) we can in no way escape the vicious circle. Here the point has been reached where one—also philosophically seen—can no longer avoid a *decision*.

In the history of Western philosophy there is that strange operation of thought called the *regressus ad infinitum*, the infinite regression. An example of this regression is found in the problem of causality, in which one proceeds from a definite given cause without reaching an end. If one does not *make* an end to this endless ascent (or better: regression) in the chain of causes by *deciding* courageously—as philosophy has done and considers legitimate—to force open the vicious circle and to accept a first, no-longer-caused cause, then an adequate knowledge is absolutely excluded.

In the face of the problem of freedom, one must, in my opinion, act in a similar way if he is to free himself from the vicious circle. It is valid, then, to accept the view that man's immediate recoil from terror and force is not a matter of his convenience, not an irrational and merely emotional reaction, and does not, therefore, reveal a bourgeois prejudice; rather this impulse reveals man and the essence of his given nature: namely, that he is a free person who possesses dignity, who must claim honor, and who has the right to be himself.

The person who makes this decision for the personal freedom and dignity of man understands at the same time the principles of secular freedom. Among modern thinkers there is no one who has thought out, perceived and spoken of the problem of freedom so frankly and radically as Albert Camus. In his great work *L'Homme révolté* (*The Rebel*), Camus establishes the fundamental dignity and right of man as a free being and formulates the basic law of secular freedom in the programmatic-sounding sentence: "The complicity and communication discovered by the revolt can live only in free dialogue." (Here is meant the revolt for the humane as distinguished from the destructive elements of all revolutions.)

Karl Jaspers, among many others, expressed himself in a similar way. In an essay called "Im Kampf mit dem Totalitarismus" ("In the Struggle with Totalitarianism"), he writes that the real struggle is "the fight for freedom within the free countries themselves. If what is fought for externally were lost within, then the battle would be senseless.[7]

Secular freedom becomes concrete for us in the political forms of democracy. Normally their philosophical assumptions are not clearly understood at all. In a frequently quoted speech about freedom, R. Guardini says: Democracy "is the most challenging and therefore the most dangerous of all political systems. This system continually grows from the free play of forces of persons with equal rights. The task of making it work is frightfully great, because there are not many who have an insight into its nature." [8]

What Camus understands by a world of "free dialogue," Jacques Maritain requires and supports in another way, proceeding from other presuppositions, but with the same intention as Camus and many others. He makes use of an old, often misused and misunderstood word: tolerance. For him tolerance does not mean only "patience" and "let be." He understands it in a much more positive sense, one could say, as an existential of being-with and "being-in-the-world." For Maritain tolerance means "human fellowship," a fellowship of freedom, of communication and of dialogue. It is only on this foundation apparently that secular freedom is possible.[9]

The numberless attempts to codify the common rights of man—such as the one Janko Musulin brought together in the volume *Proklamationen der Freiheit* (Fischer Series: 1959)—are an impressive indication that a free world worthy of men can be found only on the basis of free dialogue.

Christian Responsibility for Freedom

Nothing, as we have seen, can be proved scientifically and with conclusive assurance with respect to the nature and form of secular freedom and while it therefore involves a decision, the responsibility for secular freedom can still be discussed. In general it is good to renew our thinking of freedom continually and more basically, to speak of and discuss it, to venture into it in this way, and to love it more and more. One often has the impression that many recognize

[7] In *Philosophie und Welt* (Munich: R. Piper, 1958), p. 96.

[8] "Freiheit, Eine Gedenkrede" (lecture in Munich, July 19, 1960), in *Sorge um den Menschen* (Würzburg: Werkbund-Verlag, 1962), pp. 133ff.

[9] Cf. J. Maritain, "Truth and Human Fellowship" (lecture at Princeton University), in *On the Use of Philosophy* (Princeton, N.J.: Princeton University Press, 1957).

the value of freedom for the first time when it is threatened or lost. But now, what is the *Christian* responsibility for secular freedom in a world of free dialogue?

When we proceed from eschatological freedom, which characterizes the Christian as such, it appears that there is no visible connection to secular freedom. The Christian, insofar as he believes, is already in the eschatological reality; for this reason Paul can say: Our *politeuma*, our citizenship, is in "heaven," in the kingdom of God (Phil 3:20). In fact, the Christian cannot deny his "eschatological place" when he has to orient himself among and with non-Christians in his secular existence.

This means that the Christian, because of what he experiences through his faith, will always consider all human efforts for secular freedom with great skepticism and reserve. This he will do because he understands the temporality of earthly reality, which he always sees as something already antiquated and overcome. The Christian knows the mystery of history; he knows that man is destined for *one* end only. He also knows that this end is certainly not unworldly, a-cosmic or super-cosmic, but that it will be a new heaven and a new earth (Apoc 21, 22), in which God will be "all in all" (1 Cor 15:28).

At the same time, however, the Christian knows that he would not have any insight into the mystery of history if it had not been given to him. He knows that he has been given everything that he has. Because the Christian knows of the gift-character of his incomparable freedom, he also knows what kind of inner tragedy all human attempts to found and bring about secular freedom must produce. And insofar as the Christian cannot remove himself from the structures of the old aeon (since God himself allows the old to linger on yet and therefore wills the dialectic which characterizes the time of the Church), he does not have the right to dispense himself from working along in the Sisyphus-like task of establishing order in the midst of secular institutions.

The essential motive for this obligation of the Christian forms the truth experienced in faith that this world is the creation of God, and as such has been made worthy in spite of all guilt of man, that it is renewed in Jesus Christ, and is to be accepted more ardently than before. The Christian also knows that the part of mankind which does not belong to the chosen old and new Israel is in no way removed from the God of history, but that it bears his law within itself (Rom 1, 2). He knows that when man obeys the dictates of his religions, philosophical systems and ethical efforts, he is straining for the one God.

Therefore, in spite of all the paradoxes, the Christian dares to trust that mankind can ardently move toward the secular freedom because it is destined for the future fullness of freedom. In the meantime there has entered into our field of vision what the utopians of the last century saw vaguely: a world government united and ordered in freedom. This strain of the human heart, which enthusiastically directs itself toward the one free world, need not at all be suspect and objectionable for the Christian. But rather the Christian—with all the reserve which he cannot give up—is able to recognize and help bring about the true meaning of the human ambition for secular freedom: that freedom points to the new world of eschatological freedom which God—taking and reforming this world—will erect.

Since the Christian is able to recognize all this through his faith, he is responsible before God for the fate of secular freedom in this historical hour. His faith obliges him to strive for the world of free dialogue in which each human is capable of existing as a free person with honor and dignity. The solidarity with humanity, into which the Christian sees himself inserted, must occasionally even cause him to restrain himself, so that he does not betray eschatological freedom as well as secular freedom by a know-it-all attitude in daily politics, by a wrong idea of the relation of Church and State (caused in turn by a medieval misunderstanding of the kingdom of God), or even by military and crypto-psychological use of power. Without solidarity in the struggle for secular freedom, the Church would not only remain an unreliable partner with respect to this freedom, but, much worse, she could not give testimony to the eschatological freedom, which is the testimony of faith itself.

Here it becomes evident that the Christian's responsibility for both eschatological and secular freedom is intrinsically connected: The responsibility for secular freedom is the sign of the existence practiced and rooted in eschatological freedom. At the same time it is true that the eschatological freedom, while it makes the Christian free for the solidarity with all in the establishment of secular freedom, also preserves him from mythologizing this freedom and from a presumptuous expectation of it.

Secular freedom is exposed to many dangers today. The acutest occurs when human hope, with absolute exclusiveness and in the midst of constant disregard for death and other elementary experiences of existence, concerns itself only with the present form of the earth and comes up with the claim to have recognized with scientific exactness the nature of freedom and of being human. On account of this it also comes up with the demand to be legitimated by history and thus by humanity itself, and the demand if need be to force humanity to its happiness and to its freedom. In the face of such a radically attacking threat, a purely spiritual justification of true secular freedom is not sufficient; rather, mankind is in the fatal situation of having to use means it detests most deeply. It is important to see that this limitation forces itself upon the scene because and for the sake of the nature of secular freedom.

In this situation it will also be more clearly seen to what degree eschatological freedom remains hidden, how intensively the Christian, contrary to his better self, remains subject to the laws of the old aeon. Eschatological freedom as such cannot be defended on the level of secular freedom, but for the sake of man and creation, secular freedom needs protection from "unfreedom." The tension and conflicts in conscience which can arise here are hard, unsentimental, and hardly bearable.

According to all this, the Christian's responsibility for freedom is so strongly challenged and put under such pressure that it almost seems impossible for Christianity—today more than ever—to be able to meet it. Nevertheless, there are some grounds for confidence. When we say and believe that man is created by God for freedom and in Christ has become free for freedom, it is not a mere theoretical disclosure; rather it denotes a reality which is hidden in history but which is nevertheless effective.

More exactly seen, the basis of Christian hope lies in the salvation-history mystery of vicarious redemption. Joseph Ratzinger has emphatically shown [10] that vicarious redemption is the key to understanding history, the Church, election, and salvation: What the few carry out by virtue of faith bears fruit for history, for he who believes is one with Christ and is empowered to cooperate with him in the great work of the history of salvation. He who as a Christian

---

[10] "Die neuen Heiden und die Kirche," in *Hochland*, LI (1958–59), pp. 9–11. Cf. also Ratzinger's article "Stellvertretung," in *Handbuch theologischer Grundbegriffe II*, ed. H. Fries (Munich: 1963), pp. 566–75.

stands up for freedom individually also stands up for the freedom of all. He who as a Christian takes upon himself and bears responsibility for eschatological and secular freedom helps history and the world reach Omega Point, which means that fulfillment in which freedom is endless.

In and
II for the World

The Christian is called with increasing urgency to work in a world of dynamic change and almost insuperable difficulty. The strength which the Christian has comes from his faith that through him God continues his creative work in the universe. As Teilhard de Chardin has said:

> Any increase that I can bring upon myself or upon things is translated into some progress in Christ's blessed hold upon the universe. Our work appears to us, in the main, as a way of earning our daily bread. But its essential virtue is on a higher level; through it we complete in ourselves the subject of the divine union, and through it we somehow make to grow in stature the divine hold of the one with whom we are united, our Lord Jesus Christ.[1]

And yet, we draw back in fear from what we as Christians are asked to do. Social tensions, violence, war, famine, death—all make us wonder if we are not foolhardy to try to do more than earn a living and preserve a quiet conscience: as St. James says, "To keep oneself unstained from this world (Jam 1:27). Yet the Christian mission is more than a passive role of suffering; it is a positive command to work to bring about God's kingdom, to help restore all things in Christ.

The Christian mission in the world is a response to God's action. God is a "sending God," one who sends his word into

[1] *The Divine Milieu* (New York: Harper Torchbook Edition, 1960), p. 63.

47

the world, sends prophets and wise men, and finally sends his
Son. The Son, having done His work, returns to the Father and
sends the Spirit. Those who receive the Spirit are sent into the
world in turn to carry on the work of the Son.

Dr. J. G. Davies has pointed out the relation of mission and
shalom:

> The scope of mission therefore extends to the overthrow of
> the forces of evil that separate man from his Creator and
> stultify him so that he is less than fully human. Mission em-
> braces too the establishment of *shalom*. I use the Hebrew
> word because its rich content cannot be conveyed by a single
> term. *Shalom* indicates all aspects of human life in its full and
> God-given maturity: righteousness, trust, fellowship, peace,
> etc. This one word summarizes all of the messianic age; even
> the name of the Messiah can simply be *shalom* (Mic 5:5;
> Eph 2:14). The Gospel is a Gospel of *shalom* (Eph 6:15),
> and the God proclaimed in the Gospel can often be called the
> God of *shalom*. *Shalom* is not something that can be objecti-
> fied and set apart. It is not the plus which the haves can dis-
> tribute to the have-nots, nor is it an internal condition (peace
> of mind) that can be enjoyed in isolation. *Shalom* is a social
> happening, an event in interpersonal relations. It can therefore
> never be reduced to a simple formula: it has to be found and
> worked out in actual situations. The goal towards which God
> is working, i.e., the ultimate end of mission, is the establish-
> ment of *shalom*, and this involves the realisation of the full
> potentialities of all creation and its ultimate reconciliation and
> unity in Christ. Further we may say that God's activity or
> mission is directed towards the setting up of the Kingdom of
> God, that rule which is "already" but "not yet," that rule
> which is of God's bringing in and not ours—witness the par-
> able of the seed growing secretly (Mk 4:26–29) which without
> human aid develops and ripens, since the Kingdom is the out-
> come not of human effort but of divine action.[2]

A Christian who moves toward an understanding of his mission cannot be content with merely approving the good in
secular society and affirming his desire to establish better human conditions and a more viable human community. He must
face the intractable forces of dehumanization—poverty, race,
violence, treachery, war—and explore possible approaches for

[2] From "The Meaning of Mission," *Parish and People* (June 1966).
Quoted with permission of the author.

overcoming their destructiveness, that is, he must try to establish *shalom*.

Like the rest of mankind, the Christian is beset by poverty, violence, and suffering of all kinds. He finds the accounts of tragic misfortune as described in the writings of the Biblical prophets very instructive, especially when he compares them with the news reports from radio, TV, and newspapers. A change of names from Babylon, Nineveh, and Tyre to New York, Paris, and Moscow shows a remarkable continuity. Power politics, war, crimes of violence, grinding hunger, disease—there seems to be little change from the fifth century B.C. to the twentieth century. The chief difference is that we know more about how much suffering there is and where it is, and we are more overwhelmed by its magnitude.

How is the Christian to live and work and think as the suffering world struggles on? One tendency is to amass details, cases, and circumstances into a pile so great that we cannot see around or over it. Another is to transcendentalize this evidence until we see only a providential work of God, who knows his own purposes but keeps his reasons very quietly to himself. An alternate of unbelief is to accept suffering with grim stoicism and to refuse to believe that a God who is good would have created such a world.

The Christian's response is to try to live by the two great Amen's of God's creative will: (1) the Amen of creation, when "God saw all that he had made, and behold, it was very good" (Gn 1:31); and (2) the Amen of redemption when Jesus, having lived man's life and suffered death to the full, said, "Father, into thy hands I commit my spirit. And having said this he breathed his last" (Lk 23:46). Between these two Amen's exists the life of each man who tries to form a better world for himself and others, who battles the constant frustration of seeing failure, misfortune, and malice undermine his work. Eventually the final frustration of death overwhelms him. To this also he says Amen, looking on death, as Jesus did, as the final phase of his journey to the Father.

To work in the world today is to feel a constant sense of

crisis. Father Robert Johann points out that crisis has its uses, for it summons us to move out of routine, shallow daily activities to a more existential judgment on what we do and how we are helping to recreate the world.

Dr. Richard Shaull explores the idea that Christian existence is "revolutionary existence." The Christian must not merely exist in a historical process; he should be a revolutionary force in its dynamism, a pioneer of social change, a reformer of systems, and a creator of new structures. The Christian must have the resources of understanding, the strength coming from community, which can sustain and orient the revolution. Above all he must believe that God's work of renewal is going on in social revolution and that the future is *really open*.

Professor Alfons Auer sees the work of the Christian in a world dominated by technology as "the spiritual penetration and domination of cosmos," but he points out the difficulties along the way: the need for man to understand himself and his powers better and his position as head and center of the universe. His work is not only part of God's creative purpose but also an offshoot of Christ's redemptive work.

A critical approach to new theories of interpersonal relationships among Christians is offered by Dr. James M. Gustafson. He asks that in proposing a social analysis of community, particularly one in which Christians are assuming responsibility, that all three aspects of community be respected: cultural ethos, interpersonal relationships, and institutions. Only when Christians understand the place and value of all three elements, including the corollaries of responsibility and obligation, can new social structures be said to embody God's concern for ordering human society.

Any theology which we now possess of the Christian at work in the world suffers from an incomplete understanding of the material world, of social processes, of the malevolent forces at work in human and natural processes. One theology, often called "secularization theology," occupies an uneasy position between an older supernaturalist theology which considered material creation to be almost entirely evil, and a theology of evolutionary optimism, which views man's work as moving triumphantly to overcome limitation and all evil. When the theology of the Christian in the world develops more fully it must account realistically for all aspects of man's work, his successes and his failures, and show which of his goals can be achieved here and now and which belong to a transcendent future.

ROBERT O. JOHANN

A Sense of Crisis

Central to the thought of Teilhard de Chardin is that man is the spearhead of evolution. In and through man, world process becomes conscious and self-directing. This means that the future is now up to us. God looks to us to complete His work. He makes the outcome of creation dependent on our free response. Although He made us without us, Augustine declares, He cannot save us without us.

The obscure realization of this awful responsibility is the root of that nameless and haunting anxiety which is part of being human. All the entities beneath man run their course more or less automatically. They do what they do because they are what they are. But man, however much he too is involved in the determinisms of nature, nevertheless in his personal core stands apart from nature and above it. The very fact that he is conscious of himself and can step back from his environment to survey it, puts within his hands the power to shape history.

With man's emergence from nature, the world becomes unstuck. What happens now is no longer the simple result of what has gone before. The future—even the question as to whether or not there will be one—is henceforth a matter of decision. As Scheler has pointed out, to be man is in a sense to stand on the brink of nothingness. It is to stare into the void and know that God Himself cannot sustain us unless we decide to let Him.

From *Building the Human* (New York: Herder and Herder, 1968), pp. 68–70. Reprinted with permission of the author.

Small wonder if clear and abiding awareness of the role he is called to play is almost too much for man to stand. Small wonder, too, if he experiences his freedom less as a precious privilege than as a burden he can hardly support. Hence it is that, having slipped the bonds of nature and its inexorable routines, man immediately sets about devising new routines of his own—routines in which he can newly lose himself, can be swept along without thinking and be freed from the need to decide. From that perilous brink where nothing is guaranteed, he retreats to a contrived world where everything has its place in the humdrum of everyday life. Even his relation to God, that partnership in innovation which should be a continual challenge to spend himself in creative effort, succumbs to a deadening routinism. Religion itself is made a comfortable matter of regular, weekly observance.

All this, I say, is understandable. It is even to some extent necessary. Man's limited powers of attention make routine and habit indispensable parts of his action. Wholesale anxiety and questioning, at least when not tempered by hope, would freeze him in his tracks. Moreover, it might be argued that to set up routines and patterns, which introduce order and regularity into an otherwise chaotic world, is precisely the contribution that man is called on to make. The institution of routines could then be seen as the triumph of reason and control over irrational caprice. Perhaps. But the triumph is limited and precarious. And this we must not lose sight of.

For routines have a way of swallowing the whole of life and deadening all sense of crisis. Their mere existence is taken as their own guarantee and as an excuse for the individual to concern himself, not with the fate of the world, but with the pursuit of his private interests. The fact that they imitate nature makes our routines seem part of the given. We forget that whatever order exists in human affairs has been painfully achieved and that its maintenance and promotion remains our individual responsibility. However much we may think otherwise, our future cannot be assured without our efforts. It is guaranteed only in the measure that we singly and collectively work at it.

In recent years the world has been shaken many times by tragedy. President Kennedy's death revealed to us all how fragile and vulnerable the devices of man really are, how little they can be relied on to take care of themselves, how narrowly they separate us from the brink of nothingness that defines our condition. Christian hope reminds us that we still have a future to strive for. Despite our past failures, God continues to come to us and seeks with our cooperation to set up the reign of His peace. Perhaps we are beginning to realize how the world hangs on the response which we, each of us, give Him.

RICHARD SHAULL

The Revolutionary Challenge

Ever since the modern world began to take shape around us
with the Renaissance and the Enlightenment, the churches of the
West have tended to absent themselves from the frontlines of the
human struggle and assume a conservative attitude toward social
change. Ecumenical social thought has attempted, over the years, to
move beyond this, and it is just possible that a significant break-
through could occur. This is evidenced by the attention which has
been given to the most recent developments in the technological and
social revolutions; it is also demonstrated by a shift of emphasis in our
theological reflection on social problems. I refer to the development
of the thesis that God's redemptive work in history, as expressed in
the central doctrines of faith, calls us to work for the transformation
of society; in fact, for a new social order. To cite one example,
Professor Roger Mehl declares that "God in Christ has made all
things new and requires us to share in this transformation of the
world." The imminence of the Kingdom of God means not only
that the future is wide open but also that "the future is already present"; and the Lordship of Christ "breaks the established order, the
established injustice, and calls us to take part in the great renewal
of history." [1]

In working out the significance and implications of this eschatological perspective, we are brought to the point where we are

From *Theology Today*, XXIII (January 1967), 470–80. Reprinted with permission of the publisher and the author.
[1] Preparatory Studies for the World Conference on Church and Society, I,
52–53. Unpublished materials, 1966.

challenged to recognize, to use the phrase of Arthur Rich, that Christian existence is revolutionary existence, and that the church's service to the world is that of being the "pioneer of every social reform," without making any claims for Christianity or trying to Christianize the revolution. I realize that not every theologian will accept this interpretation; at the same time, I find myself obliged theologically to support it and rejoice in it. I see here a sign of hope that, from this point onward, those who, because of their Christian faith, find themselves called to participate in the revolutionary struggle, will be able to turn to the Christian community for theological and moral support.

I

However, I should like to attempt to push the debate a bit further. A new generation of Christians, in many parts of the world, is taking this responsibility for revolution, "for the great renewal of history," seriously. When they do so, they find themselves in a strange, new—and sometimes shocking—world, and part of a dynamic historical process. Within this situation, some issues are seen quite differently than they appear to those outside, and the specific way in which they are raised changes on the road to the future. All of our encouraging theological reflections will not be of much help to the new revolutionary unless they are set within this concrete revolutionary situation and related to the questions arising there. Our first theological task is to take that step.

This means, I believe, that we must examine more carefully precisely what is involved in bringing about social change today; i.e., what the concrete shape of the revolutionary struggle is. On this, I would like to present three points as a basis for discussion.

The first is the discovery that technology for all its revolutionary impact on the structures of modern society, has tended thus far in its most advanced stages, toward a total system of social domination and an *ethos*, which offer almost unlimited possibilities for preserving the established order. One of the major characteristics of the new revolutionary posture is the conviction that those who want to bring about a significant transformation of society are up against a total system of power and are called to work for a fundamental change in the direction and structure of that system. This conclusion, by and large, is the result of the experience of people who began by attempting small social reforms and were forced to a more radical position. In the developing world, it is now clear that development is not merely a question of rapid technological advance and industrialization, but of changing the whole complex of factors which constituted the feudal-colonial order, as has been demonstrated by the writing of the Brazilian scholar, Candido Mendes de Almeida. Likewise, the students and leaders of the poor in the urban ghettos in the United States soon find that they confront a comparable situation in the inner city and cannot solve their problems until fundamental changes occur in the whole structure. At the present moment, the civil rights movement is moving to a new stage of radicalization partly as a result of a similar discovery.

The most important new factor in all this is the growing awareness that overarching, and in some sense sustaining, all these developments, is the power of the established technological order itself. This is the reason why in recent months a book by Herbert Marcuse, *One-Dimensional Man*, has been making such an impact on this student generation in North America. His thesis is that advanced technology, together with the ideological *ethos* accompanying it, is producing a system which tends to be totalitarian. The development of ever larger economic and political units, together with the integration of the economic and political orders, create a society in which certain material needs of a large percentage of the people are met, but they have no significant opportunity to participate in the decisions regarding their own future. The system not only has tremendous power but it also reduces to ineffectiveness those forces which might otherwise bring constant pressure for social transformation. The white collar as well as the blue collar workers have a certain sense of satisfaction with the system if not a vested interest in it. The major political parties no longer offer fundamental choices regarding the structure and direction of social development; and a politics of consensus seeks to avoid deep political conflict. Countervailing power exists except where it would counter the whole system; and the whole order is so rational in its irrationality that those who oppose it can easily be portrayed as lacking in judgment and common sense. For Marcuse, these developments in the economic and political spheres are accompanied by an *ethos* of "secularity" which reduces social science to the empirical analysis of *given* structures, restricts the universe of discourse of philosophy and removes, from culture, the critical, transcending power it has often had in the past. The end result may be one-dimensional existence, without vitality, creativity or excitement; a society without power for its own renewal.

I am not prepared to evaluate Marcuse's thesis. The point I want to make is that a significant number of young people today, from widely different backgrounds, who are committed to the construction of a more just and human society, have been pushed to a position in which this makes sense to them. As a result, they are convinced that technology can contribute, in the long run, to human well-being and fulfillment only as it is challenged by revolution, and thus choose revolution as the only road they can take in working for the future of man. Moreover, it is this fact which creates a new identity of outlook and purpose between the revolutionaries in the developing nations and a minority in advanced technological society.

The second point is a problem which arises here. If we are convinced that revolution is necessary for the humanization of modern society, we must also face the possibility that the traditional type of social revolution, which aims at the overthrow of the whole social order and a total change in the structures of power, may now be practically impossible. If by chance it should succeed, it could result in social and economic disorganization that would have disastrous consequences for a long period of time.

This is stated most sharply by Professor André Philip, who cannot be accused of wanting to maintain the *status quo*. He claims that the type of action now needed "must be technical in character and in no way revolutionary or violent. Violence seems to be impossible, even apart from ethical considerations. In the industrialized countries, the technical structure is too elaborate and the different elements overlap too much for any sudden break to be made without upsetting the whole system of production and consequently impoverishing the masses." [2] Without much effort, most of us can think of any number of instances in recent history which confirm this statement.

Thirdly, for Professor Philip this means "the end of revolution." For those of us who do not have his trust in the capacity of the established order to renew itself without strong revolutionary pressures upon it, it means rather the search for a new strategy of revolution. The justification for and possibility of this search may be found

[2] *Ibid.*, II, 120.

in certain characteristics of the society now taking shape around us. Thus far, technological advance and the conservation of the established order have gone hand in hand. But as Robert Theobald has pointed out to me, there is nothing in technology itself which makes this inevitable. In fact, as technology advances, the instruments as well as the atmosphere which it creates could just as easily serve the cause of social transformation and emancipation. Moreover, the breakdown of the stable, ontocratic, authoritarian patterns of the past and the dynamic character of modern society create a new potential instability and a very precarious social balance. Sudden pressures applied effectively at the right place at the right time may have a surprisingly wide and deep impact; and small changes can set forces in motion which will produce much greater changes in the future. In this situation, revolutionary strategy is a question of developing those bases from which a system unwilling to initiate major changes when they are most urgently needed, can be constantly bombarded by strong pressures for small changes at many different points. Without such revolutionary forces in our societies today, the prospects for the future are not encouraging. But these efforts could help to keep society open and flexible, renew it in spite of itself, create a new social context for technology, and perhaps lead eventually to the type of social institution that would be sufficiently responsive to human need as to make revolution unnecessary.

In recent decades, a revolution has occurred in military strategy through the use of guerrilla warfare. Small revolutionary groups, confronted by overwhelming military power, discovered that they could fight a winning battle in some situations by means of a strategy of concentrated surprise attacks by small disciplined units with limited objectives; by maintaining flexibility and freedom of operation, and by keeping the initiative and advancing to new fronts whenever blocked on old ones. Guerrilla warfare is a military strategy; its aim has usually been total conflict and the complete overthrow of the old structures of power. But a careful examination of these movements may suggest a strategy for effective *political* action of a revolutionary type today. In fact, the formation of such "guerrilla" units, with a clear sense of self-identity, a vision of a new social order, and a commitment to constant struggle for change, inside or outside certain social structures, may offer one interesting prospect for building a new society at this time.

This limited struggle of small groups in permanent revolution is here envisaged primarily as a political strategy. To the degree that it succeeds, the temptation of the oppressed to rely on violence should be reduced. But we would not go so far as to urge exclusive reliance on nonviolent action, or insist that the Christians should have no participation in the use of violence. There may, in fact, be some situations in which only the threat or use of violence can set the process of change in motion. What is important is not whether violence is outlawed, but whether its use, when absolutely necessary, is geared to a strategy of constant struggle for limited changes in society, or is set in the context, as so often in the past, of total warfare and the total overthrow of the social order.

If the strategy we have suggested is to succeed, it cannot be a matter of isolated, sporadic efforts. It must rather include the constant formation throughout society of small nuclei with revolutionary objectives; an intensive effort at the type of education which will open new perspectives on social problems and point the way to new experiments and new solutions; and close coordination of the work being done by the various revolutionary movements.

My conclusion—in this first area of discussion—then is this: If the church is inclined to take seriously the vocation to which Professor Wendland and others have called it, then it should provide the context in which people are helped to work out a theological perspective on and an ethic for revolution. No one can guarantee that the churches or even the ecumenical movement will accept such a challenge. But we would take a great step forward if we decided really to listen to those who come from the developing nations, the representatives of a new student generation in our advanced technological societies, and others who incarnate the urgency of this concern for fundamental and rapid changes in the present order.

II

This leads to the second major issue that I should like to raise for further discussion: that of the relationship of theology to the revolutionary struggle. Professor Wendland has stated his position clearly when he argues that the Christian should work positively and critically for revolution without an ideology of total revolution and without utopian dreams of a perfect society. From this I conclude that our principal theological task is that of exposing and challenging the latent idolatry in all such movements. This is always an important task for Christians in society; it is especially important among those who are called to pay the price of a revolutionary struggle. But I am not convinced that this is our primary theological responsibility at the present stage of revolution. This is partly due to the fact that other forces in our contemporary society seem to be doing a more effective job at this point than we are. The "incognito Christ," if I may use that phrase, working through technology and secularity, has broken the dominance of old absolutes and shattered utopian dreams. Today a strong sense of the limitations of knowledge about society and of the ambiguities in a revolutionary struggle can be found among the new revolutionaries in Latin America, the new student left in the United States, and new groups of philosophers and writers in Marxist societies. All these groups may need the encouragement and support which Christian faith can provide, but our major responsibility lies elsewhere.

If the new revolutionary is to carry on a long and arduous struggle without absolutes and without utopian illusions, something quite different is called for. What he now needs are those resources of understanding and community that can sustain and orient such an effort: the possibility of believing that the future is really open, the hope that weakness can be victorious over established power, and that meaning and fulfillment are possible in a life lived in an intense revolutionary struggle. What is perhaps even more important, the new revolutionary needs those resources of transcendence and transgression which free him to break the bonds of the secular, empirical *ethos*, dream new dreams about the future of man, and cultivate the creative imagination so as to be capable of thinking about new problems in new ways, and defining new goals and models for a new society. What the revolutionary needs, in the words of Professor Roger Mehl, is "a new vision of the world and a new conception of man." Thus, the real question before us theologically is that of the vitality of the Judeo-Christian tradition, in its diverse forms, and its capacity to relate to the human situation today in such a way as to liberate old images, symbols, and concepts and create new ones that can perform this task.

Given the present state of the churches and of theology, can we expect this to happen? Each of us must answer this in the light of his faith and experience. On the basis of my own experience with revolutionary movements on two continents, I can only say that I believe it is a live possibility—on one condition: that theologians take seriously the fact of the death and resurrection of the *Logos* as indicating the only road open to us in this situation. Let me try to suggest examples of what this may mean.

III

Much of our Christian social thought has been and to a certain extent still is dominated by an a-historical way of thinking. I was reminded again of this in reading this quotation from Cicero:

> There is in fact a true law—namely right reason—which is in accordance with nature, applies to all men, and is unchangeable and eternal.... To invalidate this law by human legislation is never morally right, nor is it permissible ever to restrict its operation, and to annul it is wholly impossible.... It will not lay down one rule at Rome, and another at Athens, nor will it be one rule today and another tomorrow. But there will be one law, eternal and unchangeable, binding at all times upon all peoples; and there will be as it were, one common master and ruler of men, namely God, who is the author of the law, its interpreter and sponsor.

I suspect that for many people involved in revolution today this sounds like a voice from a far distant past, belonging to a completely alien world view. For the reality that the revolutionary knows is that of his involvement in dynamic historical existence, which is constantly being shaped and reshaped in very concrete and unexpected ways. It is not a stable, eternal, rational order, but one in which he has some slight hope of imposing order as he attempts to shape the future in the direction of certain specific goals. In other words, we are now well aware of what Troeltsch, decades ago, described as "the fundamental historicizing of all our thought about man, his culture and his values," and we cannot escape his conclusion that only the type of thought which is rooted in the raw factuality of concrete historical events can be of any use in this situation.

In recent years, there has been some discussion as to whether ecumenical social thought should give attention primarily to principles, values and middle axioms, or become contextual, or allow one to be a corrective to the other. The discussion in these terms will, I believe, produce very meager results. Perhaps our task at this moment is to recognized this fact of the radical historicizing of all of our thought, and work through the theological implications of it, allowing it to lead us where it will.

What I take this to mean is that ethical orientation can be provided only as values are translated into specific social goals, specific human needs, and specific technical possibilities and priorities. No set of abstract principles, or ideas like the responsible society, will be of much help unless we succeed at this job of translation, which will have to be done again and again in changing situations. What can make a significant contribution is an ongoing process of reflection on specific questions in the light of the perspective on history provided by the particular history into which we as Christians have been incorporated, and in the light of the shape of the new man that is coming into existence, as portrayed by one man, Jesus of Nazareth. It is out of this sort of biblical and theological reflection that the broader dimensions of thought about the renewal of man and his historical existence may be kept in the center of the revolutionary struggle. In this way, they can become an explosive ethical force, as they break the limitations which man tends to impose on his thought and actions and make real a higher order of life which stands in judgment upon all his achievements.

All this may sound very well, but the experience of many contemporary Christian revolutionaries is that the theology we have provided for them does not equip them for such transgression and transcendence in the secular order. Much of our traditional theology —as well as our ethical thought—reflects such a degree of acculturation of Christianity that it has lost its iconoclastic and transfiguring power. For a brief period in our recent past, neo-orthodoxy performed this task in a rather striking way. With its emphasis upon the Otherness of God, the Word which stands over against all human thought and achievement, the work especially of Karl Barth, it provided us with an amazing new freedom in relation to culture and society and suggested a new vision of man and of human relationships. Unfortunately, as Bonhoeffer understood, this effort ended up in a theological restoration, the restoration of concepts and terms which belonged to a very different world view and historical situation. Thus our theological thought about the world, with all its potential richness, was even more closely bound to concepts that are now largely meaningless. The experience of participation in radical historical existence through social revolution has now made this clear.

It is for this reason that many of a new generation have only the memory of a meaningful Christian faith, but no way to take hold of it concretely, or relate it to the problems of personal and social existence. It is this situation that has produced a new ferment in theology. Younger theologians are appearing on the scene who are convinced that all the old images and concepts have lost their power; they can no longer serve as bearers of the Christian message of radical iconoclasm and transcendence, or contribute creatively to the formation of a new image of man or a new style of life. Thus these men are searching for a new language which can point to this reality in a more adequate way. In the United States at least, even the wildest of the death-of-God theologians reveal this longing for a new language capable of doing in our time what our more orthodox theologies did when they were first formulated.

This search for a new language of faith is not an easy one. It requires, first of all, not a new language, but a new involvement in those places in the world where God is most dynamically at work. And involvement must be accompanied by patience, for we may have to wait for a long time until authentic new theological language and new concepts emerge. In the meantime, there is a job that needs to be done, and theology is called to do it: to keep going the difficult but not impossible running conversation between the full biblical and theological tradition and the contemporary human situation, and discover how, in this context, to point concretely to signs of hope and grace, of meaning and fulfillment in the midst of the ongoing struggle for the future of man.

Harvey Cox created something of a sensation by doing this in his discussion of the humanization of life in the secular city. A similar effort may be called for now in order to point to God's work of renewal in the social revolution. Our traditional discussions about God, his otherness and his sovereignty, may make little sense today, but we can describe the freedom, openness, and hope that are possible in a world over which he is Lord. A new generation may not pay attention to our former complicated discussions of eschatology, but they might be interested in an apocalyptic perspective on the present world that combined a sense of urgency about revolutionary change, the acceptance of the possibility of deepening crisis and tension in the present order, and expectant appropriation of new possibilities precisely in the midst of this crisis. We may not talk much about Jesus Christ, but we can point to his concrete benefits in the midst of our lives today. And out of this openness to crucifixion, a new theological resurrection may once again take place.

ALFONS AUER

The Christian
in a Technological World

Technological development has reached such a degree of intensity that it has brought about an inevitable crisis in the affairs of men. Pessimists believe that in the modern world the dignity of man must of necessity suffer more and more damage. The worker in particular is sacrificed to technological development. It is inconceivable with the advent of increasing mechanization and specialization that his work can continue to give him pleasure or develop his personality. The more advanced technology becomes, the more widespread are automation and uniformity. There is danger to one's status as a human being.

Optimists do not in any way deny the menacing dangers and existing disadvantages of the conveyor-belt and automation. But they believe that we are in a period of transition and that transition and suffering go hand-in-hand. A dozen advanced countries could be named in which a period of expansion has followed in the wake of their initial progress. And this makes the outlook rather bright. The characteristics of the new development are the abolition of strenuous physical work, a shortening of working hours, more extensive education, an increase in average life-expectancy and an improvement in the standard of living. J. Fourrastier summarized the results of the first one hundred and fifty years of technical progress with the words:

From *Open to the World* (Baltimore: Helicon Press, 1966), pp. 191–201, 212–15. Reprinted with permission of the publisher. For full footnote documentation, see original publication.

They neither degraded the human being nor forced him into the iron corset of mechanical determinism, as had been feared thirty or fifty years before. On the contrary, everything points to the fact that mechanization not only makes possible the unfettered development of man's highest faculties, but makes such a development necessary. Furthermore and above all, there is every indication that the invention and use of machinery, which for more than a century have compelled scientific endeavor to devote itself fully and exclusively to an investigation of fixed laws, and to neglect and deny all unstable phenomena, will lead to a second phase, namely a much clearer understanding of the entire world. Because of their contrasting features the laws of the machine will enable us to understand the laws of life.[1]

Here only one problem need concern us: How the Christian can and should fashion his spirituality in a world which is highly technological?

The Theology of Work to the Present Time

The French Dominican M. D. Chenu finds fault with the moralism in the current theology of work.[2] He refers to the much-cited passage of St. Thomas's *Summa Theologica*,[3] which deals with the fourfold purpose of work: the acquisition of necessary livelihood, and avoidance of the capital sin of idleness, the subjugation of the rebellious flesh by asceticism, and finally almsgiving made possible through an abundance of material goods. This reference to Thomas does not appear to be a very happy one, because in his Question entitled, "Concerning those things which are suitable for religious," Thomas certainly did not develop his complete theology of work. This would have been much too narrow a framework for his broad concept. But in view of the usual theology and preaching of the ethos of work one certainly cannot say that Chenu's criticism is unjustified. For work was seen as a form of penance and atonement, which should be undertaken in the spirit of the cross. The command of the Lord found in *Genesis*, namely, to dominate, was not overlooked, but the penitential character of work was very much in the

---

[1] J. Fourrastier, *Die gross Hoffnung des 20 Jahrhunderts* (Cologne: Deutz, 1956), pp. 8of.
[2] M. D. Chenu, *The Theology of Work* (English tr.) (Dublin: 1963; Chicago: Henry Regnery Company, 1966); cf. also G. Teichtweier, "Versuch einer Theologie der Arbeit," *Theological Quarterly*, CXXXVIII (1958), 307–29.
[3] *Summa Theol.*, II–IIae, 187, 3.

foreground. Certainly this is an important aspect of all work, and especially of technical work; but it is not the first and most important aspect, and certainly not the only one.

The inadequacy and one-sidedness of such a theology must now be obvious, since over a century and a half ago work emerged as a new reality with new goals, new structures and new functions. It was no longer of any avail to refer to the ascetic, charitable or catechetical value of work. The theological aspect would remain hidden as long as work was considered an affliction or a means of avoiding temptation. Neither did a mere reference to the cross serve any purpose, since it is not denied that from the example of the cross countless men of all ages have drawn priceless strength and patience for their work in life.

This reference to the cross was inadequate, because the "theology of the cross" is only part of salvation history; and for that reason it remained historically and morally one-sided. It lacked a comprehensive integration in the mysteries of creation, the incarnation and fulfillment of the world.

The inadequacy of the theology and preaching of work consisted also in the fact that there was no recognition of the dawning novelty of the concept of work in the technical world. M. D. Chenu was the first to elucidate this novelty within a theological context, and in so doing he rendered a great service. He demanded that the concept of work should be theologically re-appraised. Modern work is no longer the same as the work of the carpenter's shop at Nazareth, which up to the present had been accepted almost exclusively as a model in sermons on work.

What does Chenu regard as new in the presentday concept of work? It is above all the new goal: the spiritual penetration and domination of the world. In a technological world a man no longer works solely for the purpose of making a living, but rather in order to penetrate and dominate the world in a spiritual manner. The whole complex of methods, machines and men goes beyond the mere working for profit, even beyond capitalistic profit, to the realms of a higher form of world domination. According to Teilhard de Chardin it becomes a world where increasing leisure is balanced by a greater diversity of interests, so that all may be intensified, attempted and developed; a world in which giant telescopes and atomic piles cost more money and call forth more spontaneous admiration than all the bombs and cannons; a world in which the problem facing the average man (and not merely the research workers whose job it is) is to discover a secret, to establish a new force which is snatched from the atom, the firmament or from organic matter; a world in which one would rather stake one's life—as has often been done—to know and to be, rather than to possess.[4]

This universe, which is in the course of development, commands the responsibility and the support of all, the closer cooperation of men in a new unity in industry, in national and international society. Without reference to class, status or calling, men grow into a new, great community of work, into a new, universal solidarity. It may be a solidarity of fear as much as one of hope, but it is certain that the consciousnes of participating in a common work and of being a part of the whole of human nature, grows stronger and more powerful, and that this fraternal feeling will bring about, and indeed has already in part brought about, a social temperature unknown in history. This awakening of collective consciousness in human society, this advent of socialization—as it is described by Chenu—is the second new factor in the modern concept of work.

We now come to the third. Undoubtedly, the human factor has not been sufficiently stressed in the development of technical work to date. The conveyor-belt and automation restricted to an increasing degree the scope of individual effort and lessened the importance of its qualities. In the meantime, however, people began to be concerned about the physical, psychological and spiritual effects of technological progress on the individual. The critical period of reflection had begun. And there can be no question but that a new awareness of the human being resulted because of, or almost exclusively because of, even better methods of production. However, it must be admitted that the genuine cultivation of the human factor in work will in the long run bring about a spiritual and social appreciation of work itself.

To work only within the framework of the above-mentioned passage from St. Thomas Aquinas is to be considerably restricted concerning any inclusion of the new elements in the old theology of work. The same is true if one attempts to develop a biblical theology of work solely from those passages in the Bible on the ethos of work. The concept of Thomas Aquinas was much wider in meaning. His theology of work visualized clearly the cosmic influ-

[4] Teilhard de Chardin, *The Phenomenon of Man*, tr. Bernard Wall (London: 1959), p. 280.

ence of work, because it included in its scope the relation of work to the world as a whole. All the individual parts, their composition and interrelation, are directed in the final analysis towards the harmony of the whole. All individual things exist only to assist in the perfection of the whole. Man himself is a member of the entirety of the universe, and it is his lot, owing to his understanding of the plan of God, to play a decisive role in the perfecting of the cosmos. This is the view expressed in the Thomistic theology of work, and there is no difficulty in including here the first-named element in the modern concept of work, namely, the spiritual penetration and domination of the world.

St. Thomas sees also the social function of work. According to the design of the creator a mutual dependence exists between the individual and the community. The individual cannot attain perfection without the community, nor can the community without the individual. The latest development of work has shown that the social function is not exhausted by this reciprocal relationship. Technological work has brought about this "socialization." A new vision of the unity of the human race is in sight. It would appear that after centuries of divergence and division the great need for unity is felt. This presents theology with the task of going beyond the Thomistic view of reciprocal relationship and of reflecting again on the functions of work which concern the formation of society and the creation of unity, and this in terms of a great socio-theological concept.

Finally, the classical theology of work has always been aware that work does not merely help in the development of the order and beauty of the world and the life of the human race, but also in the personality of man himself. Man's resemblance to God fulfills itself only in matters of government; and the great virtues of work, which have always been stressed by theology, such as self-discipline, love of order, punctuality, responsibility, patience and objectivity among others, are merely the concrete realizations of man's likeness to God and indicate the way to man's perfection. And so it will appear to us that the modern technological world of work and the classical theology of work merge in the personal aspect of work— in the respect due to human beings. Work is an obligatory opportunity for man to perfect his personality; that is, theologically expressed, to realize his likeness to God.

The classical theology of work has dealt with all the aspects which confront us in the modern world of work. Understandably these points have not been fully developed. This was neither necessary nor possible; the conditions prevailing in former times did not call for it. But in modern times we cannot leave unattended the theology of work as it has developed to date; rather, we must confront it with modern concepts and realities. We also benefit in that it is brought home to us more clearly that the validity of what theology has to offer is explained only in the light of salvation history.

Work in the Light of Salvation History

The technological work of mankind is of its nature deeply theocentric. It represents a partnership in the creative and protective work of God, a partnership with God the creator. By creation in the Word, God has shared himself with the world as a rational basis. He has endowed man with intellectual ability in order that man may discover and appreciate the classifications and structural laws of creation. The cosmos is full of possibilities which await man in his search..., which are gradually discovered by him..., and which may be utilized for his purposes.... Technology, and natural science which is basic to it, are therefore thoroughly spiritual or intellectual activities; they receive their existence from the spiritual structure and law of the cosmos, and from the human intellect which is applied to them. Technological activity also pertains to the "explanation of God" (Nicolaus Cusanus).

Karl Barth is cautious in dealing with this partnership of man with God and with man's role as a perfecting instrument in the work of creation.[5] He fears that this might allow mankind too much independence and creative preoccupation and hence might detract from the majesty of God. This fear appears completely unfounded in a radical theocentrism to which a proper understanding of the mystery of creation is essential, even in technological matters....

It is said that in the lilies of the fields and the birds of the air man experiences a greater awareness of what it means to be a creature than in a grand piano or a television set. In contrast to Old Testament spirituality for which the "secondary causes" of nature or in history operated in the shadow of the creative "first cause," namely God, modern man is so engrossed in the efficiency of technology with all its "miracles," that the image of the God of creation

[5] Cf. K. Barth, *Die kirchliche Dogmatik*, III/4 (Zürich: Zöllikon, 1951), p. 596.

is often almost completely excluded. This is similar to the view of many Christians who believe that the creative activity of God was restricted to the beginning of the world; hence, in practice, they are infected with deism. This deistic misunderstanding can be cleared up only by making known the constant reality of the influence of God upon material things and human activity. The man who believes in creation says: "I do not start from the beginning; I start with something, at something and on something. It already has in it its being, its law, its order, its rule—a system to which I am bound, as soon as I raise my hand to it. Such admitted dependence specifies my dominion over creation and prevents me from seeing my own glory as that which is absolute. . . . Here we stand on solid biblical ground. For here work is seen as a reflection of God's work of creation and avoids any suggestion that work is something autonomous.

The further consequences of technology of which we have still to speak, the cosmic, social and personal, do not exist as independent considerations adjacent to the theocentric, but are rather included in it.

Technological activity is no longer concerned only with providing for everyday needs, but rather with the spiritual penetration of the cosmos. The lasting creation of God and human participation in creation would be without honor for God and men, if the mere management of forms, complete and perfect for all time, were the purpose of their work. But God created these forms and classifications only as "seminal powers" . . . , and thus imparted a dynamic power to the divine and human activity in the world for the duration of history. Man develops the embryonic basic forms to their completed stature and condition. And this endeavor is a constant process. It is unthinkable that a time should ever come when a man can placidly fold his arms, because he has exhausted all the possibilities of the cosmos. This dynamic understanding of creation and human participation in it does not make the original act of creation less, but rather greater than the earlier more static understanding of it. For it embraces, in addition to all existing things, all that is in the future, whether arising from nature or deduced by man. What was created in the beginning, contains all potential future change.

No matter what progress is made through simplification and automation, it will never exceed the possibilities latent in things and in the universe. Until a few centuries ago mankind had to be content with a philosophy of the world which today appears to have been summary. The less they knew of the structural laws of the material order, the more deeply did they grasp the nature of values and the content of symbols. . . . At any rate it is certain that in the meantime man has discovered to a degree never suspected the proper order in things, and has used them in the past and will use them even more in the future. . . . [T]he Bible seems to make no allusion to this dynamic element in technological work. It would be equally astonishing if the Bible contained directives on the ethics of work, which in the existing stage of technological development would have been unthinkable and unintelligible. One need only unfold the sense of the account of creation in order to find a clear answer to our problem. It is also of deep theological significance that in striving to understand the nature of technology, one arrives at an understanding of the order and structure of things, the truth of existence, which is to be found nowhere else but in the Word of creation.

Technological and economic development has prompted new social initiatives. The task of the spiritual penetration and domination of the cosmos is so powerful that it can be accomplished only by the coming together of all in a universal human community. In the beginning God created human beings as a whole, as a unity. Perhaps nothing recalls this unity ordained by God so clearly as the recently apparent oneness in hope and fear among all men on earth which has been caused by technological progress. M. D. Chenu, who speaks of this event of socialization with genuine pathos, perhaps overestimated the actual human and ethical value of this new community-consciousness. Without doubt the economic and technological progress which has forced the desire to be united as one human community, offers an ethical obligation and a real opportunity to bring this about.

Much will have happened before human beings thus forced will become aware of the dangers of a mass type of existence and react against them. The new social temperature is only tacitly admitted by many; in many other cases there is no recognition at all. But as history has proved, the intellectual mastery of such situations will usually be accomplished in the first place freely and consciously only among an élite. In this way a freer and more consciously activated awareness of community can be effected in a wider sphere. In any event, technological development has brought to mind anew the created unity of the human race, and has already looked to it as the only possibility for a successful future.

In this coordination of the technological penetration of the cosmos and its consequences for the human community, the personal aspect of human work is brought to fulfilment. The dignity of man consists in the fact that he reflects the image of God on earth. This he achieves through his mode of existence, namely, his spirituality, his freedom and his ruling position in the world. But the likeness of man to God achieves its final fulfillment only in activity. The active man rather than the passive one is the perfect reflection of God. In the same way work is the expression and the coefficient of man's own likeness to God.

A wider and indeed more fundamental significance of this human likeness to God is contained in the fact that man regards God as the all-embracing center of the universe. As God spans all things in the absolute sense—so does the human being in the relative sense. All stages of existence are assembled in him—nature, spirit and, in the created image which we call grace, even the divine life. Matter and spirit are united in man and joined to God. Through his body man is composed essentially of a joint nature, and the cosmos and all the possibilities it contains are entrusted to him and enjoined on him. Because he realizes them through his technical efforts, he fulfills his own being in which nature and the spirit are united. He becomes more a man than he was previously. His ontological position as head and center of the cosmos becomes greater existentially through his technological domination of the cosmos. Because man admits and takes seriously his incarnate nature also in its cosmic development, he fulfils his role as a being composed of spirit and matter as ordained by God and placed by him in the center of the world.

.   .   .

We know little of the final state of perfection of the universe. Yet we know enough to realize that there will be a new earth and a new heaven, and that Christ as the *pantokrator* will rule them. We have already shown that there are two views regarding heaven and the life of the chosen ones. The one which we can call "ecstatic" visualizes the elect as completely filled with the glorious majesty and love of the triune God, and so completely carried away by it that no other "activity" is conceivable other than the contemplation of God. Other theologians attribute even to the chosen ones in heaven a certain "bodily activity"—and this is said with the greatest sincerity. They argue from the earthly life of Jesus. He is the carpenter's son who carries on a small earthly trade, and he is at the same time the son of God who participates in the divine inner life. From this point of view, they do not consider it impossible that

> ... the elect, although they are living the life of the Trinity which is their greatest happiness, may also be able to develop simply and simultaneously their entire and ineffably glorified humanity in a renewed cosmos in virtue of all the potentialities of earthly transactions with which their refined and powerfully "pneumatic" bodies will provide them.... Why should not the blessed be capable of the most wonderful changes in the cosmos to enable them to pass over in a supreme development from the possible to the actual? [6]

In this way, technological activity appears to be a preparation for the final redemption. The creation, the incarnation and the descent of the Holy Spirit are not instantaneous salvific acts in the sense that being once accomplished they are like human actions, namely over and done with. Rather they establish a new beginning, and they give permanence to it. If the human being engaged in technological matters regards himself as a partner in these enduring divine works of redemption, then his work is no longer merely spiritual penetration and dominion of the world, but rather a fashioning of this imperfect and formless world to the image of that perfect one. This is achieved by the influence of certain images of the final cosmos which are located in the present, and which are designated [as part of] creation.... Material nature participates in the prologue of its inclusion in the supernatural glorious order of eternity. Therefore the divine majesty receives from it perfect praise, and the Christian finds in the service of nature an increased power of further development. To be sure, death and earthly destruction signify major alterations, and the kingdom will come from above as a completely new one. But this new kingdom is not opposed to the existing one and does not destroy it; rather does it exalt and complete it. This exaltation and completion is already in progress. The future has already begun. Recently H. Rondet has emphatically underlined this demand for a completion of a theology of work through a positive eschatology. The less platonically inclined Middle Ages had already partly over-

---

[6] G. Thils, *Theologie der irdischen Wirklichkeiten*, (Salzburg: n.d.) p. 202.

come the traditional point of view which was still strongly influenced by Greek thought.

> Now perhaps the time has come to pose this eschatological problem more directly. Is one to suppose that nothing will remain of all the works of man, but his love and the good intention which prompted their realization? What would the risen Gutenberg be if he had a body identical with his own earthly physical body but without any relationship to the invention which made him famous? What would a Christian painter be without his work, a musician without his symphonies, a poet without his poems? And is absolutely nothing to remain of the tremendous development of modern industry, nothing of the achievements of engineers or of workers? Must one then be content with the medieval theology of *solvet saeclum in favilla*, "heaven and earth in ashes burning"? [7]

Because the Christian believes in the resurrection of the body, he believes also in the completion of the technological effort in the transfiguration of the world, and also in the completion, in the communion of saints, of the process of socialization which has been fostered by technology.

In order to arrive at a theological definition of work, and in particular technological work, it is not sufficient to refer to the historical Christ and his example of work, or to his suffering on the cross, or to choose from the Bible extracts which deal indirectly with work. This approach can be fruitful if one includes the historical Christ and the biblical statements on work in a total theological concept which embraces a period from the word of creation and the Christ-event to its conclusion in the Parousia.

... Christian understanding of technological matters is not completely derived from the mystery of creation, but rather ... it gets its final directives from the message of Christ. In order to avoid all misunderstanding it must be asserted again that the order of salvation is not identical with the order of creation; both must be clearly differentiated, one from the other. This is of course possible only in the abstract, but it is necessary nevertheless. In concrete reality they are of course not to be separated. Whoever would separate their mutual involvement cannot properly understand either one or the other. It has been shown sufficiently clearly that creation without redemption is incomplete. Only in the complete realization of salvation, that is in the second coming of Christ, can it attain its comple-

---

[7] H. Rondet, *Die Theologie der Arbeit*, p. 64.

tion as creation. It is from the beginning so essentially directed towards salvation that, were it excluded from the order of salvation, it would fall short in a decisive manner of its preordained destiny. On the other hand, the complete order of salvation is not conceivable unless it embraces creation in its entirety. Because physical nature is proper to its essence, perfect physical nature is proper to its perfection. Once again, the two orders are not identical; they are distinguishable one from the other, but in concrete reality they are united. The body belongs to the head and the flesh to the Word.

From the very beginning creation is "the potential body" of the order of salvation. From the incarnation on, the activation of this potential body is in process and not only during the historical life of Jesus but for ever, because the Holy Spirit ever carries on the work of Christ through the whole course of history until the two orders converge in the completion. Then the order of creation will be the body of the Word and as such participating fully in the glory of the Word, who at the same time is the head of humanity and of the cosmos.

JAMES M. GUSTAFSON

A Theology
of Christian Community

One of the more overworked clichés about modern technological society and the churches' participation in it runs something like
this: In modern society there is a profound alienation of man from
the structures of work, politics and other aspects of life. The large,
powerful public world seems to be managed by a few persons in
the seats of power or, in the view of analysts, appears to be running not only itself, but the persons who are supposed to manage
it. The church has no way of influencing these centers of real power
in the world, for in an age of secularization its moral authority is
no longer recognized, and it lacks the modes of exercise of social
power to become a significant pressure group to countermand the
tendencies that appear to be against its understanding of what life is
meant to be. Alongside this powerful ordered public world is the
private world of person-to-person relationships, of family life and of
individual existence. It is in this sphere that some of the protests
against the alienation from the structured world take place—the re-
bellions of youth or the efforts to achieve some compensating meaningful life by concentrating on family activities. The church, we are
told, has become functional with reference only to this private
sphere. And even here its role has become supportive, therapeutic,
pastoral and even idolatrous, for it functions to give religious sanc-
tions to a culturally defined pattern of life that is itself not sufficiently subjected to theological and moral criticism.

The effect of much persuasive writing in this vein, by Marxists

From *Man in Community*, ed. Egbert de Vries (New York: Association Press,
1966), pp. 175–93. Reprinted with permission of the World Council of Churches.

and existentialists, by theologians and some Christian sociologists, by world-renowned philosophers and street-corner culture critics, has been to create a mood of hostility toward the church even on the part of many who continue to call themselves Christians. The churches are seen to be part of the problem of alienation, for they have been attending to institutional demands for self-preservation, to cheap piety and to concern only for the private sphere, none of which rectifies in the least the moral impotence of institutional Christianity. They represent religion, and this, on testimony from antibourgeois theologians, is bad. The avant-garde Christians then call us to a radical secularity that, we are to assume, overcomes the embarrassment of church life which seems to be merely pious and private in its morality, and institutional in its demands. Secularity also presumably overcomes the distance between Christian faith and the centers of power where things that really matter for the life of man are taking place.

Certain assumptions that inform this perspective need to be brought under serious question. They are both sociological-historical and theological in character. We may ask whether the division between the private and the public, the personal and the structural is not too sharply drawn, and whether significant relations do not exist between them. We may also ask, from a social-psychological perspective, where the person-forming communities are going to be in a program of action that looks with disdain upon the church and other "private" spheres. What is to shape the mind and the spirit of the person who is told to be completely identified with the "world"? What is to provide a center of his own personal existence which informs his involvement in the secular order when religion, as a historical movement influencing persons and cultures, is apparently not to be cultivated? What kind of sociological assumptions lie behind the view that Christians can be socially more effective by involvement in secular institutions, since it is through these that history is being shaped, while at the same time the institutions and the religious culture that shape the Christians are judged to be increasingly useless? Where, also, is the positive place of custom and of cultural values, of *ethos*, in this critical material? In the antibourgeois stance, have critics failed to distingush between false and suppressive moral customs and order, on the one hand, and the positive significance of cultural morality, on the other?

There appear to be theological assumptions lurking in this kind of social analysis as well. They are many, and they do not form a single consistent school. Insofar as the social analysis moves to the cultivation of an existentialist mood, one wonders if God is not seen primarily in terms of the accepter of persons, the lord who wills meaningful moments of self-realization in personal terms, rather than the sovereign ruler of depersonalized institutions as well. The mission of the church becomes focused too exclusively on the personal and interpersonal. Insofar as the social analysis leads to the glorification of the secular world, where Christ's lordship is presumably being worked out, one wonders whether that world, like the church, is not also deeply corrupted by unfaith and rebellion against God. One wonders sometimes whether we cannot rely upon Christ's presence and lordship in the church, and indeed through religion, as much as we can rely upon his lordship being exercised through social crisis and social change. There is a stress on secularity without adequate delineation of how Christians judge the secular. Insofar as the social analysis separates the realm of the personal from the impersonal, but assumes that God's dominion is pressing in upon both, one wonders whether there is not the legacy of a Lutheran theology and a Brunner theology that sees God doing work with persons through the gospel with his right hand and with institutions through the law with his left hand, in such a way that these are spatially or chronologically separated. The realms of redemption and of preservation become sharply divided, with a different ethic for each.

Debate over adequate social analysis and over theological assumptions has some significant effects on the actual life of the Christian community within the wider community. Our institutional forms and activities are guided in part by the sociological perceptions and theological interpretations. The establishment of "coffee houses" as places of ministry adjacent to college campuses in the United States, for example, is informed often by cryptosociological assumptions about what the actual situation of society is—one in which students are alienated and thus must be ministered to in terms of that alienation. It is also informed by crypto-theologies, believing that God's grace is known in the intimacies of coffee, poetry and jazz, and is not known in the course of study or in the world of "establishment." The founding of centers for discussion of vocational and political problems may assume not only that the churches as they are now organized cannot effectively speak to the world, but also that conversation about the world without embarrassing reference to theological conviction and to religious interest is the way in which God (if there is a God) works in the modern world. I do not intend to be overly critical of the new forms of witness and mission, since for both sociological and theological reasons I affirm their place in the life of the church. As many have noted, the traditional routinized activities of institutional churches in all parts of the world also certainly rest upon sociological perceptions and theological interpretations that have to be brought under question.

It is my intention in the main body of this essay to suggest an interpretation of community, based upon sociological and theological perspectives, which I hope is more adequate to sources of truth and of insight than some perspectives that are currently in vogue or are historically influential in the life of the Christian community.

The Functions of Community in the Light of God's Purposes

What purposes of God are being realized in the existence of men in community? We should have in mind all three aspects of human community: cultural ethos, interpersonal relationship and institutions. My answer to this question hinges on a number of verbs: God creates, sustains, restrains and makes possible better qualities of life through the existence of men in all three aspects of community.[1]

Common life in various segments of humanity is a means by which God's *creative purposes* bear fruit for men. What is new emerges out of the common life of the old. Human creative achievement takes place within the patterns of life in which persons are related to each other, whether one is thinking of biological procreation, development of new forms of social organization, novel patterns of art and music or scientific and technological developments. Creative work is related to the past in dependence upon it, as well as in rebellion against it. Creative persons are sustained by communities as well as by defending themselves against them. The continuities need to be stressed in an age that is preoccupied with finding discontinuities and with celebrating the novel. Underlying these

[1] This section has clear echoes of the thought of my late colleague and teacher, H. Richard Niebuhr, which I readily and gratefully acknowledge, although he would not necessarily have approved of precisely what I have done here.

achievements of men is the potentiality and purpose of newness, or creativity, which is part of God's gracious gift to men in the giving of life. Two examples will make clear how God's creative purposes are achieved through human community.

Newness in human understanding of the physical world is one of the forms of creativity that dazzle the mind. The fresh interpretations we are given, not only of the minutest possible sources of life and energy in the physical world, but also of the relations of the constellations of "universes" to each other, enable men not only to understand the natural world of which they are a part, but also to participate in it with greater intelligence and to master aspects of it for human purposes. Creativity in the world of natural science, however, is not a matter of one person in isolation contemplating introspectively or calculating on the basis of his individual observations. It is a communal enterprise. There is a community of scientists, evoking criticisms and responses from each other, building upon each other's observations and theories, in communication with each other through their own abstract symbols and words. Creativity in perception and understanding, surely in the divine providence a possibility and purpose given by God, is born of intense life in a human community.

Even where the individual appears to "break through" with radical novelty, he is participating in an ongoing community. The rejection or transformation of a traditional pattern in one of the arts, for example, does not come into being as a creative act out of nothing. It takes place as a creative virtuoso responds to the inadequacies of a tradition for the purpose of expressing what he perceives in the world, or what he feels about himself and his world. Novel forms are not *de novo* forms; they are creative responses to patterns that have been given. The discontinuities can be great, as for example in the development of the twelve-tone scale in music, but nevertheless a community is present—one over against which the new is defined; and quickly a new community is born, developing the fresh pattern. Newness, creativity, comes into being through the existence of common life.

Common life is a means by which God sustains human existence in the world. There is an ordering of existence, changing in its particular forms, to be sure, that provides for the continuity of life. Human life is sustained by the continuities of custom and belief, of values and ideas, as well as by the creative perceptions which alter the traditions of men. The ethical importance of custom and of ethos is an area neglected by many Christian interpreters of society today, probably because a defense of it seems in the West to be a defense of a bourgeois outlook, and many Protestant theologians wish above all to be differentiated from that. Life is sustained by the meaning that one person has for another in friendship and marriage, in pastoral relationship and teaching. It is sustained by the ordering of economic and political power through civil law and through institutions of commerce, police power, trade unions and family. Even when men revolt against a given institution or custom that has sustained them in the past, they seek not the absence of community, but a new community organized by a different institutional form, or by a different set of customary standards. The sustaining power of the tribe is cast aside in the aspiration that the nation will take its place as the formative community. The rigid extrinsic code morality of nineteenth-century tradition is rejected in the hope that a more meaningful morality, intrinsic to man's deepest needs or to his Christian life, will come into being. Sustaining patterns of life deserve a dignity in a Christian interpretation of community that is sometimes overlooked, particularly in a time of revolutions and when individuals find custom and tradition to be so oppressive that authentic human existence is often defined in terms of radical freedom from them.[2]

A part of the sustaining function of community is the restraints that it places on individuals and on other communities. The organized interests of one nation act to restrain the aggressive interests of another. The fighters for justice for those who are oppressed are limited in the means by which their struggle can be executed by the existence of a community that concerns itself for the preservation of civil order. The willful inclinations of the antisocial indi-

---

[2] A question is implicit here that deserves long and serious study. One gets the impression that much of the Christian social leadership and experimentation is now directed toward those who are alienated from the past and from present communities, and some of it makes for an attitude not just of criticism of "establishment," but of sheer rebellion against establishment as a prime virtue. I do not wish to suggest that particular attention to the depressed and the "outsiders" is not important, but some of it is being given to the neglect of meaningful interpretation of the significance of pattern and order for human beings, and of the ways in which old orders can be reformed to fulfill better the necessary functions of human social life. We seem to be much clearer about the oppressions of custom and institutions that sustain us than we are about their positive functions in the sustaining of human life, and thus about how these patterns themselves can be altered better to fulfill their essential moral purposes.

vidual are restrained by the existence of mores and customs, as well as by the civil law and the powers of police enforcement. The personal community of family is not only a pattern in which its members sustain each other physically, mentally and spiritually, but also one in which limits are set upon the activities of each other by the obligations of its members toward one another and toward the family as a whole.

Through communities the ordering (sustaining and restraining) work of God for the sake of men takes place. New patterns of this work come into being, and older patterns pass away. One of the mistakes of those who define "orders" of creation and preservation is that they often find a kind of revealed positive sociology in the fact that men exist within family and state, as if there were a clear pattern for these institutions ordained by God. This, as has often been seen, can lead to a false identification of an existing historical pattern with the divine order, and thus to an uncritical, conservative acceptance of a *status quo*. We have now properly learned to speak of ordering rather than orders, in the light of the errors of the past. Or to use a different set of words, community can be interpreted functionally, as accomplishing purposes needed for human life. Its particular form or order is to be judged by its effectiveness in fulfilling its morally purposive functions. God sustains and restrains life through the functions of state and family and other institutions, as well as the historical occasions for them occur; through the development of mass public education, through the work of universities and their institutes, through political parties, through labor unions and through international organizations.

Through community, God also makes better qualities of life possible for men. Indeed, while sin is not redeemed by community, God's redemptive love can take particular historical force and form through the relations that persons have with and for each other. Even civil law, as an establishment of new patterns of justice and order in human society, functions to bring new possibilities or qualities of life into being in particular societies. The order of law and the order of society can be the means by which God's love makes possible better existence both for social groups and for individuals.

Community, then, through God's creative use of it, has a high order of theological dignity in a Christian interpretation; it is not merely something oppressive, hostile to authentic life, embodying sin and prejudice. The social mission of the church, in turn, needs to be related to each of these aspects of human community, with each of the aspects of God's purposes in view.

It would be very one-sided, however, to acknowledge that the corrupt, the demonic, the sinful did not also exist in human community. At least since the time of A. Ritschl and W. Rauschenbusch we have come to understand the existence of "kingdom [or perhaps better, realm] of sin." To cite the positive significance of custom and tradition for human community in the economy of God does not imply that custom cannot be perverse and run counter to God's purposes for man. The embedding of racial prejudice within social custom is one case in point. Tradition can also be oppressive, functioning as an idol that prohibits men from responding to the call of God in the openness of the present. To cite the sustaining and even redeeming importance of interpersonal relations, of being for the other person, is not to imply that such relations cannot be demonic and destructive, cannot be the means by which perverse domination of one person over the other takes place, or the means by which inhuman servility of one person under the other is justified. To suggest the positive ethical importance of institutions and civil arrangements in the human community is not to deny the existence of unjust laws, or the magnifying of the effects of human selfishness through the use of economic and social power over workers, or over a nation. Indeed, corruption, perversion, distortion of purpose exist within each of these aspects of human community; human relations are a realm both of sin and of God's creative, ordering and redeeming presence. They are constantly under the judgment of the presence of God; they are constantly in need of prophetic criticism and reformation; indeed, they also await the full redemption that is to come. But we err if we see only their perversity, or if we fail to give them a high level of dignity in our understanding of God's work for men.

Community and Moral Action

These same patterns of God's care for man that are apparent in human community are also the patterns of mutual service, responsibility and obligation within which men are called to moral action. Christians together in the church are particularly called to interpret their existence in community as the location in time and space of their responsibility to God for human society and for other persons. To participate in a cultural ethos, in a moral tradition, is to have responsibility for that ethos and tradition. To be personally related to another is joyfully to serve the other and to be obligated for his well-being. To function as a person within an institution is to see the power of the institution as the means for the upbuilding of humanity and to acknowledge the responsibility of the institution for the preservation of justice, liberty and order in the world. The patterns of common life are patterns of service, responsibility and obligation in a Christian interpretation of community, to God and to men. They are patterns in and through which moral activity takes place.

In response to God's goodness man freely and joyfully serves not only individual neighbors, but the common life that binds men together. This is most easily seen in the realm of interpersonal relations. The other is one whom I love, one whose good I can seek, one whose presence I can sustain, one whose despair I can help to overcome, one in whose presence I have delight and joy. Existence in family life makes the details of this clear. In his love, God has given the others to me: wife or husband, and children. In their love for me, the others sustain my life and bring to it joy and delight. In response to the love of God and the love of others, freely given, faithfully given service is an expression of moral action. But service is not confined to the interpersonal.

Participation in a location of responsibility in an institution is also a call to service. Consciousness of the care of God for the human community through government and university, through voluntary associations and political parties, evokes a response of grateful service to others through these institutions. They are the spheres in which freedom, love and concern are expressed. Their own internal structures can be shaped in part by expressions of freely given love and care. They can be shaped in part to be consonant with purposes that express the Christians' response to God's goodness.

Life in community is also life in common responsibility.[3] It is the acceptance of accountability for the shaping of the values and customs that inform much of the unconscious responses and actions of the members of the human community. Community is held together by custom and tradition; good and evil are embedded in custom and tradition; custom and tradition shape the character of

[3] For a succinct account of the nature of responsibility, see H. R. Niebuhr, *The Responsible Self* (New York: Harper & Row, Publishers, 1963).

persons and institutions so that loyalties and convictions drawn from
them inform the responses and actions of persons, even when they
are not aware of them. Persons with a minimum experience of cultural pluralism within a nation or across national boundaries are
conscious of the fact that attitudes, emotive expressions of moral
convictions, words and sections often express cultural values different from their own. Part of the pattern of responsibility in community is responsibility for these often inarticulated values, customs
and traditions.

The Christian community has the responsibility to articulate and
criticize this glue of custom that holds societies together. If tradition and custom regard Negroes or certain castes as inferior and dic-
tate prejudiced attitudes and actions toward such groups, it is the
responsibility of the Christian community to engage in the alteration
of these forces. If tradition and custom sustain respect for personal
liberty and inviolability of conscience against powers that seek to
invade and manipulate men, the Christian community has a responsibility to maintain and strengthen these forces. Such forces have in
many instances no definite location: There is not always an institution that is dedicated to the cultivation of the evil or the good that
is present in an ethos. Yet through instruction, prophetic writing,
the nurturing of the minds and spirits of children and other means,
the Christian community can exercise influence in shaping the forces
that in turn invisibly shape the attitudes, responses and actions of
men.

Interpersonal relations are relations of responsibility. They exist
not merely as occasions of joyfully given service, and certainly not
merely as occasions for self-realization. Faithfulness of one for the
other is an aspect of the interpersonal. To be for the person is to be
faithful to the other person, to accept responsibility for the well-
being of the other. Through interpersonal relations, God cares for
the well-being both of the self and of the other. As active persons
in these relations, Christians interpret them as occasions of responsibility to God for the care of others. As the promises of the marriage service so vividly suggest, to be related as husband and wife
is to be related not only in freely given affection, but to be responsible for each other. Indeed, responsibility for each other is a structure of love, not merely the occasion for love. It is a pattern of
service and responsibility. Parents are located in a pattern of responsibility to God for the well-being of their children. Friendship, if

it is not confused with mere acquaintance (as it often is in the United States), is not just the enjoyment of each other, taking delight in the presence of each other; it is also the acceptance of responsibility for the needs of each other. To be for the other person is to be responsible for the other person.

The formal and informal patterns of relationships established within institutions and between them are clearly patterns of responsibility. As active agents in institutions, Christians particularly interpret them as centers of power and influence the conduct of which has moral consequences in the society, and therefore institutions are to be understood in terms of moral responsibility. This responsibility is not a thing, a substance, as it were, that institutions could have. It is rather to be articulated in detailed terms for particular institutions; for the political party, the management of a small business and so forth. Christian interpretation asks certain questions of institutions: For what is this institution responsible? How do its purposes cohere with an informed understanding of the manner and ends of life that Christians believe to be consonant with what God is seeking to say and to do? How can persons in institutions act to give direction to their activities so that the well-being of humanity is sustained and improved by the policies and activities of institutions? In the divine economy, institutions and their relations to each other are patterns of social life in and through which moral responsibility—to God, for the human community—are exercised.

Obligation—a stronger word than responsibility—also enters in. Life in community is life in a structure of moral obligations, of claims upon persons and of claims upon groups. To participate in the community of custom and tradition is to be obligated to God for its rectitude and its nurture, for its continuity insofar as its effects reflect an understanding of what God wills to do for men, and for its alteration insofar as it is a corruption of what God seeks to do and to say. To be sure, the Christian community is in a sense emancipated from cultural ethos; it certainly does not find its final righteousness and justification in its responsibility for the customs and traditions of the society of which it forms a part. Its loyalty to God gives it a position over against custom and tradition, its faith gives it a freedom from bondage to social custom and tradition. But this freedom ought not to imply that the Christian community has no obligation to God for the sustenance and cultivation of those customs and traditions which can be a means of God's governing and edifying work in the world. I have sought to make a case for the positive function of culture in the divine economy; if such a case is made, the Christian community is obligated to God, who rules and upbuilds through culture for the moral quality of that culture.

Mutual obligation is an aspect of interpersonal relations as well. Personal relations, if they are significant, exist over long periods of time and across the boundaries of spatial separation. To be for the other person is to delight in his presence; it is also to be responsible for him, to be obligated to him. In many forms of personal relationship there is a formal rite which not only confirms that two persons will be faithful to each other, but that they are obligated to each other. The marriage service is again an excellent example of this fact. There, a covenant is made between two persons, before God and a congregation of his people, which details some of the obligations that exist, by virtue not only of the freely given love of one for the other, but of the fact that this love is a faithful and responsible love. As such, it is fitting that there be an articulated, determined detailing of the structure of obligations that both express love and nourish love. Obligation in personal relations is not antithetical to love; it is a form of responsible and faithful love. Marriage is not the only interpersonal relationship in which this is the case.[4]

"Steadfastness" or faithfulness as an aspect of interpersonal relations, with the implied duties and obligations toward each other, is a part of the Old Testament interpretation both of covenant and of love. It is not a nineteenth-century or post-Kantian imposition of extrinsic rules or duties upon persons. It is part of the Christian conviction, born of God's revelation of himself, that informs the church's understanding of relations between persons. In the time of a "new morality" that comes into being under Christian auspices,

---

[4] An American is constrained to comment at this point upon the difference between the casual interpersonal relations of his society and the formalized relations of the Continent. Friendship and acquaintance have come to mean virtually the same thing for many Americans: There is no sense of being responsible for the other person by virtue of friendship, and no sense of obligation that gives the other a serious claim upon one. There are no little rites that signify a transition in the character of the relationship. By contrast, the mutual consent to move from the polite to familiar form of "you" in more traditional societies symbolizes not only that two persons are at home in each other's company, but that they virtually pledge themselves to a kind of faithfulness to each other which may entail responsibilities and obligations. The interpretation I am giving to interpersonal relationships obviously would place a high value upon such articulations of a "covenant" even if made only in the mutual consent to address each other in the more familiar forms of speech.

a morality that smacks of a kind of shallow concern with self-realization, it is perhaps even more important to see the significance of the structure of personal relations as a structure of mutual obligations of persons to each other and for the consequences of their common life.[5]

In the institutional spheres of life, the aspect of obligation is more clearly seen. Institutions have rules and laws which articulate the obligations that persons have toward each other, and the duties that they have toward the institution. But a Christian interpretation is not a mere support of obedience to institutional laws and rules; it is rather an understanding that institutions and those acting in and through them are obligated to God for the conduct of affairs, and thus obligated to the persons and society of which they are a part for the actions and effects of the state, the economy and so forth. Institutions are locations in which man's obligations to God and to other men have a concreteness, a virtually material quality, which expresses man's moral discernment and care. The Christian community is obligated first to God and then to and for the institutions in and through which duties toward God and the neighbors can be carried out.

Implications for the Mission of Church to Society

Some suggestions about the implications of this interpretation for the work of the church seem to be in order. It is not for me to spell them out in terms of practical programs, but only to indicate stresses and correctives that appear to be required in the present situation.

First, and most obvious, is the need to keep all three aspects of community in view. Those activities of the churches and other agencies that view the Christian concern to be primarily personal obviously tend to neglect the institutional patterns of society. The concern for the personal often leads to a disengagement from the realm of the technical and the impersonal. Indeed, there are theologi-

---

[5] One looks in vain for any serious discussion of obligations in the books that often are covered by the appellation "new morality," such as J. A. T. Robinson's chapter, "The New Morality," in *Honest to God* (London: SCM Press; Philadelphia: Westminster Press, 1963) and Paul Lehmann's *Ethics in a Christian Context* (New York: Harper & Row, Publishers, 1963). One suspects this is so because obligation suggests law, and law seems to be antithetical to an ethics of grace in which the "divine indicative" has such clear centrality of attention.

cal options that encourage this disengagement by judging the realms of technology, bureaucracy and other forms of organized social and economic power to be virtually demonic, and at least to be detrimental to the ends that the Christian message seems to have in view. It becomes difficult to move from the existential and the personal to the technological and institutional if one's interpretation of modern communities, in theological and sociological terms, places the weight of importance and dignity on the realm of subjectively meaningful existence. The kind of mutual involvement that develops between persons through the impersonal patterns of large-scale social organizations provides, in the light of my interpretation, both for significant, meaningful life, and for moral activity in giving direction to the course of human events. God's purposes, as discerned in the Scripture and in tradition, relate to the historical course of events, and *ipso facto* to technology, bureaucracy and other aspects of industrial societies that are of crucial importance in our time.

Second, these activities on the part of churches and other agencies that are institution- and "world"-oriented must not lose sight of the importance of the "private" and the personal as spheres that sustain persons in their institutions, and more particularly as places in which there is a formation of outlook and of values that in turn deeply affects the kind of judgments and actions that persons make in their "offices" or institutional responsibilities. The private sphere is not only a place of escape from the pressures of the institutional sphere; it is not only the location of a pastoral and therapeutic concern that can never be ruled out of the purposes of the Christian gospel. It is a place in which are formed the attitudes, reflective moral commitments and motives that persons carry into the institutional and technical world. Choices, moral judgments and actions reflect in part the commitments, loyalties, values and motivations that are nurtured and reshaped in the sphere of interpersonal existence. If an understanding of community as a process of action within orderly patterns has validity, attention has to be paid to the spheres within which moral habits, character, decisions, indeed, virtues and their opposites are shaped.

Third, the interpretation given in this essay calls for a far more extensive place for the virtues than popularly exists in Protestant ethics today. Basic selfhood is shaped in the "private" and interpersonal spheres, in the family, the congregation and other centers where the attitudes and values of persons are formed, criticized and in part re-formed. Protestant theology has for too long tended to assume that the language of the "virtues" necessarily implied an uncritical approval of bourgeois attitudes, or suggested that to take the task of shaping the conscience, or of shaping virtues seriously is to live by self-righteousness and law rather than by grace. Indeed, in societies which are undergoing rapid change, with traditional external standards in flux, it is all the more important that the basic loyalties and convictions of persons shall have a measure of stability and clarity, so that their participation in the world may receive direction and purpose.

Fourth, participation in institutions on the part of the members of the Christian community ought to be governed in part by their life of faith, and by purposes, objectives, means of action that reflect the Christian gospel and are informed by the ethical reflection of the community. Life in the church is life revivified by fresh apprehension of God as the sovereign ruler of the world, by renewed dedication to his purposes that is engendered by worshiping him, by informed conscientiousness about the responsibilities and actions in the world that are coherent with the church's understanding of what God seeks to have this world be. It is in the common life of the church that both intentions and dispositions on the internal, subjective side, and purpose and patterns of life on the external, objective side are to be engendered, fashioned, critically scrutinized and articulated. There is no doubt that the churches as we know them have been remiss in fulfilling this moral function, but we have no other historical social unit within which these functions, in allegiance to Jesus Christ, are performed.

Fifth, culture, or ethos must not be left out of the purview of Christian interpretation and action in society. It is notoriously difficult to influence, since its values and styles are developed by so many different agencies. Protestant churches, and others as well, when they have addressed the problems of culture, have often made sweeping critical attacks about "materialism" rather than finding ways in which to influence the goals and purposes that persons seem to absorb from their milieu. The place that is given to culture in the interpretation offered in this essay calls for a continuous dialogue between the Christian community and other groups, all of which are involved in the shaping of culture. There are signs that this is occurring in the critiques of movies, television, advertising, novels, business ethos and other distillations of culture that have been published under the auspices of Christian churches. Rejection of culture is largely gone as a stance of the Christian community. But apart from persistent critique of it, accompanying our constant involvement in it, we are seriously faced with the temptation to become a new generation of culture Christians, and in our critique of it we often fail in two respects: The faith becomes too readily identified only with the movements of protest against mass culture, and it begins to look as if the Christians had their stakes exclusively in the causes of angry young men; and in our antibourgeois sentiments, some of which are in harmony with the claims of the gospel, we are prone to isolate the critical concerns for culture from the daily involvements in it of unexciting, humdrum mothers, children, clerks, executives, laborers and professional people. Too often Christian critiques of culture are critiques of the Christian cultural élite who, by virtue of their own advanced tastes and training, have separated themselves from the masses whose daily involvement in ordinary affairs God uses and on whom the élites depend.

Finally, we need to find a way in which to reintroduce the idea of obligations and responsibilities without falling into the traps of legalism and heteronomy. These are the traps that ethics is most conscious of today, sometimes at the expense of the right sense of duties and obligations. Indeed, it becomes easy to slip from an antilegalism into an ethic of self-realization in which immediate fulfillment of desires, rather than deepest human needs, is the goal of life. Grace and love drive us from within to become involved in the needs of the neighbor and in the suffering of the world, but under God's sovereign rule we are obligated to take on the burdens of the world as his responsible deputies, even when inner disposition is weak. Life is to find fulfillment in the relations between persons of each sex, but the fulfillment is also one of the duties and obligations that we have toward each other by virtue of these relationships in the divine economy. Faith and love bring us a new sense of freedom, but a pattern of responsibilities and obligations exists to keep that freedom directed toward those things which are helpful and which build up. Neither we nor the world is as "mature" as we are often told, and in the absence of such maturity the necessity of rule and authority under God in determining conduct and activity is indispensable. God's concern for the ordering of human society so that freedom and fulfillment can abound is as much a part of his purposes as is his emancipating men from the bondage of false orders and outdated rules. The interpretation given in this essay calls for more detailed understanding of the church's activity in society in terms of the ordering of institutions and of the duties and obligations of persons at each place of Christian life in the world.

Poverty, Suffering,
III Death

The miseries of man's life and work in the world have been a constant Biblical theme. From the Genesis account of the universal reign of sin (chaps. 3–11) to the laments of the prophets, suffering, persecution and death predominate. The task of the servants of Yahweh was to proclaim his word and to shed their blood in martyrdom, "from the blood of Abel to the blood of Zechariah" (Lk 11:51). Their fate was to be that of Jesus in his turn: His proclamation of the Kingdom inevitably led to persecution and death. The apostles and early Christians expected and even desired persecution and martyrdom, for the realities of human life had to be faced, and most prominent among them were suffering and death.

The question raised by the book of Job concerning the affliction of the just man and the prosperity of the wicked has been a constant theme of philosophers and theologians. From Augustine to William Langland, from Aquinas to Sartre, philosophers and theologians have struggled with the problem of evil. Extensive suffering caused by natural disasters, wars, violence, and accidents of chance have spurred incessant study of the Christian dilemma: Can one believe in a God who is perfectly good and infinitely powerful, and who nevertheless permits the existence of suffering, disasters of all kinds, and an overwhelming presence of evil?

Especially since the nineteenth century, philosophers of pes-

simism and materialism have found the coexistence of evil and
an all-powerful God a logical contradiction—impossible to en-
tertain. Recent evolutionary theories consider suffering to be
a natural and inevitable attendant of the evolutionary process,
but these theories do not give much credence to the existence
of God or allow for individual moral responsibility.

To follow, even in a summary way, the contemporary discussion of the problem of evil would require volumes.[1] Yet
eventually most thinkers come to the same conclusions as Ga-
briel Marcel: Evil is not so much a problem as a mystery.
Marcel wrote:

> In reflecting upon evil, I tend, almost inevitably, to regard it
> as a disorder which I view from outside and of which I seek
> to discover the causes or the secret aims. Why is it that the
> "mechanism" functions so defectively? Or is the defect
> merely apparent and due to a real defect of my vision? In
> this case the defect is in myself, yet it remains objective in
> relation to my thought, which discovers it and observes it.
> But evil which is only stated or observed is no longer evil
> which is suffered: In fact, it ceases to be evil. In reality, I
> can only grasp it as evil in the measure in which it *touches*
> me—that is to say, in the measure in which I am *involved*,
> as one is involved in a lawsuit. Being "involved" is the funda-
> mental fact; I cannot leave it out of account except by an
> unjustifiable fiction, for in doing so, I proceed as though I
> were God, and a God who is an onlooker at that.[2]

In the world of the twentieth century it is almost impossible
to look on suffering from the outside, as a detached observer,
who is not involved. Newspapers, magazines, radios, TV, and
films have brought the horrors of war, murder, riot, famine,
and starvation into the homes of most Americans and many
other people throughout the world. If our consciences are not
aroused by reading about the suffering of others, actually
witnessing suffering involves us to a degree which is difficult
to ignore.

We are increasingly aware, even if the conscience of the
West is not sufficiently aroused to take massive action, of the

---

[1] An excellent recent work on the subject is John Hick's *Evil and the
God of Love* (New York: Harper & Row, Publishers, 1966).

[2] *The Philosophy of Existence* (London: Harvill Press), p. 9.

situation of the developing nations, the "third world." Its largely inarticulate millions are increasingly alienated, angry, and explosive in their determination to come abreast of the developed world.

The "third world" exists in a vicious circle of poverty with a poor outlook on life expectancy, health, food, housing, and education. Unless the "rich nations" move more rapidly to improve the lot of the destitute, the climate of world revolution will grow with increasing speed.

The stand of the Roman Catholic Church and the World Council of Churches has been made clear in the encyclicals of Pope John and Pope Paul and in the declarations of the World Council which stress improving the conditions of the developing nations as a primary concern. How deeply involved Christians of the West will become and what influence they will exert can only be conjectured.

It is difficult to deal theologically with the problems of poverty, suffering, and death, for if one remains on the level of innumerable concrete examples, no general principles can be developed. And, if one moves from concrete examples to the theological dimension, the impression can easily arise that one is dealing with an unreal abstraction and that the existential sufferings of real people are being overlooked.

To illustrate both points of view, this section includes an essay on poverty by Yves Congar, which is based on the Biblical background of the Incarnation. This is followed by the more sociologically oriented essays of Dr. Visser 'T Hooft and Dr. John J. Harmon. None of these three authors provides concrete solutions; indeed, solutions are outside the province of the Biblical scholar or the theologian. But theologians must always make clear that they are really involved in man's suffering and aware of the pressing need for solutions.

In one respect Christian understanding of poverty and suffering is dependent on an adequate understanding of the Incarnation, for the God who entered history has taken on the miseries of humankind. The Incarnation makes more credible the patience of an all-powerful God with human weakness, sinfulness, and malice. Christ not only suffered the consequences of human malice, he underwent the final emptying of himself in death.

Death is the ultimate challenge to optimistic philosophies. What is the worth of humanistic efforts for a more livable world for man if death claims every man in the end? Teilhard de Chardin describes death as the "critical point of our excentration, of our reversion to God" and the sufferings which attend this final "diminishment" as the "tearing up of roots involved in our journey into God." [3]

Only when seen in the perspective of a call to man to achieve his full capacity in a transcendent life of union with God is it possible to view death as an affirmation of all that man is. Christian death is an affirmation by which man reverses rebellion and accepts the final diminishment of his powers before they are reintegrated in "the divine milieu." Dr. Ladislaus Boros in his essay describes suffering as the "Christian task of transforming darkness into light." The ultimate meaning of Christian life can be described as "dying and rising with Christ." Dr. Rudolf Schnackenburg sees in Paul's understanding of baptism, and the life of the Christian after his baptism, as the challenge of suffering and endurance, which is at the same time a partial entrance into glory. The death of the Christian is also his triumph, the beginning of his long awaited "hope of glory."

[3] *The Divine Milieu* (New York: Harper Torchbook Edition, 1960), p. 88.

YVES CONGAR

God Reveals
Himself in Poverty

The Mystery of the Poor

The first thing that impressed us was that God reveals Himself in poverty. We see this in the election of Israel, the people which was the bearer of the revelation. It was not because Israel was powerful, or because it stood out as a creative force in the cultural field, that it was chosen as beneficiary and witness of the revelation. Israel was, on the contrary, small, and it was because of its smallness that it was chosen (see Dt 7:7; cf. 10:14–15; Ez 16:3–15; 1 Cor 1:27). Within Israel itself, those who were chosen to be bearers of the design of God were those whom neither superior qualities nor preeminent position marked out. On the contrary, it was the youth who were chosen in preference to the elders (see the story of Cain and Abel, Jacob and Esau, Ephraim and Manasse, David...), it was the sterile who became the mothers of the great chosen ones of God: Sarah, Rebekah, the mother of Samson, Hannah the mother of Samuel, Elizabeth the mother of John the Baptist, finally Mary the mother of Jesus, who proclaims:

> He has regarded the low estate of his handmaiden,... he has scattered the proud in the imagination of their hearts, he has put down the mighty from their thrones, and exalted those of low degree (Lk 1:48–52).

From *Jesus Christ* (New York: Herder and Herder, 1966), pp. 66–85. Reprinted with permission of the publisher. For full footnote documentation, see original publication.

The history of souls and the witness of spiritual men speak in a fashion which is so much in agreement and which is so categorical that it seems necessary for us to consider as a law of the spiritual world, one as certain as the laws of the natural world, the necessity to be and to recognize oneself as wholly without resources, so that God might lift us to Himself. Yes, truly, He fills the hungry with good things and sends the rich empty away (Lk 1:53). Is it because God is sovereign and wishes to be affirmed as such? He who exalts himself before Him (so much the more, he who exalts himself against Him), He brings low; he who acknowledges his poverty before Him, He fills.

In all of this, poverty is not a question of a purely material condition. Between the Pharisee and the publican, it is rather the publican who would, in the economic sense, be found to be a possessor. The ideal is not to be in want, but to be free in the face of abundance or of privation, as was the Lord Jesus or St. Paul (cf. Phil 4:11), and, especially, to have in one's soul the attitude of waiting and of desire, of openness to grace, of dispossession, of total and confident dependence which is the attitude of "The Poor of Yahweh." [1] Material poverty, destitution, a humbled condition constitute no more than *dispositions* which may be favorable; but they could also set up reactions of bitterness and envy, revolt and rejection, which would be as contrary to the Gospel as the hardness of heart, the self-sufficiency, the ingratitude, and the pride of a wealthy man who is dispensed, by his wealth, from putting his confidence in God. We do, nevertheless, very often find among the poor (the *Misérables* of Victor Hugo, and also those of Tolstoy, Gorky,...) the dispositions of nonpossession, of welcome and of sharing which are, as if naturally, acknowledged as proper to the Gospel. The only thing lacking to these dispositions is that they have not been evangelized, have not even been recognized as a religious attitude. Jesus Christ would have to be shown to these poor ones. He is the fullness of all that is already in His image.

The next thing that struck us was that the poor can be revealers of God. They can be a means or a way of finding Christ. We are, in fact, held back from finding this way by our attachment to certain goods, certain false pretensions, by the snare constituted by

[1] See Albert Gelin's beautiful book of that same name (Collegeville, Minnesota: Liturgical Press, 1964).

comfortable habits, by the fear of risk. But when we confront the poor, when we come into contact with them, our false security and our illusions melt like snow in the sunshine. The "glorious" and utterly vain creatures we have made of ourselves strike us as hollow and false. We take stock of the fact that, after all, we knew nothing: We were empty, we were not even apprentices. Then, if we have a touch of nobility in our hearts and some small beginning of spiritual unrest, we see ourselves as judged and we judge ourselves; we are very close to hearing the voice of truth.

Very quickly, though, we came to see that there was, on the part of Jesus, a certain predilection for the poor, that there was a certain identity, confirmed by His own words, between Himself and them.

It is quite true that we cannot, in the name of the Gospel, somehow canonize poverty in the economic sense of the word. If this were required, we would have to maintain men in that condition of poverty. But, as the Fathers, the theologians, and the popes have often said, the Gospel does not require that the poor exist so that the rich can practice mercy: It would be far better if there were no poor! The Gospel does not canonize material poverty. Still, one cannot reduce its message to an exaltation of poverty *in spirit*. Certain facts, certain statements resist any such process. Jesus Himself chose first to lead a laborious life, then a poor life, without assurance of resources. And the apostles, too, to whom it was said: "Blessed are you poor" (Lk 6:20), were next told: "Blessed are you that hunger now, for you shall be satisfied." Then there followed the curses which correspond, term for term, to the beatitudes: "But woe to you that are rich, for you have received your consolation. Woe to you that are full now, for you shall hunger." The particular insistence of St. Luke on poverty in the social sense of the word is quite well known. Still, we cannot exclude this aspect from the fourfold witness which was inspired by Him whose Gospel we know it to be. We must see it in its place.... It is also difficult to attempt to understand only in a spiritual sense the terms used to express the messianic sign. "To preach good news to the poor..., to proclaim release to the captives, and recovering of sight to the blind" (Lk 4:18; Is 61:1). The help brought to the unfortunate seems inseparable from the spiritual liberation, exactly as so many miracles show us that it was in the life of Jesus.

The parable of the wicked rich man and Lazarus is also proper to St. Luke (16:19–31). He does not say "the *wicked* rich man," nor does he say that Lazarus was a "poor man" in the spiritual sense of the word. Lazarus was, quite simply, a poor man, and it was on this basis that he received consolation. We can, therefore, ask whether there may not be, in the Gospel, a predilection for the poor as such.

Better still: In the teaching about the last judgment which is given in St. Matthew (25:31–46), Jesus identified Himself with the poor: "I was hungry and you gave me food..., I was naked and you clothed me.... As you did it to one of the least of these my brethren, you did it to me...." The just were not aware that, in doing these acts of charity, they did them for the Lord Himself. He was, then, really hidden under the appearance of the hungry, the naked, the imprisoned.

And yet, we can wonder if the teaching really goes that far. Does it affirm the general fact of an objective presence of Christ in the poor, so that in going to them we encounter Him? Or is the affirmation more detailed, more limited? Many commentators are of the opinion that the works of mercy involved—known and recognized as such in the biblical milieu—are to be exercised towards other *disciples*: "to one of the least of these *my brethren*." We can cite in support of this opinion well-attested parallels: "Whoever receives one such child in my name receives me" (Mt 18:5; Mk 9:37; Lk 9:48; cf. Jn 13:20; Mt 10:40ff.). There would then be question of nothing more than the revelation of a proper and crucial characteristic of the Christian ethic: Our acts involve a vertical relationship to God or to Christ. The text of St. Matthew on the judgment would, then, do no more than reveal this dimension of Christian behavior and apply it to acts duly recognized as done for the benefit of other Christians, members of the mystical body.

Even then we could question the way in which "the least of my brethren" was being interpreted. These words can, in fact, signify, not the special quality of disciple, but the general fact that all men were considered by Jesus as His brethren and that, among them, the "least," that is, the poorest, the most oppressed, the most despised, were particularly His brethren. This, we think, is the true meaning of the text. On the level of a theological reflection, it must be understood within the basic fact of the Incarnation, as we shall see further on. Let us go forward gradually in an attempt to probe the reasons for the existence between God (Christ) and men, especially between God and the disgraced and the needy, of a connection of such a nature that an encounter with the latter has the value of an encounter with God, and that the charity which is practiced on the human level has the value (we hardly dare say it!) of good done to God.

Our Way to God Passes through the Poor

Actually, we could even go so far as to speak of the role of things and events in this regard. Even things which are alive, but not spiritual or personal, bear vestiges of God. Man, however, bears His image. If we do no more than consider the framework of an existence in which God is in search of man and man, even without knowing it, is ordered to find God, we see that everything is, in some degree, an occasion for an encounter with God, a place for a possible visit. Everything has an "iconic" value, one to which the saints were particularly sensitive, and which Jesus perceived to the highest degree. Things are parables in potency, presenting the possibility of signifying the religious rapport and of inducing its realization. The universe, the things and the events within it, all can become sacraments of the active presence of God.

Looked at from the standpoint of our advances, there is a continuity, and thus a homogeneity, between the attitudes we assume in our encounters with things (which are, after all, the context of our decisions and contain in a real, even if latent, way the occasions for encountering God) and the fundamental attitude we assume towards God Himself. The latter attitude is foreshadowed in our habitual and basic decisions, but gradually takes shape in the exercise of our freedom, within a field of successive and mutually conditioned advances: of God towards us, and of us towards God, advances which vary according to every possible degree, every possible modality of clear or obscure awareness of what is at issue. What is important to our present reflection is that we be conscious of the encounter with God which takes place under the guise of something other than God, that we be conscious of the connection and continuity which exist in this area. This very connection and continuity have their reality in God Himself, in whose sight we are, and in whose regard we, when confronted with creatures or events, choose.

We can assume that what is generally true of our encounter with things is true also, in particular conditions, of our encounter with *persons* or with *men*. This seems to us to be true for two principal reasons.

[The first is] the mystery which every person contains. We never know *who* we are encountering. Abraham sees three men coming towards him. He shows hospitality to them. Yet the sequel of the story shows that they were three angels, three messengers of God, or even God Himself in person (cf. Gn 18, 19:1). Simon of Cyrene, coming back from the fields to make ready the Pasch, is forced by Roman soldiers to take up the cross of a condemned man who could not carry it to the end. Did he grumble, or did he accept the task with a good heart? Later, it will be made clear and his sons will be found among the Christians (cf. Mk 15:21). At the moment he did not know that he was helping the Son of God to carry the instrument of the world's salvation. We could give example after example to prove that we never know *who* we are encountering, *who* is sent to us, *who* we receive. This is true in the most special way for us who are priests. What exactly is the man looking for who knocks on my door, who sits down next to me on the train? What is in the soul of the man who comes to arrange for a wedding, the fellow who asks to confess his sins? Who are they? And how many times have I been blind and deaf, callous and dense, incapable of even suspecting, of even guessing! Yet everything witnesses to the mystery of hospitality, of openness. The word "mystery" is not too strong a word here, since it indicates that there is something beyond what is seen, something in which God is working and can be attained.

However that may be, the man whom we encounter is *a person*. This is why he lends himself in a formal way to becoming the occasion for us to declare our attitude toward God, who is *Person*. There is no other creaturely mediation which can do this in the same way. These persons are, morever, made in the image of God, and this makes of them a reflection, an echo, somehow a prolongation of God. "For we are indeed his offspring" (Ac 17:28). When we learn from the Word of God that the second commandment is like to the first, we realize to what extent it is true that, in the persons of other men, we reach God Himself. It might even be said that, in a certain sense, we cannot fully realize the love of God except in the love of neighbor. St. Catherine of Siena said that "we conceive the virtues in the love of God, and we bring them forth

in the love of our neighbor." We could apply this maxim to
theologal love itself, inasmuch as love, by its own nature, wills to
procure the good of the one who is loved. It cannot content itself
with being affective, but wills to express itself and to prove itself
in good works. But what am I to bring to the Lord that He does not
have already? The love which I have conceived for Him has, we
might say, its *locus* in the world in the love I have for my neighbor.
In this kind of created extension of God in His living images, I can
do Him the good that is demanded by my love for Him. In this
sense, God has, so to speak, given me my neighbor to love in His
place. In the Gospel revelation, not only does the love of God seem
linked to the love of neighbor, but it is somehow enveloped by it.
In the Sermon on the Mount, Jesus expresses the evangelical demands with regard to God (Mt 6:1-18) only after He has expressed
those which concern the fraternal relationship with regard to one
another (5:21-48). That this sequence is not due to editorial hap-
penstance, that it translates the sense of the Gospel doctrine, can be
seen in ten places where it is clearly shown in particular applica-
tions, most notably in the law which governs forgiveness (Mt 6:12;
18:21-35; Lk 6:36-38).

If God became man in Jesus Christ, this fact cannot possibly be
without influence on the role which is played by humanity, hence
by men, in the religious rapport. We think that there are two points
which must be emphasized here:

1. In Jesus Christ, God has united Himself to human nature,
which is really one; He has thus made of all men His brothers.
The divine decree which decides the redemptive incarnation brings
about, between men and Christ, a particular solidarity, one which
corresponds, besides, to what is called for by the very nature of the
realities involved. In virtue of this solidarity, Jesus, God-made-man,
draws men to form with Him a single object, entitled to the heritage
of God (provided men receive the gift of God through a personal
and free act of living faith). This constitutes the foundation of the
people of God under the new dispensation, which makes of this
people the Body of Christ. The solidarity which God effects brings
with it this consequence: What is done to men is done, in a certain
way, to Christ. Where disciples and the body which is the Church
are involved, this solidarity is translated in the "Saul, Saul, why do
you persecute me?" of Acts (26:14; 9:5; 22:8). This is the most

intense degree of mystical identification. In the least explicit degree, anything which is done to any human person whatever touches Christ. Within the area between the two degrees, we would undoubtedly have to situate all that might be done to the Jews. But, if our reading of the text from St. Matthew is correct, the truth is that there is, on the basis both of the decree of God and of the existential conditions of the incarnation, a particularly solidarity, a certain "juridical identification" between Christ and all those who are in need of help: the poor, the hungry, the imprisoned, the lowly.

2. "God's love (*agapē*) has been poured into our hearts through the Holy Spirit who has been given to us" (Rom 5:5). The love of which this text speaks is, as we know, the love with which God loves. In fact, the sublimity of charity is such that it represents a participation in the love with which God loves Himself and all things. When we profess that we love our neighbor "for the love of God," our profession means nothing else and nothing less. Now the love with which God loves us has assumed a way and a form which have given it a definite character and, in doing that, have revealed its deepest nature. "I am the way," says Jesus, "no one comes to the Father, but by me" (Jn 14:6). Yes, He *is* the way, the living way which He has opened for us through His flesh (cf. Heb 10:20). We know what this way, as the unique path of truth and of life, has been, and we know what it will forever remain: the way, humble and filled with love, of service of men, the way of a descent right down to the brambles to seek the sheep that is lost, right down to the dust of the earth to seek the lost coin. To love with the love with which God has loved us? This is to love as Jesus loved (and this is the "as" which is demanded by the *new* commandment, *His* commandment). It is to love with a love which seeks with predilection the little ones, the ones who are in need. All of this is bound up with the *newness* of the Gospel, which itself is the consequence and the reflection of the mission, inspired by the *agapē* of the Father, of the Son of God.

The great revelation of His Gospel is the boundless love of Himself and of His Father for the little ones whom the world scorns or condemns. When we know of the mistrust of Judaism—and of so many "self-respecting" religions—for these "unclean ones," we sense the full revolutionary character of the attitude of Jesus. We are already aware of the scandal of the Pharisees when confronted with a salvation which was too easy and was offered to every comer. Qumran now provides us with an even clearer example of this scrupulous *intégriste* piety, which thinks it is better to serve God through an isolation from all that is not itself and through a hatred for sinners.

When determining the place of all these factors in the plan of God, one cannot avoid making the following statements: The way that leads to God passes through the humanity of Christ, something which is inseparable from the love and service of men, particularly those who are in misery under all its forms. If it is true to say, with Saint John of the Cross, that "in the evening of this life we will be judged on love," it is more certain still that we will be judged on the basis of this: "As you did it to one of the least of these my brethren, you did it to me." The aim of the preceding meditation has only been to try to better understand this saying of our Master. We have seen that it supposes, between men and Christ, a link of such a nature that all men, and particularly the poor, enter as decisive elements into the realization of the religious rapport.

We first saw the poor as an occasion, a sort of sacrament of the encounter with God. We even saw them as identical, in a certain manner, with Jesus Christ. Our way to God passes through them. What we would like to do now is to prolong our meditation by considering things from the point of view of God and of Christ. We will no longer ask ourselves why men, and especially the poor, play a decisive role in the religious rapport or in evangelical behavior. We will ask, instead, what it is, from the standpoint of Christ and of God, that links them particularly to the unfortunate. What has Christ to do with the poor? What is the basis, in God and in Christ, of the kind of predilection which we have observed? It is in Christology that we must seek the light which will best illumine an entire aspect of the Gospel and, as a corollary, an entire aspect of the mission and life of the Church as well.

The Poor in the Mystery of the Incarnation

If the incarnation implies a structure which is in some way metaphysical or ontological—the subsistence of a human nature in the hypostasis of the Word, it remains, before all else, a fact of "the economy," the disposition of the will of God as it is gradually unfolded and realized in time, of which St. Paul speaks in the Letter to the Ephesians (1:3–14). The incarnation is not dependent on the necessary mystery of God, but on His free mystery. It is not dependent on the "in Himself," but on grace, on what God freely decides to be and to do for His creature. The fact that God decides to become man and the concrete circumstances or modalities chosen by God to effect this design represent positive data which are absolutely free in themselves but, once decided on and effected, present the believer with something which he must understand and imitate. This is the order of the mysteries of the economy. It is what the holy Scriptures are talking about when they say that *it was necessary that this be accomplished....*

We have here an order of realities which, considered from logical reason alone, is a free order of simple fittingness, but which, in the existential context of the purposes of God and the saving economy, is imposed upon us as a law of Christian activity. Moreover, reason, seeking an understanding of what we believe..., discovers in it marvelous and profound harmonies. The actual order of the economy then appears as astonishingly coherent, both as to the unfathomably profound nature of God and as to the profound nature of man, in the light of his present condition and of the end that is promised to him....

God, indeed, *is* Love, God *is* Grace. Grace is freedom, but its very impulse as grace makes of it a condescension and a gift which intimately correspond to the aspirations and the nature of love. Its reality as grace brings it about that God can be as well in what is low as in what is high. "How could God's deity exclude His humanity," writes Karl Barth, "since it is God's freedom for love and thus His capacity to be not only in the heights but also in the depths, not only great but also small, not only in and for Himself but also with another distinct from Him, and to offer Himself to him?" [2] He whom the heavens, whom the most sublime created spirits cannot comprehend or contain, can dwell in the lowest without its being burst asunder or destroyed. The Old Testament said: No one can see God without dying. But when God made Himself more intimately known by coming to us Himself, by becoming one of us Himself, we knew for certain that it is by seeing Him and by touching Him that one has life (cf. Jn 14:9; 1 Jn 1:1f.).

But if grace, through its character of freedom and transcendence, dwells with the low as well as with the sublime, we are forced to say that its profoundly loving and condescending nature actually in-

[2] *The Humanity of God* (Richmond, Va.: John Knox, 1960), p. 49.

clines it to come to the lowest and the most miserable. Everything which has been said about *agapē*, the gracious love of God, must be repeated here. And everything that can be said about the kingly character of mercy must be repeated as well. There is then in grace, and in God inasmuch as He is *agapē* and *grace*, not only some possibility of being with the smallest, but an actual inclination to go to the poorest, to the one who is most miserable, so as to communicate to him His Good and His Life. Everything which we have, thanks to the book of Anders Nygren, re-assimilated on the theme of *agapē* was implied in this: It is not by reason of a goodness possessed by someone whom the *agapē* loves, but, on the contrary, *because* someone is poor and miserable, that the *agapē* loves him. (Reread in this connection 1 Jn 3:16, 4:9; Rom 5:8, 8:32–39; Eph 2:4–7; Jn 3:16.)

Now all that God is in His profound being, and especially all that God is *for us*, all that He is as grace, has been supremely manifested to us in Jesus Christ. But, at first, God did not make Himself known except from afar, and through an intermediary. One day, He came Himself. In Jesus Christ, He freely manifested Himself: "Philip, he who has seen me has seen the Father" (Jn 14:9). But how, and in what form? ... When God freely manifests Himself, when He definitively reveals to us the way of truth and of life, the way which is His, the way which is Himself, what do we see?

1. He does not remain a stranger to misery. He did not assume sin, but He did assume and bear the consequences of sin: He joined men, He married our humanity in the conditions of our misery, largely conditioned by sin. It is undoubtedly true that we cannot simply attribute to sin all the miseries of men. Misery makes its own chain of being. There are certain factors, inherent in the nature of things, which by themselves create the conditions of misery: Poor soil and subsoil can hardly yield anything but poverty. Man, though, is called to free himself and to free others from misery, and sin prevents this. Sin is always the exaltation of self to the detriment of others, egoism, self-justification, refusal to share and to act as a servant in love and in self-surrender. It is also the worship of idols, of the false absolutes fabricated by men, and all the ignorance and alienation which that brings with it. Even Christianity has been and sometimes still is thus bent, although this is the complete contrary of faith in the living God, the God of the incarnation and of the Pasch. As for the history of the world, it is a history made up of the trampling of the weak by the strong, the crushing of the

little by the great, and, for the majority of men, the incredible accumulation of woes.

... The begnning of our liberation consisted in this: He who was in the light, the riches, and the glory of God (Jn 17:5) began to exist among the little, the poor, the lowly. He became a little child, weakness; He was born in a working-class family and He Himself worked with His hands; He grew up among a people subjected to a military occupation, under authorities who made no game of submission; He knew what it was to be hungry, to be in pain, to be held in suspicion, to be put on the index by the most sacred authorities; He knew contradiction; He knew, finally, the conditions of total destitution of a man accused, the defenseless exposure to accusations and to blows, to flagellation, to the horrible punishment of the cross, a punishment imposed on slaves. When we meditate on the circumstances of "the blessed passion" of Christ, we cannot help thinking that Jesus assumed it all so as to be fully *with* so many poor people who, throughout the ages, have been beaten, hanged, crucified (the five thousand slaves crucified after the revolt of Spartacus; the five hundred Jewish patriots whom Josephus claimed to have seen crucified at once).

2. The incarnation is not the pure metaphysical fact of the assumption of a human nature in the uncreated subsistence of the person of the Word. It is existentially a fact which was produced in such and such concrete circumstances, announced, anticipated, prepared for a long time, then finally realized: *"oportebat," "ut Scripturae implerentur."* Now what do we find?

We find Jesus announced as the suffering Servant.

We find him avoiding the title of "Son of David," which would have suggested the idea of a kingship of a human type, and taking the title of "Son of man." He rejects the prospects of triumphal or temporal messianism which are set before Him either by the Tempter, or by the crowds, or by His disciples and His brethren: He will be liberator by the cross, He will overcome misery by assuming it.

The most profound revelation touching on the incarnation is given to us by St. Paul in the Letter to the Philippians, 2:6–11. The fact which we celebrate on March 25th and December 25th is there presented as the beginning of a descent, even as a *kenosis*, a making-into-nothing. Yes, the beginning: to come as a tiny little child—the weakness, the total dependence which is a little baby!—is but the beginning of a descent which will only be accomplished *at the lowest point* of human existence, death. The term of the *kenosis* of Christ is the descent to hell, a very profound mystery which is essential to our faith and by which our faith takes on all its human and cosmic dimensions, its depth and its realism. . . .

This is exactly the same logic, the same economy, that we find in the great rhythmic text, perhaps a Christian hymn, of the Letter to the Philippians, 2:6–11. Adam, who existed in the condition of servant, yielded to the temptation to raise himself above his own condition to attain a condition of God, and imagined himself as an absolute independence, without subjection to anything ("You will be like God, knowing good and evil": Gn 3:5); but Christ, who existed in the condition of God, did not remain covetously attached to this dignity, but took the condition of slave, which is the condition of men, and in this very condition He abased Himself to the extent of suffering, in our place, the punishment of slaves, the frightful death of the cross. This is why God exalted Him to the extent of making Him Lord over all that He has encompassed, from the highest to the lowest.

Glory is promised to us with Christ, provided we first suffer with Him, says St. Paul (Rom 8:17). We must enter into the law which constitutes the most specific part of the Christian ethic and which has us act as Christ—or, rather, as God has shown us, in Christ, that He acts: to love *as* He loved, to pardon as He pardoned, etc. The great text from Philippians opens with these words: "Have this in mind among yourselves, which was in Christ Jesus." In this "marching in the footsteps," we are in the earthly phase, at the stage of descent and of service. To be obedient to the Christian law, which has its own intrinsic obligation . . . , is to be born with this new birth, whose final goal is liberation, which means to descend to the lowest, to begin to exist with the poor.

The poor are not only the economically deprived; they are not only the poor "in spirit." They are all those who suffer misery, in the broadest extension of the word. This extension corresponds to the sense in which Christian tradition has looked at misery: it has acknowledged the spiritual works of mercy along with the corporal, and it has practiced them, but it has not yielded to the error of believing, for all practical purposes, that either can do without the other.

JOHN J. HARMON

The Church
and the Dispossessed

In what might properly be called "the age of disincarnation,"
when Christians are more adept at analysis than action, research than
reconstruction, we need to emphasize qualities of identification and
involvement. We need to emphasize the implications of the Incarnation—*what it really means to live in a particular place, and what it
really means to make others live in their particular place.*

The place, the locus of one's life in the world, is never—for those
who have some freedom of choice—an accidental matter. Similarly,
the assigning of places to other people is not an accidental matter.
Those of us who have this excessive degree of freedom—the freedom of both choosing for ourselves and for our neighbors, by establishing ghettos for the dispossessed and ghettos for the possessors
—stand on very dangerous ground. *There is often far more involved
in such choices than we perceive or admit.*

It is out of this problem of the choice of place—of living where we
choose, and choosing where others live—that some of the Church's
chief weaknesses in her ministry to the dispossessed arise. For it is
precisely those who have this unique and unwarranted freedom
today who by and large determine the mind and ministry of the
Church toward all the dispossessed—whether racially, economically,
educationally, religiously, or culturally.

Let me develop this thought with three propositions concerning
the Church's relation to the dispossessed and one of the places in

From *American Ecclesiastical Review*, CLIV (February 1966), 73–83. Reprinted with permission of the publisher and the author.

which they commonly live, the "slums" (which I put in quotes because, like the term "race" and others often used, it is so loaded with irrational opprobrium and class consciousness as to almost make it useful only for caricature):

I. *Understanding. The dispossessed people and areas are not really understood by the Church because most of the authoritative writing and determinative views about them come from people who have freely chosen to live elsewhere, and generally don't appreciate the implications of this choice.*

The process of understanding is akin to the process of incarnation. The fact that the Lord knew his sheep was not primarily due to the analytical acuteness of his mind, but to the fact that he lived among them.

Of course, it is true that one doesn't have to become totally a part of a particular situation or people to understand deeply. After all, we can disagree with the Pharisee and say, "O God, I thank thee that I *am* as other men are"; and this affirmation helps us to understand other men and ourselves far better. But this recognition of our essential identity with all men doesn't compel us to over-identify, actually to become—more than we already are—"extortioners, unjust, adulterers or even as (that) publican."

But overidentification is not our problem today; it is rather one of overabstraction. Our problem stems from the fact that to voluntarily disassociate oneself, disincarnate oneself, from a particular situation and people is a sure sign of certain personal predispositions; and from the fact that such generally nonrational sentiments may seriously disfigure our understanding.

We generally choose to live in one place rather than another because it is "better"; "better" for many reasons, but especially "better" for the children. There are few white people who wouldn't say that it is "better" to live in Westchester than East Harlem. Regardless of the objective truth of such a judgment, if there is an overt "better" there is always a more covert "worse." (It is covert because in America, while it is proper to aspire to that which is "better," it is against our public ideology to hold that anybody is really "worse.") And in the degree to which this "worse" is hidden from our self-understanding and our rational processes in general, then it can seriously distort our views.

And this is the condition of the contemporary understanding of the "slum" and its people. Such understanding generally rests on a hidden scale of values, in which the suburb is the pinnacle and the "slum" the nadir. It's a totally irrational scale. There are, after all, those who choose to live in the "slum" precisely because they consider *it* to be "better." Moreover, one cannot talk to suburbanites without immediately hearing about all the problems of living in their social setting.

Yet even though objectively those incarnate in the suburban situation will offer the keenest criticisms of it, they still subjectively adhere to this "better"-to-"worse" spectrum. The simplest proof of this is that, having the freedom to move (a freedom the dispossessed largely lack), they don't.

Now, how do you write or talk truthfully about juvenile delinquency in the "slum," "racial problems," gangs, unmarried mothers, integration in housing projects, etc., when you've already made specific and preliminary value judgments about such people and their situation? Moreover, how do you really understand the ghetto and its people when, at the same time, you freely acquiesce in the enforcement of the ghetto system?

Let me give two illustrations of the problem:

First, the understanding of the Church with regard to the amelioration of the conditions of the dispossessed. It is remarkably gradualist, in spite of the new activism that the Civil Rights movement has shamed us into. Whenever new racial, ethnic, social, or economic groups enter a situation, they are first ghettoed in an area of depressed housing, and then gradually allowed to escape, once they've begun to conform to the dominant standards of the possessors. And this scheme—easily illustrated in American urban history and never really contested by the theology and practice of the Church—is supported by the usual paraphernalia of the gradualist ideology; chiefly the non-Biblical notion that one only gets what one deserves, the heretical boot-strap theory.

Now gradualism *per se*, as a theory of social change, is not necessarily erroneous; certainly this is precisely what we mean when we talk about the family or parish nurturing the Christian development of its members.

But what are the implications of holding such a position with regard to divisions within society without realizing that one is at the same time *withholding* oneself and one's family from sharing the persistent pain of such gradual amelioration—which always rests only on those being "graduated"? Is gradualism a position arising from a true understanding when one is willing to commit the children of the dispossessed ghetto to an intensity of pain and damage that one refuses for one's own children? Moreover, how true is such a doctrine when it becomes quite clear that its origin lies not in a real concern for the dispossessed, but rather in a concern to preserve the walls of separation in order to avoid contamination? The present tendency of northern urban public school systems, whose personnel are chiefly Christian, to substitute compensatory programs for an attack on *de facto* segregation, is just such an attempt to appear concerned about Negro children and yet still keep them safely contained.

Another illustration: It is well known that Christians outside the ghetto of the disinherited have a great deal of difficulty in accepting "interracial" marriages, and are apt to see them as at best the result of neurotic compulsions rather than normal human love. But their lack of understanding here is largely predetermined by their own prior choice of living place; for one of the most forceful reasons for living in the ghetto of the possessors is to forestall the possibility of one's own children being faced with this horrible temptation. To choose to live in an all-white ghetto means, in part, that one has already decided the merits of "intermarriage"—and without ever having really come in contact with it.

Like Lazarus and the rich man—between those who form the mind of the Church regarding the dispossessed and the dispossessed themselves, it would appear that there is a "great gulf fixed." However, it is not quite so unbridgeable as in the Gospel story: Those who presume to be knowledgeable in the matter could either choose to become physically incarnate in the condition they seek to describe, or abandon the hidden value scale—or better, do both.

Actually, in a peculiarly perverse way this gap has already been bridged. For it must be admitted that the degree to which Christians "outside" commonly misunderstand the situation and nature of those "inside" is exceeded only by the degree to which some of the latter have adopted for themselves the same caricature and scale of values! It is very much like the situation of some older Negroes in the South who, in order to survive, have in fact *become* the white man's caricature of them. It is also very much like the situation of other Negroes who, for a different purpose, *pretend* to be this caricature. So that whether through suicide or pretense we arrive at the same disability on the part of some of those 'inside"; and Christians both "outside" and "inside" are hobbled by the same misunderstanding.

It has been one of the achievements of the Freedom Movement to bring to light this self-destructive pattern on the part of the ghetto Negro; and, by offering him a way to participate in the process of fulfilling his freedom and humanity, has given him at the same time a chance to change his self-estimate. This is a radical and blessed development.

Incidentally, this system of a developing scale of values is quite comparable to the developmental prejudice which until recently hampered the Church's understanding of her Scriptures, and enticed her into thinking that the Old Testament, while necessary to the faith, was somehow qualitatively of a lower order of religion. Just as once grace was excluded from a view of the Old Testament, so it is now from our view of the dispossessed; and just as law was once considered the dominant fact of the Old Testament, so now law is considered the dominant fact of the "slum"—both its breaking and its enforcement.

This leads to my second point.

II. *Appreciation. While (a) the "slum" is generally appreciated only as the backwater of creation and the breeding ground of moral deterioration, it is (b) often in such places and among such people that God originates his most strategic advances in history, and (c) the chief forward movements today are being nurtured.*

(a) The fact is, of course, that there is a multitude of ordinary, strong people who live out their lives in a "slum" (this is one reason the word has to be used with caution): They work, raise children, and assume their responsibilities just like conscientious people anywhere.

It is not remarkable, however, that the chief public picture of them is one that conforms quite closely to the sensational newspaper headlines, which always emphasize disgrace and the machinery of the law. After all, once you accept the ghetto system on the "better-worse" rationale, then it is both comforting and necessary to have a supportive public picture; so that every derogation becomes a further justification for disassociating oneself from the wrong sort of people.

This inaccurate picture is very much like one in the minds of the killers employed by "Murder, Inc.," as described by Mr. Turkus, who prosecuted some of them:

> [They] invariably referred to their victims as "the bum," a peculiarity based on a psychology of justification. They thus sought either to soothe a fleeting flicker of conscience on the theory that killing a "bum" was excusable, or to work up a dislike for someone they were about to murder for business reasons, who might otherwise be a very nice fellow.

It is not very pleasant to be reminded that "bum," and similar terminology are terms employed not only by professional killers but frequently by professing Christians, and essentially for the same reasons.

Moreover, this distortion is abetted by confirmation coming from quite a different source and motivation. Often it is personally pleasing to those seeking to be helpful in the "slum" situation to adopt an heroic role; and the simplest way to emphasize one's own heroic qualities is to minimize the human qualities of those you're helping. I have personally known people, both volunteer and professional, who could not have survived financially or physically had they not had such a misshapen picture. This is the origin of the whole "zoological" approach, in which the inhabitants of the "slum" are treated like bizarre animals, totally controlled by their betters, who never hesitate to publicly dissect them and their problems with an appalling lack of compassion.

It is true too that some who begin on this heroic note are soon humbled and have this particular demon exorcised through exposure to a truer heroism on the part of the people they serve.

Let me illustrate this lack of appreciation through a very common stereotype: the prevalence of sexual immorality in the "slum." Now it is perfectly true that all sort of vices are found among the disinherited; St. Paul's description of the urban situation in Corinth is applicable today (1 Cor 6:9f.). But two further questions are immediately necessary: Is this condition peculiar to the "slum"; and, are there any positive elements that are peculiar to the "slum" and have been obscured?

To the first question, John O'Hara, Grace Metalious, et al., have given a definitive answer.

The second question leads me to this proposition: It is just as possible for parents to develop a strong sexual morality in their children in the "slum" as in the suburb. The reason: Both parents and children are freer to adhere to their own standards, and are less pressured into accepting the norms of the community—the very anonymity which is so often criticized in the urban situation—which allows this freedom. Opposed to this is a remark made to me with great feeling by the Rector of an Episcopal parish in one of America's poshest places: "I don't see how we can face having our children go through adolescence in this community." I have never had to say this about my four daughters who have grown up in Boston's ghetto.

Actually, of course, one can't divorce sexual immorality from the total moral picture of a community. The white suburban ghetto which fosters anti-semitism, for example, will most probably see this particular character deformation overflow into other immoralities. It was not by chance that the political immorality of the Nazi movement was accompanied by an uncommon degree of promiscuous homosexuality. Evil spirits, as the Gospel assures us, like company. And *the irony of our current situation is that those who segregate themselves off in order to cast out one demon (contact with the dispossessed) are more than likely inviting seven other worse spirits into their lives.*

(b) Historically, I am convinced that it is through the disinherited that God makes his most strategic advances.

This primary initiative coming from and through the dispossessed is often obscured by the simple fact that the historian too has the problem of not really understanding. Like the newspaperman, he writes from an opposing perspective; so that—and here the Marxists are quite right—history is generally class history. The new interpretations now appearing of the Reconstruction Period in this country are an excellent illustration; the previous interpretations were far too controlled by the endemic racism of the white middle class, which in recent years has graciously been exposed. It is undoubtedly true too that in a generation the current "riots" in northern cities will also be put in a new light; they will probably be seen more positively, as part of the general anti-colonial revolt of the nineteenth century.

Mr. Drew Middleton, in a review of his *The Sky Suspended*, is quoted as suggesting that the tenement dwellers of London, because of their "humility, their cheerfulness, their stolid, unspoken determination to continue," were responsible for saving London's name during the terror of the Blitz. If this is true, then the question to ask is: To what extent is all of history permeated with the "unspoken determination" of the poor, which, although largely unheralded, provides the major means through which God accomplishes his ends?

Paradoxically, the basic advantages of the dispossessed as agents of God come from the very fact of their being dispossessed; for it is always true that the oppressed is latently of stronger moral fiber than the one who oppresses. This is true for two reasons: first, because the oppressor debases himself by the act of oppression (and it makes little difference exactly how conscious he is of taking part in disinheriting others, since we are tainted by omission as well as commission); as Marian Anderson once said, "when you push somebody down in the ditch, a part of you stays there"; second, because the oppressed, while severely disfigured, is yet made more available to God's pressure since he has so little wordly armament and so little treasure to protect.

To overgeneralize, a good example of this moral advantage is the remarkable self-control and integrity of the American Negro. I would cite not only the whole Freedom Movement, with its remarkable discipline, dignity, and courage; but also the American Negro's keen insight in rejecting Marxist appeals in the twenties and thirties (to be "loved" as a class is just as dehumanizing as not to be loved as an individual). In the years to come it will be precisely from the Negro that America will draw her greatest strength.

But this does not mean that therefore we rejoice in oppression (any more than we "continue in sin that grace may abound"). It simply means that, following the pattern of the incarnation, we must voluntarily share the pain of the oppressed, in order to absorb and eliminate as much of this pain as possible, and so that we can become eligible to continue the work of the incarnation.

In a day when we talk much about "the God of history," it is necessary to be reminded about *this* type of historicity: God active through the outcasts, or, contrariwise, God "putting down the mighty from their seat," to quote Our Lady. God in ancient times sought his ends through the election of an obscure people who were no people, his historical climax was through human incarnation in a person identified with the oppressed of an occupied country; and he continues his work through a Church, the largest part of whose membership has always been the socially unacceptable.

If the Wise Men went first to Herod's Palace instead of the cattle shed to see the new thing that was happening, they may be excused;

for we still look only to the upper echelons of society for the really significant movers and movements of history, ignoring the fact that our ancestors were a wandering Aramean, slaves in Egypt, the harlots and sinners of Jesus' day and not many wise, powerful or noble —the weak of St. Paul's day.

(c) It is among the "weak" today that God is doing his most significant things. An excellent illustration is the "race question," which is certainly one of the main historical fulcrums of the twentieth century.

If one asked where, nationally, the chief movements toward amelioration were originating, the reply would most likely include the 1954 Supreme Court decision and the new Federal legislation; the sit-ins, freedom-rides, voter registration programs, etc., of such groups as SNCC, CORE, SCLC, and NAACP; and the leadership of people such as Dr. King, Bob Moses, members of the Mississippi Freedom Democratic Party, etc. Certainly such a list is true, and could be extended to include the pressure of world opinion, the economic pressure of the Negro, the sociological-anthropological studies which have eradicated many intellectual barriers, and the broad use of nonviolence as a means for achieving social change.

But the point is that the one source of amelioration which would probably be omitted is the one which, I'm convinced, is really laying the foundation of the new society—the "slum" in which there is racial mixture. For it is here—and not without real pain and conflict—that white and colored are actually living side by side; that some children are being raised who, though usually seen only in terms of deprivation, simply don't carry the emotional racial irrationalities of their peers in segregated all-white or all-colored districts.

It is precisely in such a "slum" that the issue can transcend self-righteous polemic and abstract sociological jargon, and become actual. People help one another, cry with one another, treat one another as human beings, and say their prayers together. Here is the true groundwork of the new society; here it is no longer a matter of talk or research or resolutions in convention—it is actual living together, with all its pains and consolations.

Of course there are racial prejudice and hatred in extreme forms here; but this we know and have been told *ad nauseam*. What we've overlooked are the new beginnings; the real heroes who absolutely refuse to abide by inhuman racial doctrines, and *quietly testify in their lives to the reconciliation Christ has accomplished between the men of the world.*

I doubt if the history books will catch much of this: but the Church must, if she is to regain her true ministry to the dispossessed.

III. *Ministry. Because the Church neither understands nor appreciates the life of the dispossessed, and also because she feels deeply guilty about their deplorable conditions, her ministry to them is very partial:*

The ministry of the Church to any people is not only a matter of exhibiting a *new* way of life through deeds and words; it is also an exposing of the Gospel as it is *already* latent in the life of such a people. After all, the world already bears the marks of the Gospel even though it doesn't perceive it (this lack of perception and acceptance is what differentiates "world" and "Church"). Part of our work is to uncover, to expose and add to the marks of the Cross and the marks of grace already implanted by Christ's work for the world.

But this is exactly what the Church finds so difficult to do—to expose the marks of grace already present—because her most influential members have already rejected the dispossessed and the place of their life as being totally disgraceful. I have heard men responsible for the direction of the Church's ministry to the poor describe them as "dregs" and "bums." The chief obstacle in the Episcopal Church to priestly vocations in the inner city is the unbelieving assumption that it is neither right nor possible to raise children in such an environment. Our perverted categories have become so overpowering that we just can't see any evidence of the Gospel already present among the dispossessed, but only evidence of degradation.

So we generally, except in a few places, relegate ourselves to either/or, a combination of two narrow ministries: a bland acceptance of the *status quo* (usually associated with either extreme sacramentalism or extreme fundamentalism), or a social service approach (usually associated with inferior theology and false heroics). The former protects the ghetto system; the latter protects our self-esteem. Neither is a full Gospel; both are very impoverished because they don't show what Christ has already accomplished and is presently accomplishing among the oppressed.

The parable of the Good Samaritan sums all of this up remarkably well. The man who went down to Jericho was not just any man. He was one of the dispossessed of his day, well known to the Priest and Levite because he'd been in and out of the Temple for years. To them he was one of the "dregs," who contributed nothing to society and lived, of course, in the worst possible section. Had he been what they considered a respectable member of society, you can be sure that the Priest and Levite wouldn't have passed him by; there's nothing quite so pleasing as helping a deserving person, who will be properly grateful. But since they neither understood nor appreciated the man in the ditch, it remained for the Samaritan to minister to him; he understood and appreciated the life of an outcast.

Now we can characterize the Samaritan in modern terms as we will. But the other two are quite clear: They are ourselves.

W. A. VISSER 'T HOOFT

Material Need
as a Spiritual Concern

Everybody knows the saying of Karl Marx that religion is the opium of the people. But he adds another, perhaps even more striking definition. Religion is, according to him, "the spiritual aroma" of the world. He sees a world full of injustice, of exploitation, of man's inhumanity to man. And above that world as a smokescreen hiding the unpleasant earthly realities is a cloudy, intangible and utterly irrelevant spiritual aroma.

Is that a caricature? Of course it is, but it is a good caricature because it emphasizes and exaggerates features which are clearly visible to every observer. Our religion has very often presented the image of a spiritual extra, an embellishment, a realm of escape, an otherworldly dimension added on the normal three-dimensional world and making no real difference to the life of that world. I once heard a Negro orator on a street corner in Harlem (New York) shout: "They tell us to turn our thoughts to heaven, but I say: To hell with heaven." In the environment of the Harlem slums which destroy both the soul and the body it was not difficult to see this point. There is in the wide antireligious reaction in many parts of the world a true insight that a religion which is just a spiritual aroma is an enemy of man.

But is this religion which Marx describes the real article? Is it the authentic faith of which the Old and New Testaments speak? Is it the truth to which Jesus gave testimony in his life and death? No,

From *The Ecumenical Review*, XIX (April 1967), 228–30. Reprinted with permission of the publisher.

whether Marx realized it or not (and as a Jew could he have forgotten it?)—he was simply echoing the judgment of the ancient prophets of Israel about irrelevant religiosity. In the first of the prophecies of Isaiah the Lord says: "Bring no more vain offerings; incense is an abomination to me ... seek justice, correct oppression, defend the fatherless, plead for the widow." And Amos (5:22): "Even though you offer me your burnt offerings and cereal offerings I will not accept them ... but let justice roll down like waters and righteousness like an everflowing stream." The prophetic message—which Jesus makes his own and fulfills—is one great protest against a spiritual-aroma type of religion.

A genuine Christianity is the opposite of a spiritual aroma; it is an explosive, revolutionary force. It proclaims that a so-called order in which some have all and more than they need and others live in want cannot and must not be tolerated because God Himself does not tolerate it. He wants his creatures to live, not to die; to realize the gifts with which they have been endowed, not to wither away. This divine revolution must begin in man himself. For a change in the outward structure of society has little meaning if men remain exactly as before. But it must certainly also find expression in radical changes in the social and economic structures.

We are now in a period in which the churches and individual Christians will have to choose between the spiritual-aroma religion and the prophetic faith concerned with justice for all men. For we who belong to the affluent part of the world have to meet a great test. The test is whether we will consider the overwhelming problem of hunger and poverty in other parts of the world as our own problem or not. I know that we are not wholly unmindful of the needs in the underdeveloped nations. There is the aid which our governments give; there is the not inconsiderable help which is given by individuals through Christian and other humanitarian bodies. But the crux of the matter is that the situation does not really improve. At a time when the rich nations become richer, the poor nations become poorer. Anyone who has travelled in Asia, or Africa, or Latin America or who has heard the real voice of these continents, as some of us did last summer in Geneva at the World Conference on Church and Society, knows that the issue becomes inescapable: either the continuation of the present trend with increasing inequality, increasing bitterness and therefore the abandonment of all hope of a tolerably peaceful international order or a radical change in relationships between the rich and the poor. U Thant has recently said that this is now world problem number one. The question becomes: Do we want the destructive revolution of despair or the constructive revolution of hope? Do we want a struggle of the have-nots against the haves or do we want to make the necessary fundamental changes together as members of a responsible world-society?

It is encouraging that the Roman Catholic Church inspired by the Vatican Council and the World Council of Churches inspired by the World Conference on Church and Society are now both seriously preparing to take up this issue of justice on a world-scale and that there is good reason to hope that they will do this together.

What can Christians do in this field? They can provide that moral force which is so badly needed to overcome the apathy, the indifference, the fatalism which now block all progress in the matter of making a new deal concerning the poverty stricken parts of the world. That moral force must prepare us to make real sacrifices, not only in the form of philanthropy but especially in the form of creating new structures of international economic and political life which will enable the poor countries to overcome their terrible handicaps. Economists of great standing tell us that it can be done, if (it is a very big "if") there is sufficient imagination and sufficient true concern for humanity in the affluent nations.

Whether we reach the moon is quite unimportant in comparison to the question whether we will help human beings to live and to live as human beings are meant to live. We must not rest until we have shown concretely that we believe in the great expectation that the hungry are filled with good things.

LADISLAUS BOROS

Suffering and Death

The problem of human suffering can be the greatest temptation of our faith and of our christian existence. How can God allow so much suffering? How can he look upon all the horror, injustice and ill-will that we experience? Why must his friends suffer just as his enemies do? Why does he not make manifest his almighty power? Why does he not help us when we feel the need for his help most keenly? Events take their course as if there were no God, as if our imploring prayer remained unheard. Gloom is not dissipated, the darkness of destiny is not dispelled, the helpless receive no lasting consolation. Often we have to look on helpless, while human beings, our friends and our neighbors, whom we love tenderly and for whom we pray in faith, are cast about on a sea of anguish and despair. What sort of God is it that permits all this and never intervenes? So the gnawing doubts multiply and undermine our certainty. They can be so strong that the whole of our faith totters, so that it seems we would be fools to go on believing. The victory of faith often consists in maintaining an "even so" of fidelity in despair, an "in spite of" in the most bitter experience.

What, then, is the meaning of pain and death? Who flung me into this painful world? Why was I compelled to live? Why did no one consult me about it? Why should I, who bear within myself an immortal spirit, why should I be tied to a body, to that which is transient, which is doomed to decay? And why should everything,

From *The Way*, VII (Winter 1967), 46–56. Reprinted with permission of the publisher.

in the end, be taken from me: my life, my friends, everything that I have built up and worked for with so much effort? Why must I go through illness and suffering, through death and through everything that goes with death, in order to reach immortality? Who answers these questions? It is Jesus Christ, who said of himself: "I am the first and the last, the living one. I was dead, but now I live for all eternity. I hold in my hands the key to death and to life hereafter." It is he who can help us to find an answer to all these torturing questions, and to win through from our darkness to his light, so that from our despair we may pass over into his joy.

This word joy expresses the inner attitude with which a Christian should approach every problem of his life, including therefore that of pain. Joy is the ultimate yardstick in christian experience. Depression—and we are thinking not so much of what happens on the surface but in the depths of our existence—is unchristian: It contradicts the spirit of the Lord. Reflection on the darker side of human life, on sickness, pain and death, ought to lead us to joy: Otherwise it is not christian meditation. Joy happens when human existence stands entirely open to Christ: He, and only he, can bring light into our darkness. To seek christian joy cannot mean closing our eyes to human needs, or turning away our gaze from human darkness, but rather to experience in its depths the contradiction of pain, and to expose it to the light of the Lord.

Every reflection on pain and death must be shot through with this vital truth: After the resurrection of Christ the destiny of the world is already decided: We are moving heavenwards. Amidst all the realities of our provisional world, what is definitive and ultimate is already in process. What we seek cannot end in emptiness; nothing can separate us from the love of Christ. So John will say insistently: "God is greater than our heart." And Paul gives an answer to all our hopes which goes beyond even the carefully calculated dreams of humanity: "When once all things are subject to Christ then will the son be with God, so that God may be all in all." In such a world there is no reason for despair or cowardice. God wants to see joyous, renewed, useful souls, souls relieved of anxiety. The Christian is to be a witness to joy in our joyless and pain-ridden world.

The ultimate questions of life, and certainly questions about sickness, pain and death are among these, must be answered from the basic insights of our faith, otherwise the answers will be superficial or simply false. Revelation gives us a basic answer to the why of suffering and death: "it was not always so," and, "it will not always be so." Once mankind lived in a state of wholeness, incapable of suffering, in a state of immortality, in paradise. And mankind will once again, in the state of eternal beatitude, achieve this wholeness, in possession of knowledge, incapable of suffering, and will live immortally, in heaven. We come from paradise and we are going towards heaven. What stands in between, the whole painful life of humanity, is therefore simply a transition, an episode of unhappiness in a world which is made for happiness.

In the beginning, man—that is to say, man as he was originally planned and made by God—was already whole, in possession of knowledge, incapable of suffering and death. He was living in a world that was "other." How was his world "other"? It was certainly a very threatening, hard and pitiless world; for man in the beginning had not yet learned to master it. And yet this man lived in a world that was "other."

What do we mean here by world? That which has two elements: the things and events which surround us, and an inner attitude, the state of man's consciousness. "World" is not a reality which is ready made. It "happens" not only out of objective situations but also out of our subjective attitude to them. Today we experience this "world" only in love and in friendship. A man who loves experiences the world that is "other." He discovers new depths and new meanings of the world. That was how it was in the state which we call paradise. Paradise was not another world; it was a world experienced in another way. We find the central moment of paradise in the third chaper of Genesis: God walked with man in the cool of the evening; they were in intimate conversation; they walked together hand in hand. This means that man was "with God"; the Lord was close to him. Between man and his creator was an "experienced" immediacy. God was a part of this man's experience; everywhere he felt God to be near at hand. That was the meaning of paradise; it was the same world in which we live, and in some ways a more threatening world. Yet it was another world, because it was experienced by man in another way, experienced in the light of God. It follows that man in paradise was whole. He possessed, as the theologians say, the *donum integritatis*: that is to say, he was not inwardly divided, not torn between desire and the realization of desire. Of course he knew nostalgia. He too was not always able to fulfill his dreams.

But, as he held the hand of God, he sensed fulfillment close to him. He knew, from his inward experience, that all nostalgia, all wishes and dreams, have their fulfillment. In this way man in paradise was whole: filled with desires, but sensing the fulfillment of his desires to be close at hand.

Paradise was also a state of complete knowledge—the *donum scientiae*. This does not mean that man knew a great deal quantitatively. The intellectual mastery of our modern technological world would have confused him. Yet qualitatively he knew much more than we do. The very little that he knew he received from the deepest ground, the very spring of all being. His world was transparent, "God-lucid": it was a veil revealing God.

Paradise was also a state of incapacity for suffering—*donum impassibilitatis*. This does not mean that man in paradise was without experience of pain. Pain is a signal which brings to man's consciousness an experience of the elements of the world that are a threat to his well-being. A man without any experience of pain could not have survived in the world. But when a man constantly lives in immediate contact with God, when he is wholly directed to the other, to God, pain cannot get out of proportion in him, it cannot take possession of his whole being; in other words, it cannot become suffering. Today we see an image of this, in love. A lover can feel pain, be troubled in soul and physically threatened; but if he loves—that is if he is accepted, with his whole being, in the beloved, then he bears his happiness with him, a happiness which no suffering can touch.

Finally, paradise was a state of immortality—*donum immortalitatis*. This does not mean that his biological condition was permanent, without change. Biological life presupposes self-development. But this development and refinement is such that it eventually reaches a state of fragility. And so, as life unfolds and is "lived out," it prepares its own destruction: It moves towards death. But this death would have occurred in the state of lived immediacy with God, without separation or rending apart. Through the power of God which was in him, man would have passed immediately into the state of perfection, into the state of resurrection, and therefore been "drawn over" into heaven. He would have experienced a dying, an agony, but not death, not the break-up of his own being. His lived immediacy to God would have produced in him an immediacy to heaven, to eternal life.

Such was human life as it was planned and created by God: not encapsulated in itself, but wholly drawn towards the holy, towards the experience of God. No matter how primitive, ignorant, menaced and liable to die this man might have been, he was perfect. Paradise was therefore a state (and whether it lasted a long time or only a moment is of no importance here) of tranquillity, of knowing, of unthreatened and fully lived being in a restless, opaque world given over to death. This life does not exist any more. Somewhere, sometime, this paradise was destroyed; and we were given over to inner conflicts, to ignorance, to pain and to death. Who brought about this state of affairs? Certainly not God. He never breaks off any friendship. In some way or other—we cannot say how and when— man told him: "I will live with you no more." This "no more" destroyed what was most beautiful and most alive in this man—his immediate relationship to God; and so it destroyed man himself. He could no longer experience God immediately; so that all his desires and dreams were empty; he gave himself over to ignorance; and thus pain grew in him and overflowed his whole being and became suffering: and thus death came out of dying.

The wonder is that God did not leave the matter there. He did not abandon man. He "permitted," it is true, that the eruption of pain should no longer be halted in us. In his despair (it is hard to find another word) he took suffering upon himself and came down into our death. As man went away from him, he came nearer to man. The whole history of humanity consists in the approach of God to us, ever nearer and nearer, and in God's gift of a new immediacy with himself: He himself became man in order to bring back the whole of man. He took upon himself fragile being, our threatened state, our creaturely ignorance, our pain and our death. Since man no longer wished to be with God, God became man, so that he could be with man.

We do not know why he did this. Love does not have to provide reasons; it gives itself without question. That is why it is love; and God is love. It is not simply that he loves: Rather his whole being consists in love. He loves and he does nothing else but love. To love and to be, in him, are one. He would cease to be (which is an impossible, indeed a meaningless supposition) if he no longer loved. By becoming man in Christ, God brought to completion the second act of creation. He makes heaven possible for us again. So creation is not yet perfected. It is still in process of being perfected. It will end only when man abandons himself again to the immediacy of God, when he enters once again paradise, which from now on is called heaven.

To be able to understand our life, we must know, in the sense of inwardly experiencing, and also make credible for others, that human life is directed to heaven. The world will be perfected only when man enters heaven. We are not yet alive in the proper sense of the word. Our life is only beginning, a becoming, a growing towards heaven. Illness, suffering and death belong to this state of transition. We know today that the cosmos is the product of an evolution that has been going on for millions of years. It evolved from its original state towards life; and life is perfected as man's mind is formed, and as this mind takes possession of itself in its recognition of God and in its giving of itself to him in love. Union with God draws the whole cosmos towards eternal fulfillment. This fulfillment is, in the end, a definitive, God-transparent cosmos: heaven. God created the world by lending it the power to rise towards him throughout its long development over thousands of years. The world is pointing to heaven. The end is the true beginning. According to the original plan of creation, the world should have passed over from paradise to heaven without any destruction, suffering or death. As things are now, because Christ became man and conquered death, and opened the way to heaven once more, the world moves infallibly and indubitably towards heaven.

But what is heaven? We do not know precisely. In the Bible this radical fulfillment is referred to as "the new heaven and the new earth." John describes this new world in his apocalypse, his "secret revelation." He speaks of oceans of glass, of streets made of gold and crystal, of doors fashioned of rare pearls, of walls built of glowing precious stones. The dominant motif in this description is the sense of power, of the humanly unattainable. Paul, too, stresses this "otherness" of heaven: "Eye has not seen, nor ear heard, nor has it entered into the heart of man, what things God has prepared for those who love him." And yet heaven is already very close to us. With the resurrection and ascension of Christ, heaven has already broken in upon our world. The powers of the world to come have already taken possession of us. Christianity considers the resurrection of Christ not simply as the private destiny of our Lord, but at the same time as the first sign that everything in our world has already been transformed radically, decisively, truly. The Easter event is not an isolated and limited fact in the history of salvation, but the sacred destiny of the whole world. Through his resurrection, Christ has spoken his effective and creative word upon the whole universe. It has already begun: "See, I make all things new." Though heaven is far from us, it is also close to us, radically related to us. The Christian lives in this tension. He is already in some sense in heaven, but in a heaven which is not yet constituted fully. In a similar way, the disciples on the road to Emmaus experienced the reality of the risen Lord. Jesus joined the two disciples who had left the brethren gathered in the upper room. For a long time he went along with them and spoke with them. But they did not recognize him. The Lord always appeared in this way after his resurrection, discreetly, as a hungry man, as a gardener, as a traveller, as a man on the shore of the lake. It is in this way that heaven is close to us. It appears unobtrusively; we catch its reflection, as in a mirror.

Christ promised to everyone a share in his own happiness in heaven. He promised what people most needed: eternal water to the samaritan woman, bread of eternal life to the people of Capharnaum, an abundant catch to the fishermen, to the shepherds, large flocks and pastures ever green, precious pearls to merchants; and to all of us an eternal banquet, a constant marriage celebration—which is a symbol of unending happiness in 'possession' of the person we most cherish in our life.

It follows that heaven is life lived intensively and completely. Not a world of ideas, grandiose but bloodless and dehydrated: but rather the fullness, the elevation of our sensible perceptions to eternity, in which they can grasp God as a gift. In heaven the ineffable gift for which the Church prays will come to pass: *accende lumen sensibus*, as we sing in the *Veni Creator*. The light of God will overflow in all our senses. What the mystics and all deeply religious men have experienced in innumerable mirrorings will come to pass: God will be seen, heard, tasted and enjoyed by us. Thus in heaven everything that is intellectual will be in the realm of the sensible, and everything that is sensible will be in the realm of the intellectual—including God himself. And man will indwell in the whole of reality, in a world made whole.

Heaven, then, is the definitive, ensconced, indestructible closeness of God, a participation in God. Our being can never full grasp or plumb the infinite depths of God's being. Hence, even this fulfillment is constantly a new beginning, a movement towards still greater fulfillment. Heaven must be understood essentially as a boundless dynamism. The fulfillment itself will so "expand" our souls, that in the next moment they can be filled still more by the being of God. We are therefore eternal seekers afer God. God remains ever greater than our limited being. A God that we had finally "got hold of" would be no God. Throughout our earthly life we seek God in order to find him. In eternal blessedness, even after we have found him, we continue to seek him. Here, he is hidden, so that man may seek after him, in order to find him. And he is incommensurable, so that we have to seek him even after we have found him. Eternity, then, will be a constant moving towards God. In heaven everything static is turned into a boundless, progressive, advancing movement towards God. Fulfillment is eternal transformation, a state of ceaseless and uninterrupted life.

Pain, sickness and death must be considered in this context. These are the real perspectives of human life. We are not forever given over to suffering. Our inner distress, our inner dissolution do not last forever. We are moving towards heaven. The suffering and need which afflict us here are provisional: in the deepest and last analysis unimportant. And yet it is still our task to protect those whom we love (and we have the duty to love as many men as possible) from all that depresses them and makes them suffer: that is, to make easier for them the way to their final happiness, to heaven.

We are all committed to oppose suffering. That is the first demand of the Christian's love of his neighbor. As long as it is possible, the Christian will offer every consolation; as long as it is possible, we must fight with God against evil. Our first task is service of the suffering brethren, for Christian existence is built upon our neighbor. As a Christian I have to help my abandoned and suffering brothers, and in that I am a Christian. A Christianity which is not concerned with the urgent task of love of the poor and the abandoned is empty chatter. The didactic point of the cure of the paralytic at the pool of Bethsaida, is that he had nobody to help him (Jn 5:1–9).

It is the most terrible experience of a human life when a person has to say: "I have nobody." As long as there is anyone in my environment, among the people who are accessible to me, who has to say "I have nobody," then I am no Christian. My eternal happiness depends on understanding Jesus' parable of the judgment: "Come

you blessed of my Father, possess you the kingdom which is prepared for you from the beginning of the world. For I was hungry
and you gave me to eat" (Mt 25:35). This is not symbolic language. It must be understood in all its hard truth. It is true that
spiritual need, inner imprisonment and hunger of soul, are also hard
realities. Somebody who has never once in his life given something
to eat to someone who is hungry, or drink to someone who is thirsty,
or never harbored a stranger, clothed someone who was naked,
visited the sick, or consoled a prisoner, will not come into heaven,
and so is not inwardly a Christian; he has understood nothing of
Christianity. He has missed its reality. A man becomes a Christian
not first of all because he finds ecstasy in his prayer, not because
he knows a great deal about laws and prescriptions, but through the
selfless service of his abandoned brethren in everyday life: of those
who are saying: "I have nobody." Whoever goes out and helps a
poor man, or even simply a man who feels abandoned, will one day
hear the word of Christ: "You are blessed. I have prepared for you
a kingdom from the beginning of the world. You have been a
Christian."

But who is my neighbor? When Christ was asked this question he
replied, not by any abstract working out of the concept of neighbor, but by telling the story of the good samaritan. The essential
point of this story is that my neighbor is the one who has only me
to help him. The whole attitude of the Christian is summed up in
that: Do what no one else will do in your place; be ready; develop
an openness of heart; be open to the sufferings of others. If you have
this attitude, then one day you will meet the man who has nobody,
apart from you; and then you must take him upon yourself; stay
with him, not pass by, tend him. It is almost impossible to bring out
in a modern language all the shades of meaning in the story of the
good samaritan. This is especially true of the point which concerns
us here. In the first two cases, those of the priest and the Levite, the
text says: "He saw him and passed by." According to the Greek
text it should rather be: "He saw him, halted for a moment without
knowing what to do, and then went on." Christian life concerns
itself especially with this moment of hesitation. I have to develop in
myself an inner readiness to overcome this moment of hesitation,
when specious reasons occur spontaneously, to let me off lightly.
There is also the fear: "If you bend down over this man, you will
have to share in his suffering; but that will be very wearisome. It

is better to pass by." Our eternal destiny can be decided in this decision to "pass by."

It is at this point, of course, that we can begin to penetrate the invincible mystery of suffering, as we come more closely to conform ourselves with the compassionate love of the Christ who fights evil with all his strength. In sharing his life, I share this struggle: As a Christian I may not give up the struggle before I have tried every possibility. Otherwise, the Christian religion would indeed be an opium for the people: it would collapse under the weight of the enormous problem of suffering. It is one of the greatest scandals in the history of Christendom that repeatedly Christian love of the neighbor was not strong enough to cry out against exploitation—the situation in which men were shackled in poverty and misery by other men.

God calls us to help him in the fight against evil. He has not spirited away pain and suffering from our lives. The Christian suffers, is hungry, struggles, like all other men. But hunger, suffering, struggle and death for him should have another sense. They should give him a chance to pass through his suffering to God, through the darkness into light.

To bear pain and illness patiently belongs to the genuinely Christian task of transforming darkness into light. Through the cross came the decisive choice for mankind. Through the suffering Christ endured there, the world received its spiritual transformation. If we want to transform the world into heaven, then we must take upon ourselves the suffering, the need and the care of men. The Christian vocation is to suffer; and, at the same time, to be convinced that we are moving toward eternal happiness. In this way the life of the Christian is a life of joy; and we have an answer to our most desperate need. Our bodily illness, our creaturely suffering, do not represent for us a threat so much as a task. Physical pain borne in a Christian way diminishes the amount of suffering in our world. When we take the suffering upon ourselves, we save others from disaster. We bring heaven nearer and we begin to transform our lost paradise.

The same principle is to be applied to interior suffering, as to physical pain: We are called to take human need upon ourselves, so that it gradually diminishes and disappears, until our world is transformed into heaven. This is the pattern Christ set in healing the man who was deaf and dumb (Mk 7:32–37). Having tended to his bodily needs, he showed him a way out of spiritual suffering. He said to him: "Be opened." This is the first and fundamental answer of Christ to our spiritual need: "Break out of the narrow circle of your self-isolation and your egoism and begin to say something good to your fellow men. It does not matter how clumsily or inadequately you do it; if you would be a man, live outside yourself and begin to listen to others. This means to be with them without counting the cost, to be there for them: What you suffer from most of all is that you are a stranger in the world of your fellow men. Open yourself. You will not lose anything. You will begin to be and only begin to be as you open yourselves for others, as you lose yourself for others; free yourself from yourself." This is the essential answer of Christ to our human suffering. We suffer from the fact that we are not fulfilled. Christ says to us: "The other is your fulfillment, go towards him, open yourself."

Again, the healing of the ten lepers (Lk 17:12–17) was for Christ an occasion to provide us with a wonderful help for our spiritual needs. He says to us: If you want to be happy, be grateful. Do not take for granted any of the gifts of life—above all, life itself. The person who can say "Thank you" confesses his own littleness, admits that he receives his true reality as a gift. Only in this way can a man be truly saved: saved from himself, no longer locked up in his own ego. So God cries out to us: "Cease to be in love with yourself. Let yourself go. Confess that you are nothing, that the little that you are you have received as a gift."

Then there was the sign in the city of Naim (Lk 7:11–15). Our Lord released a mother from her despair. He gave back to her all that she had lost. When we think that our life has been of no use to anyone, wasted on trivialities and frivolities, all our longings unfulfilled, Christ says to us: "Have no fear, I will pay it all back to you. There is no dream and no desire which remains unfulfilled. You have lost nothing, least of all what you have renounced. Go forward calmly in self-forgetfulness. Lose all for others. Even if you have lost all, you will receive all back again from me." So Christ draws us out of our spiritual narrowness and out of our obsessions and sense of failure. This is salvation: salvation from ourselves, from our own suffering.

In the end human pain enters so deeply into our being that it becomes the power of separation and of death. One's whole being collapses. In death man experiences a radical powerlessness and destruction. Is there an answer even here? "Yes," Christ says to us: "I possess the key of death." It is only in the moment of death that a man can finally lay aside the otherness of his own being and become sufficiently master of himself to encounter Christ completely, with every fiber of his being. It is in this confrontation that he is able to make the truly real decision.

According to this hypothesis,[1] in the moment of death, every man is given the possibility of deciding for or against Christ, with complete freedom. Notice that we say "in the moment" of death. We are not speaking of the moments immediately preceding death or of after death; but of the precise moment when the soul abandons the body. Then it awakens to its full spirituality, and understands all that created spirit can grasp. It sees its whole life summed up in a single whole, and discovers God calling and leading. It is impossible in this moment to ignore Christ. Man must decide once and for all—for all eternity, which will be nothing more than a development of what happens in this moment. Here he is faced by all he has sought for, grasped at, longed for. And through it all there gleams the light of the risen Christ. He is no longer confused by his environment, all that in his world or in his past gave him a distorted image of God. He is able to make a really true judgment, and decide for total rejection or total embrace of Christ.

The objection to this hypothesis—that if it is true, why bother to live in this world according to Christ's pattern—is a specious one. Only I can provide myself with the certainty of making the right decision in this truly crucial moment. I alone am the measure of the sincerity of my desire to be converted to Christ. So it follows that the decision I would wish to make in the future I must begin to make now, with all that is in me. Every postponement of it will be a decision against truth and myself. Nothing can guarantee, except my own responses now, that I will transform everything in the moment of death. If we understand this, we begin to penetrate Christ's constant advice: "Be sober and watch." So many of us during our earthly existence wander at a distance from the truth. So many of us pass God by, dominated by people, things and events, by our own desires and dreams. All these things hold a man, scarcely leaving space for God in his thoughts. To enter heaven, men must have the possibility of standing before God and deciding for him.

[1] Fr Boros has developed it fully in *The Mystery of Death* (New York: Herder and Herder, 1965).

Before this can happen, all that a man was and had, all that he has made and clung to, that is not God-like, must be taken away. All the masks must come off, all the roles he has played, before self and the world alike, must cease. Here is the moment of decision, when he is liberated from all that prevented him from seeing God face-to-face. It is in this moment that he stands at the center of the cosmos, before the glorified Christ. On his brow the sun gleams, his eyes are of fire; his face sparkles more than beaten gold and his hands hold the stars. Christ took upon himself the agony, the dying and the death, so that every man who has to pass along the road of death might encounter him; so that every man, at least in death, could make a free and definitive decision in his regard.

Thus Christ made us capable once again of recovering the nearness of God and of entering into endless happiness, the name of which is heaven, the real beginning of all things.

RUDOLF SCHNACKENBURG

Dying and
Rising with Christ

Our existence in the world is constantly threatened by sorrow, privation, and death, as well as darkened by sin and guilt. Religion reveals its power to overcome the desolation and darkness of human life. And Christian faith is especially efficacious in this direction, for Christ himself trod the way through death to glory. In the Pauline epistles we see exactly how profoundly the Apostle grasped, theologically penetrated, and personally applied this revelation of God in Christ to his life. The Pauline notion of dying, and rising with Christ is a principle that possesses great value for Christian existence in general. Although we meet related expressions in most of Paul's epistles, we properly understand this Pauline notion only when we carefully study the passage on baptism found in Romans 6: 1–11. Proceeding from this point, and thus from the basic concept of sacramental "dying and rising with Christ," we shall concentrate on broader statements proving that this notion is a central theme in the whole of Pauline thought—one that penetrates his personal life and becomes as well a model for every Christian's existence.

Dying and Rising with Christ in Baptism

It is hardly possible to treat exhaustively Paul's well-known text on baptism (Rom 6: 1–11), which is filled with many exegetical

From *Present and Future* (Notre Dame, Ind.: University of Notre Dame Press, 1966), pp. 101–21. Reprinted with permission of the publisher and the author. For full footnote documentation, see original publication.

problems. We can only discuss the most important parts and attempt a more accurate translation:

> Do you not know that all of us who have been baptized into Christ Jesus were baptized into his death? We were buried therefore with him by baptism into death, so that as Christ was raised from the dead by the glory of the Father, we too might walk in newness of life. For if we have grown together with the likeness of his death, we shall certainly grow together with that of the resurrection. We know that our old man was crucified with him so that the body of sin might be destroyed, and we might no longer be enslaved to sin. But if we have died with Christ, we believe that we shall also live with him.

We shall try to steer away from the interpretations of other scholars and simply present our own explanations in a positive way.[1] In this context the Apostle refutes an objection to his teaching on grace. In the preceding chapter of Romans (5:12–21), Paul teaches that, because God's grace would abound with the coming of Christ and because it would by far surpass the damage wrought for mankind by Adam, less prudent men might conclude: "Let us remain in sin, so that grace might abound" (6:1). Paul rejects this false and dangerous conclusion with the objection that we are once and for all dead to sin and are committed to a new life for God in Christ. In order to reinforce his argument, Paul refers to baptism and invests it with a new and deeper interpretation. His readers know that they have been baptized into Christ and now belong entirely to him. Paul, however, remarks even more clearly that in baptism they have been baptized into the death of Christ and that they have died to the malice of sin. In this connection he always understands sin to be a power that formerly dominated us, a power to which we have died through this baptism unto death and which we have completely thrown off.

The Apostle probably refers to the symbolism of baptism as it was then administered: A person was totally submerged in water so that he disappeared in it. But this liturgical symbolism represents a much more profound reality, namely, that we are incorporated into the death of Christ, who died definitively to the power of sin for all of us. We recognized this return to Christ's death when Paul in verse 6 remarks unexpectedly, "Our old man was *crucified* with

---

[1] For a fuller discussion see R. Schnackenburg, *Baptism in the Thought of St. Paul* (Oxford and New York: Oxford University Press, 1964).

him," that is, with Christ. Hence, when we disappear under the water's surface in baptism, it symbolizes a mystical union with the death and burial of Christ. Along with the external event occurs an interior event with consequences for our salvation: We are crucified with Christ so that our "old man," who was a slave to sin, is destroyed. Moreover, we also know by faith that Christ did not remain in the grip of death but was raised from the dead by the power of the Father. "The death he died, he died to sin, once for all, but the life he lives, he lives to God," Paul remarks in verse 10. Thus, we also die with him, that with him we might live to God. That is the meaning of the "newness of life" in which we should walk. This passage refers primarily to our moral life but involves more than simply a moral attitude. There is an actual participation in the life of the risen Christ. This has begun for us in baptism and will reach its final perfection only at the moment of our own resurrection. This eschatological perspective is revealed in verse 8, "But if we have died with Christ, we believe that we shall also live with him."

Up to this point everything should be clear. It is more difficult, however, to grasp the nature of this union initiated in baptism, by which we enter into the death and resurrection of Christ and so with Christ himself are crucified and raised from the dead. In verse 5 we come across a mode of expression that is concise and difficult to translate: "For if we have grown together with the likeness of his death, we shall certainly grow together with that of the resurrection." The Apostle obviously wants to express the whole reality of the event, of our actual union in the death and resurrection of Christ. To "have grown together" is a vivid image for a close union. The Vulgate in this instance did not translate *complantati* accurately enough, that is, to "have been planted together." The Greek version is even more arresting: We have been drawn entirely into Christ's death so that we ourselves have died with Christ, and with him have been crucified. This lays the foundation for solving the difficulties involved in our consideration of just how we can "grow together" and share in the likeness of the long past death of Christ on the cross.

This is best explained by noting that Paul had previously developed the typology of Adam and Christ (5:12–23), and regards Christ not only as an individual, but also as head or progenitor of the whole of a new mankind, namely, of all who believe in him. Now, according to Semitic thought, the progenitor represents the whole of those followers or that posterity united with him, so that he acts on behalf of all who are still to come and who share in his destiny. Thus, Paul states: "Since one died for all, therefore all died" (2 Cor 5:14). Through baptism we have been included in the destiny of our spiritual progenitor, Christ. We have undergone the same thing he has, and we have done so in union with him. Not only does our Christian faith witness "that Christ died for our sins according to the scriptures, and that he was buried and that he rose again on the third day according to the scriptures..." (1 Cor 15:3f.), but also all who believe in him, all who have been baptized unto his name and who thus belong to him testify to it. We, too, have died with Christ, have been buried with him, so that we might also rise with him. Baptism is the saving event allotted to each one of us, which at the same time unites us to the community of Christ, wherein we receive new being "in Christ" ($\dot{\epsilon}\nu$ $X\rho\iota\sigma\tau\tilde{\varphi}$). The Apostle clearly indicates this at the end of the passage in Romans, "So you also must consider yourselves dead to sin and alive to God in Christ Jesus" (6:11).

In Colossians we find the same thought expressed, namely, that in baptism a sacramental, actual dying and rising occurs: "In Christ you have been circumcised with a circumcision made without hands, by putting off the body of the flesh in the circumcision of Christ, and you were buried with him in baptism. In him you were also raised through faith in the working of God who raised him from the dead..." (2:11f.). But a comparison of Paul's thought in Romans and Colossians reveals a certain theological refinement: In Romans Paul says that as a consequence of our baptism we should lead a new life with Christ, and that we shall (one day) also live with him; but in Colossians Paul says that in baptism we have *already* been raised from the dead. This advancement in thought depends, most likely, upon the situation for which the epistle was intended. In Romans Paul's main consideration was the moral conclusion that since we no longer in any way belong to the power of sin, we *should* lead a new life. In Colossians Paul opposes a heresy by stressing that we have already obtained our salvation in Christ: Now we already possess, at least in a hidden and preliminary way, the life of the risen Christ, or, as Paul himself says at the beginning of chapter 3, "You have died and your life is hid with Christ in God; when Christ, who is our life, appears, then you also will appear with him in glory." These are fine distinctions. In the earlier epistle the emphasis is laid upon "dying with Christ," and the future rising from the dead appears to be withheld, whereas in the later epistle this future hope is already more firmly anchored in the present. Objectively, the thought in both epistles hardly differs: There is already in baptism a "dying and rising with Christ," although our own bodily rising from the dead first happens at the end, on the last day.

Salvation has been bestowed upon us fundamentally and radically in baptism, a salvation in Christ and totally bound up with Christ. Our union with Christ, our sharing in his course and destiny, is most forcefully emphasized in these statements that constantly reiterate acting "with Christ." From the moment of baptism the Christian sees himself as a person crucified and raised from the dead with Christ. In this fundamental sacrament God himself has touched us with his grace. We will now consider how Paul draws far-reaching conclusions for the whole of our Christian existence.

Dying and Rising with Christ in our Temporal Christian Existence

Because the Christian is bound to Christ as closely as possible, Paul sees in our dying and rising with him a law or rule governing our whole Christian life. This assimilation into the destiny of Jesus Christ, our Lord, is realized in a twofold manner: In the moral endeavors of the Christian and his temporal condition.

Moral Life as a Dying to Sin

In the epistle to the Galatians the Apostle remarks, "They who belong to Christ have crucified the flesh with its passions and desires" (5:24). The context is one where Paul underscores the necessity of decisive moral endeavor. He does not, however, simply enjoin an ethical imperative, but places this imperative within the new life of the spirit that has been given us: "If we live by the spirit, by the spirit let us also walk" (5:25). In the former he does not enjoin an imperative but says: "You *have* crucified the flesh." Finally, he turns his attention once again to baptism, in which our former self, bound to the service of sin, has been crucified with Christ. He means that just as our dying and rising has its origin in God, we *should* respond in our life by crucifying our flesh with

Christ—or to phrase it even better, we should have crucified it for our whole lives. This same idea weaves its way throughout the whole of Pauline ethics: Whatever you are, whatever you have become because of God's action, must be made a reality right now in your temporal existence. To paraphrase it more concisely, Paul places the moral imperative on the plane of the objective fact of grace.

But what does it mean "to crucify the flesh"? The Greek concept which we translate by the word "flesh" ($\sigma\acute{\alpha}\rho\xi$), is difficult to explain. It does not mean simply the bodily aspect of man, or even in a more restricted sense the sexual desires of man. It is much more comprehensive: the inclination toward sin of the whole man on the temporal and bodily plane of existence; that painful, destructive inclination we all experience. Among the "carnal" desires Paul lists not only the bodily or carnal instincts, but also those desires that we would preferably designate as vices of the "spirit" for example, dissension, anger, strife. Paul contrasts the "carnal" man with the "spiritual" who is driven on and led by the Spirit of God. "Walk by the Spirit, and do not gratify the desires of the flesh. For the desires of the flesh are against the Spirit, and the desires of the Spirit are against the flesh; for these are opposed to each other, to prevent you from doing what you would" (Gal 5:16f.). Here, by "Spirit" is meant the divine, Holy Spirit who from baptism fills us and moves us. Thus, we also learn to recognize the unique character of Christian morality, which takes up moral endeavor because of God's strength and the Spirit of God who has been bestowed upon us. We need do nothing more than permit ourselves to be moved by the spirit of God, and without resistance accept his promptings.

The fact is, however, that after baptism the Christian still finds himself living in his former body and is still exposed to temptations. Paul, employing the terminology of his time, speaks of "passions and desires." Contemporary man primarily understands "passions" to be strong emotional forces that can be employed for both good and evil. The Apostle, however, has in mind passions that impel man to sin. He sees man realistically, strikingly inclined toward evil acts, and he holds the power of sin accountable. Moral life is not without its battles, and so he readily employs corresponding images: "Let not sin therefore reign in your mortal bodies, to make you obey their passions. Do not yield your members to sin as instruments of wickedness, but yield yourselves to God as men who have been brought from death to life, and your members to God as instruments of righteousness" (Rom 6:12f.). Sin is seen as a power set upon war, which will imprison and enslave us, in order at the end to pay us our "soldier's wages" with eternal death (6:19f., 22). This power knows how to force its entry by means of desires and passions in us, it attracts us by using what is forbidden "you shall not covet" (7:7ff.), and it can gain the upper hand in us if we do not oppose it in the strength of the Holy Spirit.

The notion of dying and rising with Christ in our moral life also stands in the background of Colossians: "Mortify your members, which are on earth, immorality, impurity, passion, evil desire and covetousness..." (3:5). In a previous verse the Apostle mentioned that we have risen with Christ, and that we should seek the things that are above (v. 1). "Set your minds on things that are above, not on things that are on earth" (v. 2). Later, he resumes speaking about baptism, in which we have "set aside the old man with his deeds," in the way an old piece of clothing is set aside, and in which we "have put on the new man, who is being renewed in knowledge after the image of his Creator" (v. 9f.). There is, therefore, a moral "dying" and a moral "rising," which consists in having our home in heaven, in union with the risen Lord, and in the striving for the "things above." But in his admonitions the notions of "mortifying" and "crucifying" our old self with Christ assume greater importance. "Rising" and drawing near to Christ act more as a motive by which we persevere under the moral struggle that is necessary even at the present.

Thus, obsolete as it sounds, this admonition to "mortify our members" has a deeper and more positive meaning. We adhere to it only to commit ourselves to the crucified and risen Lord, in complete self-surrender to his person and destiny. It is not so much an ascetic training or struggle, but rather *a personal following and fellowship —transposition of the discipleship of Jesus in his earthly life to the continuous union with Christ, our exalted Lord.* This will become clearer as we consider yet another aspect of this idea.

Dying and Rising with Christ in Our Temporal Destiny

The Apostle has made even fuller use of this notion in relation to the Christian's temporal course and condition. His own experience collaborated in this, that is, his apostolic existence during which he was constantly subject to suffering, persecutions, and dangers (1 Cor 4:9–13; 2 Cor 6:4–10, 11:23–33). In a life constantly threatened by death, he saw that he was a follower of Christ, who had preceded him along a way of suffering and death. It is not, however, merely a matter of imitating Christ—merely a re-enactment of Christ's fate—but it is at the same time a profound inner union with him. For this reason Paul develops ideas that have not mistakenly been termed a "mysticism of suffering."

In this connection one of the most significant passages is 2 Corinthians 4:10–18. After the Apostle has glanced back at his painful but unbroken existence, he remarks: "Always bearing about in our body the dying of Jesus so that the life also of Jesus may be made manifest in our bodily frame. For we the living are constantly being handed over to death for Jesus' sake, that the life also of Jesus may be made manifest in our mortal flesh" (vv. 10–11). Paul's sufferings are a manifestation of Jesus' death, are the "sufferings of Christ," as he says in the same epistle but in an earlier chapter: "For as the sufferings of Christ abound in us, so also through Christ does our comfort abound" (1:5). Paul is then convinced that he must sustain the trials and pains of his office as an apostle, not only for the sake of Christ but also in union with his Lord, so that Christ's sufferings might be visible in him. He lived in the conscious awareness of his weakness and his hardships, and that in him Christ crucified vicariously revealed his sufferings to the world.

But the Apostle does not concentrate solely on the thought of suffering and death. For him the cross and Jesus' resurrection forge an inseparable unity. Thus, he knows with the assurance of faith that Jesus' life will some day also manifest itself in his body, namely, as he remarks to the Philippians, that Christ upon his return "will change our lowly body to be like his glorious body" (3:21). He sustains Christ's sufferings for the sake of Christ's future glory. We know by what follows in verse 14 that in the passage from 2 Corinthians Paul is thinking of the glorification of the body at the resurrection: "We know that he who raised up Jesus will raise us also with Jesus." Once again we meet the typically Pauline expression "with Jesus." It is noteworthy that in this context Paul invariably speaks about "Jesus" and not about "Christ." He is reflecting on the once crucified and now risen Jesus, in whose death and resurrection he is incorporated, so that, if he is to share in Jesus' resurrection at the moment of eschatological perfection, he must first in his own temporal existence assume these sufferings with Jesus.

Finally, he indicates his apostolic and missionary convictions when, in a characteristic turn of his thought, he states in verse 12: "Thus death is at work in us, but life in you." Through his own suffering in union with Jesus, Paul wants to be a cause of the Corinthians receiving the fullest possible measure of the strength and glory of their risen Lord. In Colossians he writes even more pointedly: "I rejoice now in the sufferings I bear for your sake; and what is lacking of the sufferings of Christ I fill up in my flesh for his body, which is the church" (1:24).

Even though Paul's "mysticism of suffering" expresses thoughts that are very personal and particularly meaningful to him as an apostle, he is nevertheless convinced that every Christian must resemble his suffering Lord. He expresses this most concisely in a passage from Romans, where he calls us "heirs with Christ": "We suffer with him that we may also be glorified with him," and he adds, "For I reckon that the sufferings of the present time are not worthy to be compared with the glory to come that will be revealed in us" (8:17f.). The course from suffering to glory, determined by God for Jesus to follow, becomes a rule of life for every Christian. It is not only a general law of our human, temporal existence, but it is imposed by reason of our close association with Christ—one with him, we must follow this course with and in imitation of him.

In a frequently quoted text from Galatians, the Apostle resumes his consideration of this notion of our Christian existence: "I have been crucified with Christ; it is no longer I who live, but Christ who lives in me" (2:19f.). From what moment is Paul constantly crucified with Christ? If we reflect more closely upon this passage (which here we cannot do at length) Paul could only mean that moment in which he became a Christian. And although he speaks in the first person singular, he means, nevertheless, every Christian who from the moment of baptism and through baptism has been signed by Christ's cross. To express it even more precisely, the Christian is one who has been drawn into the event of crucifixion. At the same time the life of Christ, the risen Lord, becomes operative in the Christian: No longer is it his own ego, but Christ himself living in him, as Paul remarks in an unparalleled formulation.

In this passage, and in others as well, we recognize that the Apostle regards Christ's resurrection as a power already present in the Christian. He speaks about this power which he receives as an apostle from his living Lord, when he declares to the Corinthians that he must take a more forceful stand on the occasion of his next visit: "Christ is not weak in dealing with you, but is powerful in you. For he was crucified in weakness, but lives by the power of God. And we are weak in him, but in dealing with you we shall live with him by the power of God" (2 Cor 13:3f.). Likewise, it is the risen Christ who consoles and strengthens him in the trials of his apostleship: "We are afflicted in every way, but not crushed; perplexed, but not driven to despair; persecuted, but not forsaken; struck down, but not destroyed" (2 Cor 4, 8f.). As contemporary men we should perhaps like to ask whether the Christian faith is only a religion of suffering. But we would misunderstand Paul if we thought that he valued suffering in itself or that he could visualize himself as a Christian only in suffering. The opposite is the case. For every human life does entail trial, distress, as well as pain, and the Apostle teaches us that suffering with Christ is necessary for this temporal order, so that one day we might rise from the dead and obtain life with him. The keynote dominating Paul's temporal existence is joy. Nowhere is this more explicit than in his epistle to the Philippians, written while he was a prisoner in jail; the expressions "to rejoice" and "joy" occur fourteen times. Among them, "But even if I am made the libation for the sacrifice and service of your faith, I am glad and rejoice with you. And in the same way you should be glad also and rejoice with me" (2:71f.). His constant prayers for the Philippians are filled with joy (1:14), and at the conclusion he admonishes them once more, "Rejoice in the Lord always, again I say, rejoice" (4:4). Union with Christ the Lord brings a profound inner joy. Paul counts all else as worthless in comparison to the knowledge of his Lord, a knowledge that surpasses all things. He strives to know him, to share in his sufferings as well as in the strength of his resurrection, and to be conformed to his death so that he might also rise from the dead (3:10f.).

After examining these texts, one thing should be clear, namely, that a vast program for life lies in the conception of suffering with Christ that we might be glorified with him and dying with Christ that we might rise with him. In this connection we shall now devote our attention to the aspect of eschatological fulfillment when we shall rise with Christ, live with him, and reign with him.

Our Future Rising with Christ

Even when writing to the Thessalonians, in the oldest of his extant epistles, Paul uses words with added nuances: "Since we believe that Jesus died and rose again, even so, through Jesus, God will bring with him those also who have fallen asleep," (1 Thes 4:4). The expression "with him" occurs in both Judeo-apocalyptic and early Christian tradition. In the book of Daniel we read about the "coming of one who appeared as a Son of Man" (7:13), and we later read about the "people of the holy ones of the most high" (7:27). In both places it is said that power and dominion will be conferred: in the former upon the one who is like the Son of Man, and in the latter upon the people (7:27). It is still uncertain in Daniel what relationship exists between the "Son of Man" and the "holy ones of the most high," whether both signify the same thing or whether "the Son of Man" is at the same time an individual and collective form, a representative of all the People of God. In the book of Enoch it is somewhat clearer: "The just and chosen ones will be saved one day and will then no longer behold the countenance of the sinner and the unjust. The Lord of spirits will then dwell above them, and they will eat *with the Son of Man*" (Ethiopian En 62:13f.). The eschatology of the early Church had already applied the "Son of Man" to Jesus and understood the "chosen ones" to be those trustworthy Christians who would reign with him. Thus, the Apocalypse (20:3) tells us that the martyrs would come to life to rule for a thousand years with Christ (μετὰ τοῦ Χριστοῦ), remarking further (20:6) that they will be priests of God and Christ who will rule for a thousand years with him. The entire early Church, however, was familiar with this idea of an eschatological reign with Christ, and it appears to have belonged to her catechesis (Mt 19:28, 25:34; Lk 22:29f.; 1 Cor 4:8, 6:2; 2 Tim 2:12; Apoc 3:21). Paul simply expresses a common doctrine of the early Church, but at the same time permeates it with his own notion of dying and rising with Christ.

The meaning of the words "God will bring us with Jesus" is clear even in the Jewish and early Christian background. At the end of this temporal order God will permit Christ, the Son of Man (Paul, however, avoids this expression, which is misleading for his Hellenistic readers), to appear before the whole world in power and glory, and with him those who belong to Christ, in order that they might live and rule forever with him. Further in the course of his instruction Paul, again employing older apocalyptic language, says to the Thessalonians "For the Lord himself will descend from heaven . . . then we who are alive, who are left, shall be caught up together with them [i.e., those who have been raised from the dead] in the clouds to meet the Lord in the air, and so we shall always be *with the Lord*" (4:16f.). We should not take exception to a mode of expression that employs old images and is bound up with an earlier cosmology. What is decisive is that we will then be united with the Lord forever. At that moment the purpose of all our presently imperceptible fellowship with Christ on earth will be reached, for if we have followed him in suffering and death, have been one with him and conformed to him, we will also share in his heavenly glory and be one with him forever. That this consummation of the final days will be allotted to us in virtue of Jesus' role as Savior and in virtue of our union with him, is clearly indicated by the Apostle: "Since we believe that Jesus died and rose again, even so [οὕτως] through Jesus, God will bring those also who have fallen asleep" (4:14).

We have seen earlier that Paul's hope and longing in his suffering are always directed toward the future resurrection. The fact that he has such strong faith in our suffering now with Christ so that we might one day be "glorified" with him (Rom 8:17), deserves closer scrutiny of his great chapter on the resurrection (1 Cor 15). Here Paul once again leans upon the parallel of Adam and Christ: "For as in Adam all die, so also in Christ shall all be made alive" (v. 22). Toward the end he states even more clearly: "Just as we have borne the image of the man of dust, we shall also bear the image of the man of heaven" (v. 49). The risen Christ, the representative and leader of redeemed mankind, exhibits in his glorified form the example for all men who belong to him and who have been called to the fullness of salvation, and he himself leads them to this fullness of salvation. Christ, the Second Adam, has become "a life-giving spirit" (v. 45); as the raised, living, and exalted Lord he pours out his spirit, the divine "Spirit" of life, upon all who believe and are united with him. In baptism we receive this divine Spirit who dwells and operates in us, until the day when he will also effect the resurrection of our bodies.

In Romans Paul remarks, "If the Spirit of him who raised Jesus from the dead dwells in you, then he who raised Jesus Christ from the dead will give life to your mortal bodies also through his Spirit who dwells in you" (8:11). At the same time it is clear that our future resurrection is a profound mystery of faith, and that we may in no way represent it according to temporal conditions and analogies. It will be a new creation from the divine Spirit of life, who has already been given us, Paul says, as "first fruits" or as a "pledge," a guarantee (Rom 8:23; 2 Cor 1:22, 5:5). Because Jesus as the glorified Christ possesses the fullness of the Spirit and permits him to descend upon us, he is also called the "firstborn among many brethren" (Rom 8:29) or "the firstborn from the dead" (Col 1:18). Our hope depends entirely on Christ, who has been crucified and buried, but who has been raised from the dead by the power of his Father. An old article of faith, taken up by Paul, maintains that Christ was "put to death for our trespasses and raised for our justification" (Rom 4:25). It is in him and through him that we have the guarantee of our own resurrection, and thus we, too, will be raised from the dead and glorified "with him."

IV War and Peace

No issues of politics or religion have provoked more soul-searching among Christians and non-Christians today than the growing violence of modern war and the decreasing possibility of lasting peace. The discussions of theologians in this field, while voluminous and laden with tensions, often seem remote from what is happening to wartorn, mutilated countries and their homeless, starving peoples. Talk of a "just war" and "limited nuclear warfare" seems more and more unrealistic in a world in which the major powers possess a nuclear arsenal with enough force to destroy the human race.

In such a situation the advocates of pacifism and nonviolence clearly have an advantage, for the realities of the nuclear situation make a nuclear war equivalent to global suicide. It has been suggested that the best attitude for Christians is to "de-theologize" the situation, i.e., to discuss the practical political and military aspects, which are generally in a state of rapid change and development, and to ignore the theological, moral issues.

However, wars continue to take millions of lives. Devastation becomes more widespread; savage wars of nationalism or social revolution increase in Latin America, Africa, the Middle East, and southeast Asia. The ideological struggle continues to erupt in eastern Europe and Asia. Men who are forced to comply with militaristic systems which accelerate ever more rapidly toward nuclear destruction, eventually realize that moral decisions must be made. If what these systems require men to do or submit to is evil, then men understand that they are called in conscience to join in protest, demonstrations, draft resistance, violent assaults or guerrilla warfare.

What has the New Testament or theology to offer the Christian conscience in this complex, emotionally charged atmosphere? The statements on warfare in the New Testament originated in an age when warfare was a limited, small-scale event which recurred periodically. Yet Rome's conquest of the known world in the first century A.D. brought into being something resembling modern warfare. The well-documented destruction of Jerusalem by Titus, and the subsequent mop-up operations at sites such as Bethar, Herodium, Masada, Machaerus, and the cave of Bar Kochba (all of which have been verified by archaeologists) seem to have foreshadowed modern "search and destroy" missions. Christians who had escaped from Palestine and converts from North Africa, Greece, and Asia Minor understood that warfare was not glorious, but a cruel process of slow or swift destruction. For them "Blessed are the peacemakers" had the impact of a positive, emphatic command.

The entire New Testament concept of peace is larger and broader than the mere absence of armed hostility. As Father John L. McKenzie shows, the Biblical basis of peace rests on the rich background of the Hebrew word *shalom*, which can mean "wholeness" or "health" and includes all that is needed for man's well-being. In the New Testament *shalom* came to be a characteristic of the messianic era, and meant the salvation brought to men by the death of Jesus. It did not preclude the idea of struggle to bring about a better human existence, a world-order here and now in which men might try to achieve their destiny.

Professor John J. Lally, looking on the reality of the needs of today, calls for a more complete theology of interpersonal conflict in situations in which conflict must be part of the struggle to achieve a just social order. The paradox of "Christian conflict" within religious groups or among differing social organizations will be a continuing phenomenon if the longing men have for dignity and freedom is to become reality. Struggle and revolution between rich nations and poor nations, between haves and have-nots, will grow in volence until the means of decent human existence have been achieved throughout the world. Whether the means to a just world order will be violent or nonviolent, an evolution is occurring; conflict will assuredly be an element in this evolution. Nonviolence, too, contains a dimension of conflict and has claims upon the thinking of all Christians.[1]

Dr. Gibson Winter looks at the Christian and theological roots of the nonviolent technique of demonstration. He thinks that those who take part in demonstrations must make a decision for or against the injustice of the situation; many will identify themselves with the human revolution which is sweeping across the globe. To such acts of decision about human rights, the freedom movement has called Christians. Many will show their belief in human dignity and freedom by protest and demonstration; others will try to gloss over injustice and destitution.

Not only the cessation of armed conflict but the constant pursuit of peace must be a preoccupation of Christians. Dr. Alva Myrdal of the World Council of Churches outlines the political, social, and legal steps which must be taken before a lasting, peaceful world order can begin to take shape.

The freedom and peace which Christ has won for men may not be realized in time. Limitations of human greed and sin may mean that lasting peace can be achieved only with the final coming of God's kingdom. But a Christian of the twentieth century cannot turn aside from the issues of war, social justice, national sovereignty, and international community without feeling guilty if he has not made the greatest possible efforts to achieve peace and international justice.

[1] For an excellent study of nonviolence, see P. Régamey, *Non-violence and the Christian Conscience* (New York: Herder and Herder, 1966).

JOHN L. Mc KENZIE

A Biblical Concept

The Roman historian Tacitus, composing a fictitious speech which he put in the mouth of a British chieftain resisting the Roman invasion, made the Briton say of the Romans: "They make a desert and call it peace." This is the earliest known gibe at the *pax Romana*, and it was uttered by a Roman. But it was not the first nor the last time that men have played cynically with the word *peace*; and possibly the reason for choosing it as one of the biblical themes treated in this series is the desire to play with it—or possibly to speak about it while we are still in a position to do so.

Any biblical handbook points out that the Hebrew and Greek words for peace as used in the Bible have a far wider meaning than our own English term. This distinction should not be exaggerated; we apply the words *peace* and *peaceful* to any condition in which tranquillity reigns. Augustine defined *universal peace* as the tranquillity of order. It is hard to define the quality of peace in positive terms; we think of it as the absence of disturbance, of noise, of violence. Thus, we can even speak of the peace of the grave, which is a violent paradox; an Israelite would not use it. To us the tranquillity of peace implies inaction; when things are peaceful, nothing is going on. The ancient Israelite, like the modern Israeli and the Moslem, greeted his brother with the wish: "Peace to you," or more literally, "Peace be upon you." This is not a wish that the brother

Reprinted from *The Living Light; A Christian Education Review* III (Summer 1967), 77–80, published by the National Center of Confraternity of Christian Doctrine, 1312 Massachusetts Ave., N.W., Washington, D.C. 20005. Reprinted with permission of the publisher.

may have rest. Peace between groups is the absence of strife. Peace to us in our day is the absence of war, but it is really more than that: It is absence of enemies, and this we think can be achieved only through war.

The Hebrew word *shalom* by contrast has a very positive content. One meaning of the verb related to this noun is "to finish" or "to complete"; it is the word used to designate the payment of a debt. It is a state of "accomplished" well-being. It is less the absence of disturbance than the absence of fear; thus, it is security, and it is related in meaning to that Hebrew word which can be translated both "salvation" and "victory." The messianic king is "the prince of peace" (Is 9:5), a title which we like to give Jesus. But this well-being is not regarded as the result of war and victory, although the passage from Isaiah, just quoted, does allude to the termination of strife by the defeat of enemies. One must recall another line of the same book which calls peace "the work of righteousness" (Is 32:17), the line which Pius XII adopted as his motto. The line sums up much of Old Testament theology: There can be no true peace, whether we think of peace as tranquillity or as well-being, that does not repose upon righteousness. "There is no peace for the wicked," to quote another contribution to the same book of Isaiah (48:22, 57:21).

Thus, God is the true author of peace, as he is the true author of righteousness, and there can be no genuine peace apart from God. There can be intervals of tranquillity, there can be the cessation of war for a time with no reference to God; but that peace which is the fullness of well-being is not within the reach of man working by secular means. Jeremiah speaks of false prophets who proclaim, "Peace, peace," when there is no peace (6:14, 8:11): They say that all is well when there is no righteousness. True well-being is achieved only in that harmony which man experiences when he is in harmony with God.

Shalom, we have indicated, is a more positive idea than our own idea of peace; it is not repose and inaction. It is rather that condition which permits fullness of action, even if it is described as a man sitting under his vine and fig tree with none to terrify (Mic 4:4). There is no romance of war in the Old Testament; war is a part of the human condition which interferes with life in one's family and in one's people, with the cultivation of the soil and the exchange of goods and services. This is the productive work by which life is sustained and enriched. The Israelite asked little when he asked for peace, no more than the chance for him and his fellows to realize the potentialities and the opportunities of their lives. They did not share and did not understand the demonic desire for conquest which moved the Assyrians. Once in their past they had known this desire in the reign of David, but the peace which David's conquests had brought had long since been shattered, and we see no serious thought that it could be regained by the same means. Ultimate and lasting peace would be wrought by God.

Was the Old Testament hope of peace entirely eschatological, postponed to a distant future when the arm of the Lord would do things which he had not done in history? This is the sense in which Israelite prophets and poets look to peace. Since perfect peace cannot be expected without perfect righteousness, they were compelled to an eschatological hope. But this did not mean that something less than perfect universal peace lay outside hope and was not desirable. If God really cherished righteousness, then he could make his peace rest upon the righteous even in a disturbed world. But this leads to the acknowledgment that peace is not only the work of righteousness, it is identified with righteousness; in a wicked world nothing but righteousness secures peace, and peace may be no more than conscious righteousness. If peace be understood in this way, we may be on the threshold of self-righteousness.

At this point we encounter the peace of Jesus Christ. He is called "our peace" in Ephesians 2:14, but the meaning here is a bit surprising. He is called our peace because he is the means of uniting Jews and Gentiles in one people of God. Peace here is reconciliation between Jews and Gentiles and between men and God (2:16). It is the end of disorder and the creation of true well-being; for the basic disorder of man is sin, and true well-being consists in union with God. In this union man fears no evil, not even death itself, which is unable to destroy true well-being. Jesus could proclaim peace at the same time that he blessed poverty and mourning. The peace which he gives his disciples is not the peace which the world gives (Jn 14:27). This peace can be maintained even when all the elements of the peace of the world are lacking. It is peace both in the sense of well-being and in the sense of tranquillity of order, but the tranquillity is interior, not exterior. It is not produced by an exterior agent nor can it be destroyed by an exterior agent.

Such a peace could be confused with the Stoic ideal of "apathy," that attitude which allowed the Stoic to preserve his "peace of mind" in suffering and iniquity because he did not allow himself to become involved. The peace of Christ does not rest on disengagement from one's fellowman, and it is, of course, engagement which threatens peace. But the Christian engagement does not threaten peace, it secures peace; for the Christian engagement with man is an engagement with God. If it is anything else, it is not a Christian engagement. The peace of the Christian cannot be taken from him by his fellowmen because he loves them, deeply and persistently; in his love he finds peace. He knows that in loving them he most surely loves God, and this is his security. If he ceases to love or if he restricts his love, his peace is lost.

Jesus called the peacemakers "blessed" (Mt 5:9). Those who call him master and Lord and bear his name must, like him, be messengers of peace. In the first place, this means that they try to communicate to others that peace of Christ which is conferred on us by the saving act of Jesus and is cherished by Christian love. But the beatitude uses the term "peacemaker" in a more specific sense, the sense of one who reconciles men with one another. To halt strife may not lead men directly to Christian love; but to permit strife or, still more, to promote it certainly does not lead to Christian love. Jesus himself said that he came "to bring not peace but a sword" (Mt 10:34; Lk 12:51). The fact that Jesus is a cause of division does not make him any less a messenger of peace and unity. He recognizes sadly that the world does not want his peace, is not ready for it, has never been ready for it, is not ready for it now. He still proclaims his peace and not the peace of the world, and his peace in the affairs of men takes the external form of reconciliation. It is not in his gospel nor in his spirit that his followers have so often preferred to seek the Roman peace which makes a desert. In these involved and tortuous human relations, the Christian is sure that he is faithful to the mind of Jesus when he promotes reconciliation; he is not sure when he does anything else.

We spoke of the eschatological peace as the ultimate hope. This still remains a hope, but the New Testament does not suggest that it should be a hope so deferred that it becomes hopeless. Until it is achieved, the Christian is to be a peacemaker, always moving in the direction of eschatological peace, never accepting strife and discord as an inevitable part of the human condition, and still less accepting it as a means of improving the human condition. Each effort, however limited, however personal, rolls back a little the reign of hatred, which is the reign of sin and death, and moves man ever so slightly towards the reign of God. For when man hates his brother, he is incapable of loving God (1 Jn 4:20).

JOHN J. LALLY

A Theology of Conflict

"Do not imagine that I have come to bring peace to the earth; I have come to bring a sword, not peace" (Mt 10:34).

Many Catholics believe that interpersonal conflict—between persons, between a person and institution, or between groups—which ruptures peace in the Church, in the community, or in the family, is "the work of the Devil." But I am convinced that the avoidance or stifling of such conflict often is a sign of immaturity and a block to the Spirit.

In Christianity, peace among men, harmony in the community, have traditionally been held to be both fruits and hallmarks of Christian life and have been closely linked to the central virtue of love (*caritas*). The bases for this in Scripture and in the liturgy are many and well-known. However, in the development of doctrine, particularly in the Roman Catholic Church, the emphasis on harmony, especially within the Church, became excessive. As a result, Church teaching about human relations came to be one-sided. Love of neighbor became too tied to peace, tranquillity, order, stability and often, at least indirectly, to security and the status quo. If change were deemed desirable, it was to be brought about gradually, with a minimum of confrontation between those with sharply differing views. Revolution, in thought or society, was not recognized as a legitimate means of change.

Examples of this tendency occur in much traditional Catholic

From *Commonweal*, LXXXVI (December 15, 1967), 355–58. Reprinted with permission of Commonweal Publishing Co., Inc.

spirituality. In the *Introduction to the Devout Life*, for example, St. Francis de Sales implies that although a Christian must resist evil and correct the faults of those for whom he is responsible, he must nevertheless *always* do so peacefully and gently; it would be better if he never expressed even a just and reasonable anger. In the social encyclicals, the Popes stress the goodness of class harmony to the practical exclusion of class conflict (even nonviolent) as a legitimate means of striving for human rights. And gradualist theology traditionally has opposed dialectical confrontations, a stance that has hampered the development of doctrine. (As John P. Sisk has indicated in a recent essay in the *National Catholic Reporter*, this over-emphasis on harmony, order and unity in the Church has been in large measure due to the reaction of the Church as institution to recurrent perceived threats to its existence.) In short, the place of interpersonal conflict in Catholicism has been greatly overlooked, neglected or avoided by the Church, at least until Vatican II. Even today much of the resistance to criticism, debate and struggle for human rights in the Church indicates how common pre-conciliar thinking on the subject is. Nevertheless, parts of the New Testament and findings from the modern sciences open other vistas upon Christian life and love. For, although complicating them and introducing an element of paradox, interpersonal conflict seems to be integral to the Christian mission and message, to Christian life and, indeed, to all human life.

Psychoanalysts, following Freud, claim to have established that the child inevitably experiences rivalry toward his parents or parent-surrogates and his siblings (if he has any) during the "oedipal phase." Moreover, it is held, these childhood conflicts are essential to normal human development. Similarly, psychology shows that the adolescent's natural strivings for identity and independence invariably bring him into some opposition to the hitherto recognized authority of the older generation. Conflict is also natural in adult relationships. Its expression can act as a kind of safety device that prevents the inner build-up of smoldering resentments which can be more destructive of human relationships than the conflict itself. A West Coast psychotherapist, discussing the inevitable disagreements and quarrels in marriage, has said that we must remove the shame from them, that we should not repress conflict, but channel it, sticking to the disputed subject and trying to resolve the disagreement with logic rather than invective. In marriage, some disputes can be expected. The real harm is done when their causes are not worked out, but magnified into abiding hatreds.

A recent collection of anthropological essays, edited by Paul Bohannan, provides fascinating analyses of conflict in various cultures throughout the world. Bohannan, himself an anthropologist, says that conflict is useful; that, indeed, society is impossible without it. Sociologist Lewis Coser in *The Functions of Social Conflict* makes the same point. Coser affirms that social conflict, as has been generally assumed, is often destructive. His main thesis, however, is: "Far from being only a 'negative' factor which 'tears apart,' social conflict may fulfill a number of determinate functions in groups and other interpersonal relations. . . ."

Coser then goes on to clarify what he sees as the functions of social conflict in discussing sixteen basic propositions, distilled primarily from the work of Georg Simmel. For example, from one proposition concerning in-group conflict: Within pluralistic societies (built on multiple group affiliations, each of which involves its members' personalities only segmentally) the crisscrossing of intergroup conflicts tends to "sew the social system together," one such conflict cancelling out another, and thus to prevent disintegration along a single primary line of cleavage. Thus, the stability of bureaucratic structures may be accounted for in part by the fact that a multiplicity of conflicts between various bureaus and offices prevents the formation of a united front, for instance, of low-status against high-status members of the hierarchy. Three other propositions relate to conflict with out-groups or enemies and how it tends to increase the internal cohesion of a group.

In his research on small groups at the Harvard Laboratory of Social Relations, Robert F. Bales has found that task-oriented group activities tend to generate rivalries and tensions among group members. This necessitates periodic group activity oriented more or less directly to re-establishing members' feeling of solidarity or integration with each other in the group. This bit of theory can be extended to social phenomena outside of the laboratory; for example, the office party after the strains of meeting a big deadline.

Finally, the experience of all of us tends to corroborate the thesis which this presentation of findings from the behavioral sciences is intended to illustrate: At least some conflict between men is normal, natural and quite often necessary and functional. By this I do not mean to say that such conflict is, in itself, necessarily good. But it does seem that any ethics or morality based on or in accord with natural law must take these things into account—as should, especially, a Christian theology for which "grace builds upon nature."

Beyond the assertion that at least some interpersonal conflict is natural and healthy, Christ's life and words clearly demonstrate that at least some conflict with others is also an integral part of truly Christian life. The mission of teaching and bearing witness to him which Christ entrusted to his followers would result in antagonism and even persecution. In the face of such opposition, his disciples should not retreat, but rather persist in their mission even though it cast them as defendants before the high tribunals and seats of power of the world. But He assured them that they would not have to do this alone. In such encounters the Spirit would assert the Word through them. Excellent illustrations of the understanding of this in the early Church are found in the post-Pentecostal activities of the Apostles, as recorded in Acts, and in the mission of Paul to the Gentiles.

Scripture indicates, too, that conflict with those outside of the People of God is not the only kind Christians must expect. As Gregory Baum has recently suggested, Jesus' struggle with the high priests, pharisees, and sadduccees—the legitimate authorities of the ecclesiastical establishment of the time—is a kind of prototype which, for the Christian, is applicable to every institution, including the Church, insofar as un-Christian patterns are present in it. Not unrelated to the spirit of this is Paul's resistance of Peter to his face over Peter's reluctance to admit into the Church Gentiles who weren't first received into the Jewish community.

In spite of these and other New Testament bases for "Christian conflict," many Catholic clergy and laity tend to see interpersonal conflict within the Church always as evil or weakness, never as involving virtue or being natural and necessary to the development of a Church that is human as well as divine. Although dialogue—which has the connotation of being both peaceful and officially sanctioned by the Church—is looked upon as an interaction between persons, when conflict within the Church is considered, it is often made acceptable only on condition that the opponents be disembodied and that it take place solely in the realm of ideas. According to this way of thinking, conflict should be between ideas, never between men.

Yet, in defending this position, even its proponents necessarily find themselves, although arguing *about* ideas, nevertheless arguing *with* those who disagree with them—persons. Catholics are often forced into such an unrealistic and artificial position and into such sophistry because, as I have suggested earlier, in effective, traditional Catholic theology the concept of love (*caritas*), as applied to personal relations within the Church, has been too closely identified with the concept of peace or harmony between Catholics, thus leaving conflict between them virtually incompatible with love.

In a Catholic magazine a priest recently wrote that, in the Church, conflict between persons ". . . is in opposition to its basic spirit, 'Love one another as I have loved you.' . . . When Christ told us to love our enemies, He certainly presumed that we would be loving our fellow Christians." But Jesus also certainly implied that sometimes our fellow Christians would (even should) be our opponents. The rest of the Scriptural quotation which begins this essay is: "I have come to set a man at variance with his father, and the daughter with her mother . . . a man's enemies will be the people of his own house."

Is interpersonal conflict which is entered into in the spirit of Christ in opposition to his law of love (or is other conflict necessarily so)? Was Christ ever lacking in love in his conflicts with his enemies? St. Paul might have been a bit uncharitable to St. Peter when he resisted the imposition of Jewish prescriptions upon Gentile Christians. Even saints' reactions can be exaggerated. But Paul obviously was acting predominantly in and with the Spirit of Christ. In spite of differences like that, and, paradoxically, sometimes because of them, the early Christians were known for "how they love one another."

Indeed, love of neighbor often requires the Christian to enter into conflict with others in the Church. An example of this stands out in some recent words of Bishop Fulton J. Sheen: "The mission of the Church is to participate in Christ's sufferings in the world and to have a kind of *lover's quarrel* with those members who would not feel the pain of the stripes on the backs of others" (italics added). But if in the minds of many Catholics love is so tied to harmony—or even, by extension, to the status quo—that conflict becomes a bad or dangerous thing, then the demands of love (or of justice, or of truth) probably will go unheeded. The current shock and disturbance among many Catholics over the increasing amount of criticism and other conflict in the Church since Vatican II is partially due to this way of thinking. In such a situation, merely responding to the critics with public pleas for more charity is likely to reinforce the notion that such critics are necessarily uncharitable. Catholics need to learn that love does not always require harmony and that unity is not achieved only by uniformity nor is it incompatible with quite a bit of conflict with others.

So far, conflict in the Church, theological disagreement, criticism of policy or action, the struggle for human rights through persuasion, debate and even boycott, strike or other kinds of pressure (moral, academic, political, economic, etc.) are the kinds of conflict I have had in mind. They are all nonviolent. Indeed, for more and more Catholic thinkers it is difficult to conceive of violent conflict as being Christian regardless of who the enemy might be. Nevertheless, traditional Catholic teaching has permitted the use of violence in self-defense and in a just war. I see nonviolence as *the* Christian way, but I am not convinced that violence by the Christian is never called for—at least, as the lesser of two evils. (Pope Paul's brief discussion in *Populorum Progressio* of the right to expropriation and of revolution in the developing nations is worthy of consideration in this connection.) This is truly a difficult subject. What is disturbing, however, are the inconsistencies, past and present, in Catholic thinking as well as in Catholic practice about the relations among love, peace and conflict. For example, many American Catholics, including bishops and other clergy, support a war which, even if we prescind from the question of its justness, is violent, while they have shied away from or opposed not only violent, but also nonviolent conflict in the struggle of the American Negro for his just rights.

By now the need for a complete, integrated Christian theology of interpersonal conflict should be apparent. Such a theology would have to deal in detail with all forms of interhuman conflict: "Christian" and other, violent and nonviolent, with others within the Church and outside of it. In order to do this adequately we should examine and draw upon the Scriptures and scriptural scholarship, doctrinal and moral theology (Catholic and non-Catholic), non-Christian religious thought (Gandhi's, for instance), the work of behavioral scientists (including Marx's contributions in sociology), and also Church history, philosophy (especially neo-Whiteheadian process philosophy), and the social action of such men as Martin Luther King and Saul Alinsky, as well as any other sources of knowledge concerning conflict. (A truly complete theology of conflict should also include a thorough treatment of the place in Christian life of psychological conflicts, tensions and crises of growth *within* individuals. But that complementary subject is beyond the scope of this article which deals only with conflict *between* individuals.)

Since Vatican II, more and more Catholic thinkers have been writing in a positive way about interpersonal conflict (especially its nonviolent forms). In the United States, for example, Father Andrew Greeley, a sociologist, in an essay in his *The Hesitant Pilgrim*, stresses the functions of social conflict and criticism in the Church, especially as prerequisites of change and of growth, and concludes that such conflict should be institutionalized by Church leaders for the sake of the welfare of the whole institution. In *The Respectable Murderers*, Msgr. Paul Hanly Furfey indicates the need for a theology of disobedience applicable to relations with authorities inside as well as outside the Church. Fr. William DuBay in *The Human Church* argues forcefully that, inside the Church and out, man generally is not *given* his rights, but rather has to win them from those in power through the exercise of some power of his own. The French author, Pié Régamey, in *Non-Violence and the Christian Conscience*, has presented an excellent general theological treatise on nonviolence, which in its positive aspect includes what I would call nonviolent conflict entered into in the spirit of Christ. However, more writings such as these, as well as others which link them together theologically, are needed.

The Paradox of "Christian Conflict"

I concede that recent disagreements and conflicts between liberals and conservatives in the Church have often been petty, intramural quarrls, lacking in charity and seemingly oblivious to the world outside the Church. Still, the same may be said of many attempts to preserve harmony, which can be preoccupied with a desire "not to rock the boat," and can be based on dishonesty and cowardice. For Christians, like anyone else, tend to act out of mixed motives and are in constant need of personal reformation and renewal in love. Yet it is true that, as necessary as conflict often is, it requires more effort to approach it in a spirit of love than it does to establish or preserve peaceful relations. But we must believe that if Christ asks us to love our neighbor, including our enemy, He will provide us with the ability to do so.

Let me emphasize that I favor interpersonal conflict when it is necessary and called for by, or at least is compatible with, the spirit of Christ; not for its own sake or when it is the product of willed hatred of persons, excludes love of one's opponents or is offensively personal.

A practical point, recently suggested by Fr. Greeley, might be considered here. In dialogue with those of different values or opinions, it might be better tactics to attempt first to stress the things agreed on rather than points of conflict until some trust is established. Greeley says that in practice "... the revolutionary yapping at people's heels may frighten the person being yapped at into some sort of Thermidorian reaction and indeed do more harm than good in the long run to his own cause."

"Christian conflict" and "Christianized conflict" do involve paradox. Conflict with persons does not easily blend with loving and accepting them. Man's heart yearns for peace, not conflict. Peace is a dominant theme in Christ's life and teachings and in the liturgy. What then of Christ's and the Church's prayer for peace? I would suggest that the perfect peace of Christ is eschatological; that, *in via*, harmony in human relations inevitably alternates with conflict in a kind of dialectic—conflict always involving striving toward a new harmony, which itself is subject to change through further strivings and conflicts—but that a certain abiding interior peace, even in the midst of conflict, is possible.

Perhaps the application of the Bales' model, mentioned above, to the Christian *in via* can provide an insight here. Participation in the Lord's Supper should help to reestablish the Christian's solidarity with his brothers after the demands of the Mission have generated some tensions and rivalries between him and them, as well as to refresh his love for them and to renew his spirit for the resumption of the Mission.

Finally, an efficacious theology of interpersonal conflict can thrive in the Church only when supported by a favorable social climate and favorable structural or institutional conditions. The creation of such a climate and such conditions (for example, a plurality of bases of power within the Church) itself involves conflict. We cannot, then, escape the fact that as Christians, as human beings, we must face life and act—whether that action requires conflicting or peaceful relations with our brothers. But always that action should be in the Spirit of Christ, who is Love.

GIBSON WINTER

A Theology of Demonstration

The freedom movement is one of the most significant events of our time. It is a part of the global struggle for human rights —the human revolution which is transforming societies in every area of the world. Among African peoples it means an effort toward liberation from colonialism and exploitation; for us it means a step toward actualizing the American dream of equal opportunity in opposition to the forces of racism and the vicious circle of impoverishment.

Most of us are in agreement with the ultimate concerns of the freedom movement, or at least we find it difficult to deny their legitimacy within the American tradition. We accept the principle of self-determination among other nations when that right does not interfere with our national interests. However, demonstration on behalf of these rights has become increasingly disturbing to many Americans. Middle-class churchmen are more and more troubled by the explosive forces which are mobilizing in community organizations. Bureaucrats are troubled by the foreign policy judgments of university faculties and students. Southern liberals give lip service to the rights of the Negro people but resent the aggressive expression of those rights in nonviolent demonstration. Politicians in the northern cities extol their own contributions to civil rights but became apoplectic with indignation when Martin Luther King led movements in the northern ghettos.

From *The Christian Century*, LXXXII (October 13, 1965), 1249–52. Copyright 1965 Christian Century Foundation. Reprinted by permission of the publisher and the author.

The demonstration is direct action: Moving outside the normal channels of legislative and judicial process, it makes its appeal directly to the mind and conscience of the people and even the world. The demonstration risks disorder and even violence, confronts the promiser with his word and asks for satisfaction.

Demonstration and the conflict it evokes have much to teach us as Christian people. We are often troubled by such direct action because we think of Christian love as peace without conflict. For most Christians in the United States the mark of the church is absence of conflict—this negative state is the goal of congregational life and poses a direct antithesis to the achievement of justice by demonstration and direct action. Thus the forces of the human revolution throughout the world are confronting the churches with a choice between an embodiment of love as demonstration with the risk of disorder and a preservation of a modicum of harmony by avoidance of conflict. Challenging Christianity at is very roots, the freedom movement in the United States is leading us to a clarification of the meaning of faith and love. If we can come to terms with this challenge, our faith will be illumined and the meaning of the Christian movement enhanced. By the same token the depth of the freedom movement can be plumbed when it is seen from the perspective of Christian faith. Thus the clarification and enrichment can be mutual.

In entering this dialogue between the freedom movement and the Christian movement—using the term "demonstration" as a key—I wish to distinguish the two movements. My position is that they are distinct, though in their genuine expression they celebrate a common cause—a human world of interdependent existence. So far as the freedom movement expresses this cause it embodies the Christian hope in our time and becomes a genuine expression of the Christian commitment. So far as the Christian movement is faithful to its authentic source and commitment, the freedom movement can properly rejoice in the collaboration of Christians in its struggle. This reservation about the identification of the freedom movement with Christianity is much more a criticism of the Christian movement than of the freedom movement. Any embodiment of love as demonstration is authentically a disclosure of reconciling power in history, but we Christians are too wont to attach labels long after the authentic embodiment is "past history."

Decision and Commitment

Criticism of the freedom movement usually emerges as disparagement of the motivation of those participating in demonstrations. It is customary to attribute participation to impulse, adolescent rebellion, desire for excitement and even hope for public attention. The truth is that demonstration starts and ends with a process of decision-making which touches a person's fundamental commitment. To be sure, the initial decision may be impulsive, even casual; at the start participants rarely sense the significance of their commitment in a demonstration. It soon becomes evident, however, that the process was only begun by taking the plane or bus: Decisions pile up at each step of the way.

The members of the University of Chicago divinity school faculty who marched in the demonstration on Selma provided a good example of this process. Whatever the initial decision which brought them together, when they heard the announcement of a federal injunction against the march as they were traveling from Atlanta to Selma that morning, arguments for and against participation began coming from every direction. The arguments continued inside and outside Browns Chapel; they not only continued up to the moment of joining the march but were still going on when the troopers stepped back and opened the road to Montgomery. One theologian noted that by the end of that morning he had heard every argument in the Jewish and Christian traditions on the place of the law.

Our indecisiveness and lack of commitment are revealed to us in the process of decision-making. We realize how unprepared we are for these decisions—how much we have depended on our routine and the world at hand. We discover too that we are our commitment—that our identity, who we are, and the ultimate direction of our lives are really one because we are no longer simply deciding for this or that cause, but the cause is judging us.

Demonstration is the boundary situation par excellence, because it dramatizes in a few moments the decision-making for and against others by which our identity comes into being within our friendships, cliques, school, work and nation. In each of these situations we are becoming who we are, but the ultimate implications of the decisions are often obscured by details or the sheer extension of

time in which the decision comes to fruition. Our true being becomes manifest in the commitment which the freedom movement
evokes. We see *who* we are in what we are *for*. We see what we
need in the way of faith and power by our lack of courage to be
for that in which we believe. One student expressed this so well
when he described his compulsion to make a telephone call as a
sheriff's posse descended the capitol steps in Montgomery to close
in on a demonstration—he is sure that if there had been a telephone
booth at hand he would have sought refuge by stepping in and
starting to dial.

If we can say that demonstration begins with impulse, it is the
impulse of total being in which our existence suddenly comes to
focus—the impulse to manifest our own being as ultimate commitment. The current epoch in the freedom movement began with a
woman's refusal to move to the rear of a Montgomery bus. After
200 years of indignity to and exploitation of her people, a Negro woman asserted her independence—she expressed her freedom,
made her demonstration. That embodiment began to work in her—
to evoke dignity and commitment. That manifestation of freedom
brought freedom to life. Thus an hour of decision brings the grace
which actualizes an authentic identity. That group of faculty—
hardly the crusader type—did march. That student did stay in the
line. That courageous woman did find a response among her people;
her impulse did move through decision to ultimate commitment.

Openness, Guilt, Forgiveness

Outsiders often accuse demonstrators of self-righteousness, yet the
common experience of participants in the freedom movement is a
sense of guilt. This guilt is certainly related to the lack of courage
and commitment which most people experience in demonstration, but
it is more closely linked to the feeling that one should have done
more—that one has done so little. A woman who went from Chicago to Selma participated in picketing and was jailed just before
she was due to return home to care for her four children and her
husband; she finally accepted an opportunity to plead guilty and be
released. It was obvious that she had done far more than most people in expressing her commitment, yet later she felt deep guilt over
having let the others down by pleading guilty.

Perhaps the guilt that accompanies demonstration comes not

merely from awareness of our inadequacies (though this is real) but from the awareness of others' needs. An abyss of human needs opens before us once we begin to respond to those needs. We can never do enough; our contribution is so small in this ocean of suffering; we assume limited liability in a situation where some can set no limits to their liabilities. A teacher marching in Montgomery told how she had not been allowed to teach after her participation in the bus boycott. Realizing the price which some must pay for openness to others, we are assailed by guilt for our own limited openness. Indeed, many of those who seem closed to others' needs, who turn a deaf ear to the freedom movement, may well do so because they sense the abyss of need and pain which awareness will uncover. In a faculty seminar some years ago one professor refused to discuss or even consider the problems of racial integration which many of us were discussing. A few years later, as a member of the faculty of the University of Mississippi, he resigned in protest over the administration's refusal to deal honestly with the integration of the school. Perhaps on that earlier occasion he had sensed, far more than the rest of us, what it would mean for him to listen—what it would cost to accept this problem as part of his human obligation.

Openness brings awareness of guilt. Love discloses lack of love. Seeing another's need awakens us to our lack of concern. At this point, demonstration touches the depth of our human condition— the lovelessness of the very love which we proffer. But this is not its last word. Our gift is accepted graciously—our measured grace is accepted with a generous spirit of thanksgiving. We receive forgiveness and acceptance at the very moment when our real inadequacy and guilt become manifest to us. This is perhaps the way in which the freedom movement and the Christian movement are most closely identified in their authentic moments—both evoke a response of love which they cherish and raise to a level of ultimate significance by weaving it into the fabric of human interdependence. What a shock it is for white participants to discover that they are at home only in those Negro communities which they once feared as strange and unknown. What grace we find in being received with such openness and generosity by those whom the white man has exploited through centuries of our Western history. Here the forgiving community—the holy community—begins to find authentic embodiment, and walls are indeed broken down.

Inclusiveness and Relativity

Christian people are being confronted with demands to commit themselves to action in the freedom movement, and they will be pressed increasingly for decisions on other phases of the human revolution around the world. Soon decisions must be made about treating the Chinese people as citizens of the human community. Soon we will have to decide whether we are to continue in the suppression of every liberty which does not fit into American economic interests. How can we judge the substance of movements like the freedom movement in this world revolution? Granted that decision for the movement manifests freedom, that openness to the needs of others can bring to light our need to be forgiven and thus can evoke communities of forgiveness. The Nazi movement stamped our age indelibly with the awareness that movements of demonic character can evoke courage and empower heroic sacrifice. At this stage in the dialogue, Christian sources and experience can shed light on the depths of the freedom movement. Christian participation can bring a significant judgment to today's revolutionary movements. There are two criteria for authentic expressions of love in the Christian experience, both relevant to a continuing scrutiny of both the Christian movement and the freedom movement. These criteria can be roughly categorized as "inclusiveness" and "relativity." They sharply discriminate between the Hitler movement and the present thrust of the human revolution.

The first criterion is the inclusiveness of the vision which a movement embodies. The Nazi movement actually gained much of its power by the demonic force with which it excluded many people from the human community—Jews, Russians, gypsies, Jehovah's Witnesses, non-Aryans of all kinds, etc. The appeal of this movement to many Americans in the thirties came from this very exclusiveness. The Christian movement in its authentic roots attests a human unity embracing all but the negation of that unity, and even the negation finds its fulfillment through the actualization of human unity—even Selma finds its fruition in a new commitment to equal opportunity on the part of the American people. Christian participation as Christian and not merely as "church" is essential from both the Negro and white sides, since the freedom movement always walks the borderline between human inclusiveness and Negro nationalism. Demonstration embodies authentic love as it proclaims human unity in an inclusive vision, even while it opposes that which denies this unity. Every movement is tempted to seek a spurious power by accenting its own definition of human society at the expense of human community. The freedom movement as well as the Christian movement needs to be evaluated again and again by this criterion of inclusiveness.

The criterion of relativity is closely identified with the vision of human unity, since every movement is relativized by a claim which exceeds the scope and vision of our historical creations. A genuine movement is ready to sacrifice itself for the cause which it serves, acknowledging the partiality of its own vision and embodiment. Some movements arise with this commitment and then in later phases set their own survival above their cause; spurious movements are characterized by their identification of their own expression with the cause which they proclaim. The Nazis were willing to see the Europe to which they were dedicated go down in ashes if Hitlerism itself could not be saved; Europe without a victory of Hitlerism was inconceivable. The cause and the movement were equated. By contrast the authenticity of the nonviolent demonstration is repeatedly manifest in its risk of its own leadership with each new demonstration. Perhaps the greatest present danger to the freedom movement is its hesitation to endanger its leaders and its temptation to set their safety above its cause. This is the kind of problem with which every authentic movement continually struggles. Awareness of the partiality of its vision and expression is the mark of an authentic movement.

In the years ahead Christians will be called ever more urgently to identify themselves with the human revolution which is sweeping our globe. They will have to make decisions in each new situation; they will risk pain and guilt from the realization of inadequate participation in meeting the needs of others throughout the world; they will have to make their judgments about movements that demonstrate an inadequate vision and they will have to risk their own understanding of the Christian movement as they embody it in other historical forms. To this extent the freedom movement and the human revolution are part of our destiny and our freedom as Christians in this period.

Demonstration or Concealment

Demonstration brings evil to light; it ends the quiet frustration which oppressors equate with law and order. Fear of demonstration is actually fear of the evil which we hide; the Nazis cremated their victims in obscure corners of the Reich as we conceal our brutal suppression of rights on dusty Alabama roads and in garbage-strewn alleys of Chicago's west side. Demonstration destroys the design of concealment; it names the conspiracy of deceit by which we bring on embittered violence. Concealment deepens the bitterness by attempting to hide inhumanity in the guise of human peace; demonstration risks an inadequate peace as it brings to light the authentic claims of humanity.

The paradox of demonstration is that it evokes conflict but in the same effort overcomes the conflict with forbearance and love. The paradox of concealment is that it suppresses conflict but foments chaos and riot by its hidden brutalities and injustice. Demonstration risks exposure to the light of day—embracing alienation in the name of a more authentic vision of human community. Oppression battens on darkness—risking riot and violence in anticipation of further gains from cherished injustices. Our fear of authentic demonstration is a proper fear, but it needs to be placed in its fuller context: All men should have a healthy fear of the light, for their deeds are evil; on the other hand, they should tremble at the conspiracy of silence, for darkness breeds the violence of despair.

Thus demonstration and concealment are the alternatives which we confront when injustice has incubated the protest of a new generation. Unhappily for our future, these alternatives are not clearly seen by many public spokesmen. Evangelist Billy Graham slips into Alabama after a year of struggle by civil rights groups and gives comfort to the segregationists by extolling love without demonstration—as though there would be gospel without the cross or a Voting Rights bill without Selma. The President of the United States, in the wake of the Los Angeles riots, equates the violence of rioters with the brutality of the Ku Klux Klan; in a masterpiece of legerdemain he equates an effect with its cause—the cry of despair and bitterness in the Watts district is equated with the brutal suppression marking 100 years of injustice. One could as well equate the rush of the Nazi victim against the electrified barbed wire with the truncheon beatings of the storm troopers; by no stretch of the imagination is a violent act of despair to be classed with the suppression which created that despair. The Los Angeles rioter is the victim of years of brutal suppression; the hooded Klansman is the instrument of that suppression. Both the Klansman and the despair which he creates are the work of concealment; the alternative to this inhumanity and chaos is to be found in the demonstration of the authentic claims of freedom.

The American people owe a profound debt to the freedom movement and the demonstration which it has evoked. This movement counters the threat of an Armageddon between white and yellow peoples with a vision of human community which transcends color. A movement which started with little more than a gesture—a seat on a bus, a meager sandwich in a cheap restaurant—stirs the deepest aspirations for human dignity and peace. The freedom movement has had the courage to grapple with a comprehensive vision of humanity; to this extent it can disclose to Christians the substance of their human commitment.

ALVA MYRDAL

The Road to Peace

The message in this personal statement of mine is that the Road to Peace is a long and arduous one. It must be made through several stages. I cannot bring myself to believe that even all the churches in the world could [harmonize] mankind over night, and thus introduce peace on earth because they would have assured us that there would be peace, and peace only, in our hearts.

The final goal of peace which we must strive towards with all our might should, however, be clearly circumscribed. It is peace in the sense of settling conflicts without recourse to collective violence. It is peace in a disarmed world. It is peace under a world order of law. It is peace ensuring justice and freedom for all. It is peace built on constructive cooperation.

Personally, I find it helpful to envisage the way ahead in three phases, well knowing that they should not be considered as consecutive but dovetailing into each other. While in our daily practical work more concerned with the immediate, we must also lay the groundwork for the stages to follow. Often enough, advance might turn out to be more easily achieved in a direction belonging to a stage we have provisionally placed in the more distant future. Our vision must constantly be kept clear along the complete road. I would nevertheless give the priority of our tasks as first concentrating on disarmament, secondly on solving certain outstanding politi-

From *The Ecumenical Review*, XIX, No. 2 (April 1967), 183–86. Reprinted with permission of the publisher.

cal problems in various regions of the world, and thirdly as establishing a world order of law.

The most immediate aim is to satisfy an impatient world by reaching agreement on some concrete disarmament measures. Even if they be only partial, and perhaps infinitesimal in comparison with the "general and complete disarmament," to which we have in the UN solemnly pledged ourselves, they are necessary for laying foundations of confidence between states, hitherto largely lined up along a cold war wall of partition. The measures most thoroughly prepared are all focussing on alleviating the threat of nuclear war, leaving for the time being the whole sector of conventional armaments unregulated. The first aim is to dismantle the arsenals of nuclear weapons. No states, no generals, no human beings can be trusted with the possession of the means of mega-murder. To reduce the dangers, the first steps must be in the direction of containing the nuclear potentials in our world.

In the actual disarmament negotiations, proceeding at Geneva in the Eighteen Nation Disarmament Commission after mandates laid down by the UN General Assembly, the issues revolve around three measures of "freezing" the nuclear situation. They include proposals for "non-proliferation," i.e., hindering the *number* of nuclear weapon states to grow, for a "comprehensive test-ban," i.e., hampering the *qualitative* development of the nuclear means of mass destruction, and for "cut-off production of fissile material for weapon purposes," i.e., curtailing the *quantitative* build-up of nuclear arsenals. Together, agreements on these measures would amount to a rather definitive locking of the spiralling mechanism in the nuclear arms race and, consequently, to considerable relaxation of the tension between states and of the anxiety of our generation.

As the nonaligned nations see it—and probably most non-nuclear weapons states—the responsibility for cutting back the nuclear proliferation in all three directions indicated, should devolve on both nuclear and non-nuclear weapon countries, not least on the great powers. I cannot but wish that the World Council of Churches, as well as all organizations of true good will, would support this demand. A "non-proliferation" agreement is valuable *per se*, as is also the establishment of nuclear-free zones, because they hinder further states from "going nuclear." But the major feature of measures to keep nuclear weapons within bounds must be restrictions on the great powers to use them, produce and develop them. They are the ones who already possess gigantic stock-piles of means to kill, yes "overkill," humanity.

Progress on a comprehensive test-ban and on an agreement to forbid production of nuclear material of weapons grade are, therefore, of immediate urgency, as they would entail sacrifices of freedom of action also on the part of the great powers. A ban on further "proliferation" alone would only involve such sacrifice on the part of the have-not countries, thus not achieving anything perceptible in the world of realities. A ceasing of underground explosions would, as would the closing of plutonium plants and installations for the enriching of uranium, on the other hand achieve this. Thus, it becomes highly important to use all possible influence on public opinion to win support for these demands.

A second phase in our effort to build a sane world would have to be concerned with attempts to solve specific political problems. The most important of those outstanding may be regarded as leftovers in the pursuit of decolonization. Our era is one where "European" world power and "white" domination simply have to cede. The great task ahead is to achieve the peaceful solution of numerous problems of this order, but solve them in their local, or possibly regional, setting, without taking recourse to great power intervention. Such intervention might seem efficient in the short run, but we know that it is void of constructive force, yes, void of staying power for the next era of history. All good forces must now be directed to help the many newly independent states, largely with populations of non-European origin, to lay their own foundations for safety of progress and of prosperity.

The situations which will have to be met are going to be very different in different parts of the world. In Latin America, the problem most pressing will probaby be the one of equalizing economic opportunities and broadening political participation. In Africa, the most urgent tasks refer to a cessation of racial strife, while other efforts must take the shape of educational up-tooling and evolution of productive resources. In Asia, the problems are even more tragically pressing; the growth pains of that region, containing some very large and very poor nations are there further complicated by internal strife and war. We might predominantly attempt to assist them by widening the chances for constructive UN cooperation and by alerting public opinion through all voluntary organizations. To the political problems for which regional solutions must be sought belong also those of Europe, both eastern and western Europe. As I find it more difficult to visualize the role of voluntary organizations in this context, I leave that issue after only making this brief note as a memento.

The function of organizations like the churches on the type of political problems indicated is predominantly to help keep public opinion well-informed of true facts and thus both more rational and more fair than it often is, particularly in lands geographically and culturally distant from the scene of conflicts. A constant concern must be to counteract false beliefs, rumours, appeals to aggressive nationalism, irrational and dangerous as such factors are. We must all strive to enhance the prestige which countries might gain if they succeed in widening democratic rule and in making economic progress, and also help to diminish the prestige they pursue in terms of victories, revenges, domination over nations or groups. Not by arms, but by harvests shall ... power be measured. ...

We must, of course, also work right from the beginning for the third phase, for the great future of an international order of peace, freedom and justice. My impression is that these ideals are in reality kept very much alive precisely by activities of organizations such as the World Council of Churches. Such pressure as you can exert for the ultimate ideals is indispensable. But these are, admittedly, long-term propositions. A fairly generous time scope should therefore be allowed for more research on these long-range problems. To construct durable solutions, where new legal rules, new forms of practical cooperation, and new dimensions of an internationalized education will provide the foundations, should be the object of such research as well as of popular discussion.

Here I have taken the liberty to clamor for more attention on the intermediary stages, where our positions already now have to become quite specific. It is my firm belief that strong stands can be taken on these issues by the very persons and organizations who are not and do not want to become partisans to particular issues. As a matter of fact, the world needs more than ever nonpartisan challenges to many of the issues of the day, bedevilled as they often are by having become the object of narrow national or group interests, or of a sheer desire to preserve prestige. Progress and peace can only be assured by making our approaches more truly international.

Hope and
V the Unknown Future

The dominance of existentialist philosophies has for a long time helped to focus man's attention on the present, on the existential moment in which he is living. What man must undergo *now* is the compelling test of his "relevance." A gradual shift to a wider historical consciousness, particularly in theology, has enlarged man's outlook to include the horizon of the future. Wolfhart Pannenberg was one of the first to restate the problem of revelation: "Only a conception of the course of history actually connecting *then* with *today* and *its future horizon* can provide the all-embracing horizon in which the limited present horizon of the interpreter and the historical horizon of the text are fused." [1] In Pannenberg's thought God's revelation in time (especially in the ministry of Jesus) is constantly carrying forward the manifestation of past event in present consciousness, which is also "open toward the future."

A theological understanding of the future must be developed with special emphasis on one's understanding of man, of the movement of history. Two concepts of man have strongest claim to attention at present—the Marxist and the Christian.

The Marxist understanding of man has evolved from a primitive determinism which characterized dialectical materialism, to

[1] Quoted in James M. Robinson, *Theology as History* (New York: Harper & Row, Publishers, 1967), p. 91.

a new position. Interaction with concepts of cultural evolution and Christian hope has moved some Marxist thinkers into the field of humanistic materialism. In the humanistic concept man, by the use of reason, imagination, energy, and productiveness, can transform the face of the earth. In spite of the inadequacy of any one man or group of men the collectivity of mankind will realize its goal of humanization of the universe.

The articles in this last section return to the theme of man's self-understanding with which this volume began. The relation of man and social process are discussed by Roger Garaudy and Johannes Metz. Their discussion is a concrete evidence of the new relations between Marxists and Christians which have come about since the second Vatican Council. After some "dialogue about dialogue" and whether it is possible for Christians and Marxists to take part in realistic and fruitful discussion, some results are already forthcoming.

Professor Garaudy, the foremost Marxist theorist in France, shows his openness to Christian thought by accepting the concept of man's transcendence in the sense that his powers can change and transform natural processes. He denies that the Marxist concept of man destroys the individual person in the totality of mankind. Rather, Christians should understand that Marxism, like Christianity, has a "development of doctrine." It was Marx who first articulated the basic problem of our century: how to think through the law of change, and master it. Marxist doctrine itself recognizes that development occurs and ideas must be expressed in language suitable to our time.

Professor Metz in his reply shows a readiness to accept ideas which Marxism has adopted—especially that of a revolutionary attitude toward the world. But he thinks that the Christian revolution is one which works toward something radically new, something which is not merely an evolutionary extension of our own possibilities. Christian hope is not only a patient expectation but it is also a call to intense struggle for human rights and dignity. Professor Metz castigates Christians who do not respond to the call for decisive involvement in the quest for justice and peace. Belief in God's promise does not do away with the radical human quest of world order but intensifies it.

Modern worldviews are for the most part evolutionary. Although the type of evolution which is espoused may differ, the communist, humanist, and Christian ideologies presuppose that an evolution, cultural as well as physical and environmental, is taking place. For Christian thinkers the writings of Teilhard de Chardin have had a strong influence. Karl Rahner develops a doctrine of Christ within an evolutionary order in which Christ is himself not only part of the cosmos but is its highest point. The Incarnation is the peak of cosmic development and the necessary moment of man's movement toward God. Christ is the human reality which makes possible each man's response to a transcendent future.

The transcendent future is called by different names among Christian thinkers. Among Biblical scholars it is the Kingdom of God; among theologians it may be the *eschaton* or fulfillment of history, the eschatological future. How each man responds to God's call to involvement in bringing about the *eschaton* differs according to the individual's personal decision and the needs of his society. A topic which has caused much controversy, especially among Roman Catholics, is that of priestly celibacy. Father Eugene Maly, noted American Biblical scholar, sees the rationale of celibacy as coming from a radical devotion to the eschatological future. The Christian collaborates in building a future which harmonizes with man's potentialities and dignity. One who is a celibate *and* a Christian is a living sign of the goal, as well as of the work to be done in achieving that goal.

The problem of the future is hidden in the conflicting forces of social, material, and spiritual movements which surge around us and inspire or threaten the human community. One question which constantly recurs in theological and popular literature is: What is the meaning of God for us today? Is he a person, a myth, or the ultimate reality? Father Robert Johann responds to the demand for a relevant answer with a concept of God which is philosophical and theoretical, yet at the same time intensely practical, in other words, "pragmatic." God and

human community go together in his answer: Where the sense
of God is lost, the possibility of human community decreases.
For better or worse, the making of community within a world
order is related to a religious meaning, a sense of God.

A new influence on discussions of where world order is going is the work of Jürgen Moltmann, *Theology of Hope.*
Repercussions of Moltmann's thought are affecting thinking in
such diverse fields as technology, politics, and ethics. Moltmann has attacked the predominance of the Bultmann-existen-
tialist interpretation of the New Testament. As he describes it:
"The debate over demythologizing was terminated when there
was uncovered in the Christ-event an integral connection between the promisory history of the Old Testament and the
revolutionary history of Christian mission." [2] In Moltmann's
thought, it is not so much the "now dimension" of existentialist confrontation with God's action here and now (what he
calls "the God of epiphany") which is important, but what is
contained in the expectation and dynamism of the future ("the
God of the promise").

An important influence on Moltmann's thought is the work
of a philosopher of Marxism, Ernst Bloch. In his mature work,
Das Prinzip Hoffnung, published in 1959, Bloch declared that
the key to the future stems from the "radiation" of man's
spirit which comes from the promise of a utopian state. The
"radiation" gives an unshakable hope in the utopian future.
Although Bloch's approach is secular and humanistic, he drew
ideas from the Old Testament prophets. Because of his orientation toward religion, Bloch did not draw much response
from the Marxists. But Christian theologians found his ontol-
ogy of "not-yet-being" in direct relationship to the Biblical
framework of promise and fulfillment. Moltmann, Pannenberg, and Harvey Cox hailed Bloch's thinking as a new source
of interpretation of the Christian mission.

It is fitting to close this section with the introduction to
Moltmann's book, which he calls "a meditation on hope." Moltmann's work and the stimulus it has given indicates that Bibli-

[2] "The Theology of Hope Today," *Critic,* XXVI (April–May 1968), 23.

cal thought and the secular world—even the Marxist world—are contributing to a developing world view. Barbara Ward Jackson declared:

> In the great struggle of ideas in our time, only the communists act on the belief that we must have one world order, and that the new world will be a communist order. The communists have accepted the scientific revolution and its consequent drive to world unity. Western democracies have yet to realize that life must be lived on a world-wide scale, that reality now includes the unity of the human race.[3]

Jürgen Moltmann is helping Christians to see their calling in the context of evolution toward a world order based on Christian thought. He declares that God's power and call is the force which urges on the Christian's work and his orientation toward the future. The Christian receives not only one call, but many:

> The callings, roles, functions, and relationships which make a social claim on man always appear in open multiplicity. Always man stands in a multi-layered network of social dependencies and claims.... Our modern society lays open to man a multitude of chances and demands of him elasticity, adaptability and imaginativeness.[4]

To give man confidence in being able to meet the demands of the world of today and the future is the role of Christian hope.

[3] From "The Task of World Order," an address given in Minneapolis in March, 1960.
[4] Moltmann, *op. cit.*, p. 333.

ROGER GARAUDY

Christian-Marxist Dialogue

In philosophy a reign is coming to an end: that of existentialism, which has lasted a little more than a third of a century. Existentialism presented itself before the world as an exasperated form of individualism, stressing subjectivity, the responsibility of man, the trial of human choice. To this indispensable assertion of necessity, so visible in forced submission to the strict discipline of war time, in the totalitarian grinding of Hitlerian fascism, in the tragedies of an officialized socialism denying particularity, existentialism sacrificed rationality and objectiveness, scientific strictness and revolutionary discipline, as if history were made up only of the fresh arising of free individual projects.

This rebellion of the subject inspired a generation of men who under the conditions of war and occupation could retain their own dignity only by negation and revolt. It became not only a conception of the world but a fashion which at the time of liberation and for years after was spread to literature and even to manners. When the time came to build, the philosophy of existence betrayed its theoretical and practical impotence. Then came the ebb tide; ideas began to move the other way round. Till then the magic word had been "subjectivity"; henceforward it was "structure." To this reversal we can perhaps find a parallel at the beginning of the twentieth century, when the romanticist theme of the "organism" was opposed to the master word of the eighteenth century, "mechanical-

From *Journal of Ecumenical Studies*, IV (Spring 1967), 207–22. Reprinted with permission of the publisher.

ism." It was not only a matter of fashion but a need born of deep disappointment and vital experience. The disappointment issued from the failure of the philosophers of existence to establish the human science. Appealing exclusively to the subject, they felt dispensed from trying to find objectivity in human relations, whereas the structural analysis of objectified human relations, in the field of linguistics, for instance, revealed its fruitfulness and showed the possibility of constituting real "human sciences." The task was to try to find the structures and give form to them; to erect systems including institutions, works or creeds, which would at the same time allow for explanation and foresight; to establish that if some properties are present others are necessarily linked to them; in a word, to give human science a position which should not be inferior to that of the natural sciences in its ability to explain or in its practical efficiency.

The temptation was great to pay attention solely to this privileged moment of human reality, a moment of the objectified reason of structure, and to deny even the reality of any other moment.

To the theoretical disappointment brought about by the failure of the philosophers of existence is linked a vital and still more general experience which accounts for the present seduction of the structuralist undertakings, which goes far beyond the field of human sciences and philosophy into literature and perhaps soon into manners. We speak of the terrifying power not only of the mass media for the diffusion of culture—press, publicity, radio, television, cinema —but also of those who make use of them to determine the behavior of individuals for economic, moral, and political purposes. This fact has created circumstances where the most visible aspect of individual behavior is its "structuration" by prefabricated schemes. From the use of publicity with a view to creating conditioned reflexes it reaches to the creation of sentimental stereotypes through the crystallizing of mass political reactions according to prefabricated formulae. The moment of creative historical initiative taken by the individual acting as a responsible subject and actually participating through his decision in the opening of a new future falls thus in the background. If we consider only the surface of things it seems in effect that the whole of history may be reduced to the dialectics of structures having their own efficiency, so that one hardly feels the need of moving from structure back to the human activity that gave it birth.

Religion and Marxism

Against such a trend of theoretical and practical inhumanity Marxists and Christians together have to defend man's fundamental values. Marxist atheism, which is also the atheism of the twentieth century, is essentially humanist. It does not start with a negation but with an assertion: the autonomy of man. Consequently it rejects all attempts at depriving man of his creative and self-creative power. As early as 1844, Marx laid stress on this, "Atheism no longer has any meaning, for atheism is the negation of God and through this negation it lays down the existence of man; but socialism has no longer any need for this middle term.... It is man's positive self-consciousness." That is to say, humanism has no more need to define itself through the negation of religion (and therefore in relation to it), than communism has to define itself as the negation of private property (and therefore again in relation to it).

Without doubt, Marxist atheism is heir to the battles for the liberation of man and his thought conducted by the atheists of the eighteenth and nineteenth centuries. It is also heir to the humanism of Fichte and Hegel, reinstating man in the possession of powers traditionally transferred to God. Heir also to Feuerbach's humanism, it opposes a religion which separates man from the best part of himself by projecting his hopes and his virtues into God. What distinguishes Marxist atheism specifically is that unlike its predecessors it does not look at religion merely as a lie fabricated by despots or as a pure illusion issuing solely from ignorance. Marx and Engels have spoken to the same human needs to which religion responded in an obscure way. Religion is at the same time, noted Marx, the reflection of a real distress and a protest against that distress.

A reflection of man's powerlessness and distress, religion appears as an ideology of explanation and justification of the existing order. It is almost constantly utilized as a weapon of domination, making it possible to teach the masses that the established order is willed by God and that it is best to leave it to him and to resign oneself to that order as an obedient and submissive subject. The dogma of original sin has been used to such ends. Saint Augustine in his *City of God* wrote: "God introduced slavery in the world as a punishment of sin. It would be therefore to stand against his will to suppress it." The Church has constantly sanctified all class dominations —slavery, serfdom, salary system—as willed by God, and the latest references to the "social doctrine" maintain this fundamental orientation. Karl Marx summed up this undeniable historical experience in this clear-cut formula: "Religion is the opium of the people." But with the moment of reflection there is the moment of protest. This aspect of religion makes it not only an ideology, the search for an explanation of unhappiness and powerlessness, but also a search to find a way out of unhappiness; not any longer a way of thinking but a way of acting, not an ideology but a faith, a way of standing before the world and of behaving in it.

Here the phenomena are complex. This faith has expressed itself in very different ways in the course of history. Marxists do not deal with religion in general, in a metaphysical and idealistic way, but as historians and materialists. They seek to know how, under historical circumstances which must be scientifically analyzed in each case, faith can play a positive and progressive part. This simply means that if the famous formula "religion is the opium of the people" corresponds to an undeniable historical experience, today still very widely verified, the Marxist conception of religion is not to be reduced to this formula.

The thesis according to which religion in all times and places diverts man from action, work, and struggle is flagrantly in contradiction to historical reality. Pointing to what in religion is a reflection of a real distress and what is protest against this real distress, Marx suggests a method of analyzing the real human substance obscured by its religious form: to study in each particular historical case the real social relations in which the imaginary reflection as well as the protest originate and to analyze the demand to go beyond these relations (even if this demand is turned away from its militant point of social application and directed towards the heaven of personal salvation).

What has Christianity, whose role was so important in our civilization, contributed to our conception of man?

The basic and constant feature of the ancient wisdom of the Greeks and Romans was to situate and define man in relation to a totality of which he was a part, whether a part of the cosmos or the city, the order of nature or an order of concepts. From Thales to Democritus the world was conceived of as a given fact. Man could know it in its ultimate reality and by this knowledge reach the highest dignity possible to him: the consciousness of his fate and happiness. From Plato to the Stoics it is again knowledge which frees man and leads him to self-control and bliss, using diverse conceptions of ultimate reality, which may be tangible or intelligible, an order of nature or an order of concepts.

At first Christianity represented a break with this Hellenistic conception of the world. Continuing Judaism, it substituted a philosophy of being. In this philosophy of act the leading motion was not that of "logos" but that of "creation," and man was worth something in that he was conscious no longer of what he was but of what he was not, of what he lacked. In Saint Augustine, man is not measured in the dimension of the earth and the stars, nor according to the rules of the city or any universality. He exists, not as part of a totality of nature or of concepts, but in his own peculiarity, as subjectivity, as interiority, dependent on the call of the God who lives in him and wrests him from any given "order." "We go beyond the narrow boundaries of our science," wrote Saint Augustine (*De Anima et ejus origine*, L. IV, chapter VI, 8). "We cannot get hold of ourselves and yet we are not beside ourselves."

To this conquest of subjectivity and interiority primitive Christianity, by its violent reaction against pagan wisdom, readily sacrificed the rationality so patiently won by the esthetic and rational humanism of Greek thought. In the fourth century Lactantius, in his *Divine Institution* (II, 5) contrasted the free divine will to the necessity of the Stoics, to their conception of order and rationality. The world was not the necessary development of a rational law but the bestowal of love.

From this new conception of the world followed a new conception of man. He no longer aimed at being great by making himself equal by his knowledge to the supreme law of the city and to the eternal order of the cosmos. He drew his infinite value from being like God, a creator in his own right capable of giving and loving, on the threshold of an absolute future. That future was no logical continuation of the past or a moment of a given totality but the possibility of starting a new life by answering the call of a God who is no longer totality, or concept, or a harmonious and complete image of the human order, but God as a person, a hidden God that no knowledge is able to convey to us and to whom only faith can give us access, although always in agony and doubt. Greek and Roman antiquity on the one hand, and Jewish and Christian antiquity on the other hand, thus brought to light two demands of humanism for rational mastery of the world and for a historical and properly human initiative.

The problem and the program of humanism in the Western tradition would be henceforward to hold both ends of the chain even if we were to be rent by it. The Renaissance failed in this. For once again the two were separated. With Humanism there arose once more all the Greek and Roman ambitions of mastering the world in a rational mathematical, technical, experimental way. In the Reformation were reasserted all the Jewish and Christian anxieties born of the divine and infinite vocation of man in the midst of his irremediable limitation; they may be seen in Luther's theology of sin and grace and Calvin's doctrine of predestination.

The first great synthesis was undertaken by the classical German philosophers and particularly by Kant and Fichte, who brought the two ends of the chain nearer. They saw the necessity of a rational law, without which neither science nor the world can exist, and the freedom of man's creative action, without which there can be neither moral initiative nor responsibility, without which there can be no history.

But once more the chain was broken, for the synthesis had not been carried out. The balance of knowledge and liberty wished by Goethe and his Faust remains a dream and a promise, the finest dream and the finest promise of humanity but still a dream, forever revived and forever postponed. The divergence springs up again, on the one hand with Hegel's stately rational system of nature and history and on the other hand with Kierkegaard's affirmation both of a subjectivity fundamental in its peculiarity and, at the same time, of transcendence.

Christianity in effect has posed the problem of transcendence as at the same time the problem of subjectivity. This is, in fact, its specific way of entering upon the problem of subjectivity. Transcendence is a dangerous expression for it is loaded with a past heavy with confusions and obscurities. Traditionally this notion means belief in a world beyond, in the supernatural, with the irrationality, the miracles, the mystery and finally the deception those notions carry with them. Does transcendence thus understood mean that we must not ask ourselves what need, what question, what experience faith in transcendence and the supernatural answers?

The claim upon transcendence, the actual human experience that man, though belonging to nature, is still different from things and animals, this belief that man is forever able to progress, is never complete. As Marx explained it, once a specifically human work appeared, a work whose law was its own aim, man rose above all other species of animals and began a historical evolution, the rhythm of which is not paralleled in biological evolution. Here we have to do with a qualitative leap, a real outgrowing, "a transcending" (in the strictly etymological sense of the term) in relation to nature. Man belongs to nature. But out of him, with culture, a superior level of nature appears. Such is the real human substance of this notion of transcending. But transcendence as known to Christianity is an alienated expression of nature outgrowing itself and moving into culture. That man, the very one who himself crossed the threshold, should have been so filled with wonder that he conceived another order of reality than that of nature, a super-nature, a beyond full of promise and menace—this is the typical process of alienation. To elaborate a conception of transcending which will not be alienated is therefore to show—and dialectic materialism admits this—that this possibility of initiative and creation is not the attribute of a God but, on the contrary, is the specific attribute of man which differentiates him from all other animal species.

This conception of transcending allows us to single out another aspect of the Christian contribution: the sense of subjectivity. If for Greek humanism man was a fragment of the universe and a member of the city, Christianity after Judaism laid stress on the subjective moment of man's life, on man's possibility of starting a new future. Between the action of the external world and the action of man who goes towards the external world to cope with its threat there stands consciousness on its various levels: anguish and effort, search and dream, hope and love, risk and decision. Such is subjectivity. Christianity has accumulated a rich experience on that plane from Saint Augustine to Kierkegaard, from Pascal and Racine to Claudel; but at the same time, adopting afresh neo-Platonic themes of renunciation of the external world, it developed fatalism and submission.

Love

Along with self-transcending and subjectivity, love is one of the most unquestionable contributions of Christianity to human formation. If we have not already mutilated man by excluding all subjectivity and true interiority in order to reduce him to a mere product of social structures, entirely determined by them; if on the contrary, with Marx we have shown that what is stifled and crushed by the structures of capitalism is precisely a human reality always developing historically but not entirely created by the present structures, one which can therefore be a protest against these structures, then we shall be able to understand how unavailing protest leads to the projection of love which is the opposite of this brutal world and whose reality lies in another world, in a "beyond."

This love has found wonderful artistic forms of expression within which to be expressed, from the poetry of courtly love to Tristan and Isolde, from Saint Teresa of Avila to Racine, from Marceline Desbordes Valmore to the "Fou d'Elsa," from Éluard to the "Soulier de Satin." Moreover, a specifically Christian attitude towards love could not really be mingled with the variant Platonism which opposes "the beyond" to this world and demands that man should part from this world, turn one's back upon it in order to emigrate to the "beyond," God. This dualism, this idealism, this disembodiment, is on the contrary characteristic of heresy from "docetism" to the "Cathari," while the essential Christian teaching, even if contaminated by Hellenism or Gnosticism, is founded upon incarnation and implies very different relations with the "neighbor." It means to deal with every human being as if Christ, the living God, were standing before us. The love of man is one with the love of God. That is why the Mystics, according to tradition which dates back to the Song of Solomon, evoke divine love with the very image of human love, as particularly appears with Saint Teresa of Avila.

It is necessary to insist upon this cardinal aspect of the Christian inheritance. Provided we distinguish the specific contribution of Christianity from that which renders it "a Platonism for the people," (Nietzsche) the new dimensions and the meaning that Christianity has given to love constitute the most fruitful contribution ever made to man's continuing creation of himself. This is what can be most deeply integrated with the Marxist conception of the world and of man. To demonstrate this, it is sufficient to compare the Christian conception of love, "Agape," with the noblest conception of love of Greek humanism, Plato's "Eros."

The Platonic conception of love, the "Eros" of the "Symposium" and "Phaedrus" is characterized by a movement which lifts us towards the supreme being or good by wresting us from the earthly world. Eros makes us rise from love of the beauty of bodies, to love of the beauty of spirits and hence leads us by an ascending dialectic to the love of beauty in itself, finally to carry us altogether away from the world of other men, out of time. It is a yearning that nothing in the real world can fulfill, a yearning inconsistent with the everyday world of men. The other is therefore not loved for what he is, but for what he conjures up of another reality. In this love there is no "neighbor." The other is only an occasion of rising towards a reality which is incommensurate with the other himself. Therefore each loves the other only for himself. What he loves is not another but love itself.

Before Christianity's teaching of "Agape" had been influenced by Hellenism, by Platonism and Gnosis, and later by Millenarianism; by "the imitation of Christ" and certain forms of courtly love, and by hypocritical condemnation of the flesh and by contempt for the world which we still find today—before all this, the central experience of the incarnation of man-God, and of God-man meant a radically novel transition from the love of love to the love of the other. It consisted in having given an absolute value to the other and to the world through Christ's incarnate love. In the fundamental Christian, that is to say Christ-centered doctrine, rising to God in no way implies a turning away from the world, since the living God can be met in every being. It is what Cardinal Bellarmin in the sixteenth century would call "rising to God by the ladder of creatures"; what in the twentieth century Father Teilhard de Chardin called "going beyond by going through," "transcending by traversing." In "Evolution of Chastity" he wrote that "it is in carrying the world along with us that we make progress into the bosom of God" and he suggested that we find a heaven for our natural activity in the faith of Christ.

The possibility that Marxism might thus incorporate Christianity's essential contribution to man, its conception of the world and of man, is sometimes called in question. For instance, it is doubted that Marxism can furnish a theoretical base to an acknowledgment of the absolute value of the human person.

Criticism of Marxism

Two recent essays written by Christian authors who are well-informed in Marxist philosophy and particularly open-minded towards Communism testify to the difficulty. They are Pastor Gollwitzer's book, *Marxist Atheism and Christian Faith* and Father Girardi's *Umanesimo Marxista ed Umanesimo Cristiano.*

The basic objections can be reduced to the following. Gollwitzer writes:

> With Marx, the human species takes the place of Hegel's absolute spirit. In both cases, Marx as with Hegel, if the individual has sense and reality only in relation to the totality which gives him his sense and his reality, the accomplishment of the individual means his total absorption in the process of accomplishment of the species. The law of the species destroys the power of man as a person.

Father Girardi puts forward a variant of the preceding question. He says: For Marxism the absolute is not man but mankind. By this subordination to a higher end man has no other value than that which he draws from his end. Father Girardi sums up all his objections into one: The Marxist conception of practice and revolution as absolute value and criterion of value does not seem to be reconcilable with the principle of the absolute value of the person.

These three objections rest upon a conception of Marxism mixed with either Hegelianism or pragmatism. At their root is a double confusion. First, the erroneous identification of Hegel's absolute spirit with Marx's human species. Marx did not merely reverse Hegel's system by saying matter where Hegel had said spirit. Marx reversed Hegel's method (another problem that we do not have to deal with here) and thoroughly rejected Hegel's system and even the Hegelian conception of the system. Marx mentions neither absolute knowledge nor the notion of the end of history. Here lies the capital difference between a closed system and an open method of endless creation.

Marx does not conceive a closed totality granting a place to each of its parts. That would be a totalitarian, fascist, and even racist interpretation of the human species or of the nation, in which the individual has no sense of reality other than that of the whole to which he belongs. Marx conceives reality as a continued creation of man by man. Communism is not the end of history but the end of the brutish pre-history of man. It is the beginning of a properly human history made up of all the initiatives of each human person who becomes the center of creation in every domain from economy to culture. In the "Communist Manifesto" Marx defines Communism as an association in which the free development of each conditions the free development of all.

When this is grasped the second confusion on which these objections rest is set aside: the confusion between end and means. Marxist social revolution is neither an end in itself nor an ultimate end. The ultimate end of all our actions, of all our fights as communist militants, is to make a man of each man; that is to say, a creator, a center of political initiative and of creation on the economic and political plane, on the plane of culture and love, on the spiritual plane. Without any doubt, social revolution (the abolition of the system of private ownership of the means of production) is, if not the ultimate end and the criterion of all value, the absolutely necessary condition of the development of the person. Preaching about spirituality but disregarding the major condition of its realization, speculating about the ends but keeping silent about the means, is a lie, a hypocritical exaltation of the human person which in fact contributes to the perpetuation of the historical conditions of his debasement. What is the Marxist theoretical foundation of the absolute value of the human person? The Christian misunderstanding of Marxism begins with Marx's own formula: "A being is his own master; he is free when he owes his own existence to himself" (manuscripts of 1844, p. 38). According to Pastor Gollwitzer this would emasculate a conception of liberty and of man, for it would isolate man both from the world of things and the world of men, and would commit him to stark solitude.

This objection is founded upon a mistaken reading of Marx. Marx defines the individual by "the whole of his social relations." It is a mistake to believe that for Marxism man does not exist, that what exists is "a whole of social relations," that for Marx there are no centers, no subjects who create meaning, no men to make history. This conception has long been held by the opponents of Marxism. Marx explicitly excludes this interpretation: On the contrary, he insists on the contradiction, characteristic of all class systems, between the personal life of man and the economic and social system which aims at making of him a mere support of production relations.

This is precisely what differentiates Marxism from all previous materialism in which subjectivity was misunderstood in that it was seen only as a passive reflection of a given internal world, ready-made in its mechanized structure. This is the very kernel of the problem of liberty, of Marxist humanism, the two-fold problem of subjectivity and of the relation of man with man and of man with the world. For man, the mover of history, is not an abstract subject, a Hegelian spirit. The individual for Marx is defined by the whole of his social relations just as the object is defined infinitely, inexhaustibly by its relations with the totality of other objects. The reality with which the physicist has to deal is already, as Lenin wrote, inexhaustible. How much more inexhaustible is the human reality which with life, conscience, society has crossed so many other thresholds of complexity!

The thesis that matter on all its levels is inexhaustible should be linked with the thesis that work produces radically new forms of material being, in which the future of ends pursued plays an active part and creates infinite possibilities. Let us add to this that those nuclei of beings, each of whom is thinking, creating and acting on another, fully exist only in reciprocal exchange and dialogue; they enrich one another endlessly. To grasp this is to understand the richness of the Marxist conception of Liberty, and the fact that it is based on an acknowledgment of each man's value as an active being and a creator.

Respect for the Human Person

That man who is for a Marxist the supreme being is not "an abstract idea of the future man"; he is "the neighbor in his concrete character," that very man whose understanding and love are for another man a constant source of human enrichment, that very man without whom I could not really exist, for I can fully develop only through what he brings to me. It would be too impoverish and caricature Marxism to imagine that it conceives only abstract statistical relations between men, and that it forgets the relations of man with man, that it forgets love in its most personal and deepest form.

Therefore it would not be fair to identify Marxism with a messianism or to think that it undermines the foundations of its own humanism. It could not justify the respect owed to each human person unless it gave no other sense to any man's life than that of serving as a means to the realization of the ends of the human species. It is not fair to say that Marxism evades this problem or that to invoke the function of the individual life "in the service of the species" is in contradiction with the humanist spirit. Such a criticism would apply only to a positivist distortion or a mechanist interpretation of Marxism.

But conversely, just concern with considering men as individuals, with respect for their person and for its infinite value, should not paralyze the effort to devise a more human organization of social relations. In this indispensable battle, the problem of means is posed in exactly the same way for Christians and for Marxists. Christians cannot avoid it: We never have the choice between violence and the absence of violence. We are already embarked upon life: Whether we abstain from commitment or whether we strike a definite attitude in either way, choice plays its part in the relations of forces. To condemn the violence of the rebelling slave is to be party to the permanent violence of those who hold him fettered. If Christians accept military service—and they have not refused it since Constantine—why should they not fight in a Resistance movement or in a revolution? Since they accept violence as soldiers while they reject revolutionary violence, it is not the means they reject but the revolutionary end itself.

History has taught Marxists to recognize the specifically religious component of anticommunism: It comes from the confusion between ethics and logic and from the attempt to deduce political and social forms from faith without acknowledging the autonomy of the secular world and the necessity of using strictly scientific means to pass judgment on a system of social relations or on a political regime. The Communist reproaches institutional religion for siding with counterrevolution. Is it certain that the Church rejects Marxism first of all because it is atheistic? Is it not rather because Marxism is revolutionary? A true dialogue is possible only if to be a Christian does not necessarily mean to be a champion of the established order.

Christians do not refuse all violence. They believe in the waging of just war; therefore, when they refuse in the name of respect for the human person to be party to the requisite violence in the battles for man's liberation, it is difficult not to suspect that they use respect for the human person as an alibi and that in reality they share in the silent violences of conservative and oppressive powers.

The dialectic tension between the individual and the totality, between the ends and the means, which makes a tragedy of each action exists as much for the Christians as for the Marxists. One erroneously disregards this tension when one opposes Christianity as it should be to Communism as it is.

The question is not to sacrifice each man's freedom, his life, and the sense it has, to the Moloch of an abstract future but to pass, according to Éluard's saying, "from the horizon of one to the horizon of all." The living and real community of men, each of whom is for the other an inexhaustible spring of richness and questioning, is so deeply the basic reality that in perspective of Marxist humanism each person can fully blossom only if he bathes in it and receives warmth and life from it. But we can never forget that the relations of exploitation and oppression with all the forms of alienation they breed in any class system precisely hamper this human intercourse. It is the struggle against these obstacles which is our first objective. In a communist system "the question of the meaning of existence will still be put and the heart of man will keep its unfathomable depths." But that also demands that we should lead a fight against everything in our class system that makes man poorer and mutilates him by alienating him. This fight can be victorious only if it is the common fight of all those who care for the future.

Dialogue

If we do not want to come to a mechanical encounter between two closed futures Christians and Marxists must become aware that we cannot mutually know one another without becoming different. That implies first that we should not consider ourselves as the unique holders of a truth given once for all, ready-made, and definitive. It is the very nature of Marxism to consider itself thus historically. Engels stressed that

> ...materialism would have necessarily to take a new form with each great discovery marking a date in the history of sciences. Lenin many a time recalled the necessity of this constant renewal. We in no way consider Marx's doctrine as something complete and untouchable. On the contrary, we are convinced that it has only laid the cornerstones of the science which socialists must further in all directions if they do not wish to fall behind life.[1]

Any attempt to shut Marxism into a closed system of principles or laws is contrary to its very essence. Contemporary theology seems also to be turning to the idea that the primary conceptualization of faith in the forms of Greek thought was only one of the possible cultural forms of this faith.

The same major facts of our century which compel us to reconsider Marxism in the spirit of our time have led Christians to fundamental meditation upon the significance of their faith and the his-

[1] Lenin, "Our Program," in *Selected Works* (New York: International Publishers Co., Inc., 1967), IV, 217–18.

torical forms in which it was expressed. Among the more lucid
Christians it is manifested by an effort to dissociate what is fundamental in their faith from the out-of-date conceptions of the world
in which their faith was traditionally expressed. More and more the
distinction between these becomes necessary. On the one hand religion may be regarded as an ideology and a conception of the world,
a cultural form taken by faith at given periods of historical evolution. On the other hand lies the faith itself.

A contemporary Protestant philosopher, Paul Ricoeur, writes:
"Religion is the alienation of faith." [2] The problem of the distinction
between faith and the historical transient cultural form it has taken
is strongly posed by a Catholic philosopher, Leslie Dewart, in his
latest book: *The Future of Belief.* Leslie Dewart first recalls that the
universalization of Christianity from St. Paul to St. Augustine was
conditioned by its Hellenization. A new conception of the relations
of man and the world arose as Christianity was born from Judaism.
But this conception adopted a pre-existing cultural form: that of
Greek thought, which introduced into Christianity its own ideal of
perfection, that is to say "immobility." This Hellenistic influence
led to the petrification of dogma. Centuries later the rediscovery
of Aristotle strengthened that trend, and medieval scholasticism
emerged as the language in which the Catholic faith has been expressed to our day. The Christian conception of God was always
more or less contaminated by Parmenides' conception of true being,
whether in the form of Plato's idea of the good, or Aristotle's primary cause and motionless mover, or Plotinus' idea of the one. The
scholastic philosophers have contented themselves with distinguishing essence and existence but in maintaining that for God essence
identified itself with existence.

Outside this typically Greek way of setting the problem, the
ontological argument no longer has any meaning. Now the Greek
way does not answer to anything in living contemporary thought.
From parallel endeavors to make up a non-Cartesian theory of
knowledge, non-Platonic ethics, non-Aristotelian esthetics, comes the
constantly renewed attempt to conceive non-Hellenic theology.

Maurice Blondel, at least in the first version of the "Action," was
perhaps one of the pioneers of this new apologetic. But the most
prevalent tendency to escape the Greek conception of the relations
between being and intelligibility was expressed in the attempt to

---

[2] *De l'Interpretation: Essai Sur Freud* (Paris: Editions du Seuil, 1965), p. 159.

theologize the philosophers of existence: the resurrection of Kierkegaard, the blossoming of the "dialectic theology" of Karl Barth, and
the theological variants of Jaspers and Heidegger from Bultmann to
Father Rahner testify to this effort. Our time above all wants a
philosophy founded upon creative development. This is no doubt the
reason for the impact of Father Teilhard de Chardin's work upon so
many Christian consciences. He has posed a basic problem for his
Church and indeed for all men of our times, namely the basic
problem of our century, the very problem that Marx set for the first
time a century ago and which he began to answer: how to think
through the law of change and how to master it.

Marx's discovery has produced the deepest transformation of the
world that history has ever known. The question that Father Teilhard put to Christians requires of them nothing less than an inversion
of attitude towards the world. He recalled the basic aspect of Christianity often obscured by a latent Platonism: that ascending to God
does not imply turning one's back upon the world but rather participating in its transformation and its construction with a more lucid
mind, with more intense activity and a more vehement passion. In
such a perspective God is no longer a being nor even the totality of
being, since such a totality does not exist. Being is totally open to the
future to be created.

Faith is not the possession of an object by cognition. St. John of
the Cross said that faith does not meet an object, but "nothing."
He evoked "the experience of the absence of God," and added in
his *The Ascent to Mount Carmel:* "one can ascertain whether somebody loves God in truth or whether he contents himself with
something that is lesser than God" (*Works,* p. 691). The transcendence of God implies its constant negation since God is constant
creation beyond any essence and any existence. A faith which is
only assertion would be credulity.

Doubt is part and parcel of living faith. The depth of faith in a
believer depends upon the force of the atheist he bears in himself
and defends against all idolatry. "We are atheists," Justin wrote,
"yes, we confess it, we are the atheists of those so-called Gods" (I
Apology, 1).

We thus reach the highest level of the dialogue, that of the integration in each of us of that which the other bears in himself, as
other. I said earlier that the depth of a believer's faith depends upon
the strength of the atheism that he bears in himself. I can now add:

the depth of an atheist's humanism depends on the strength of the faith he bears in himself.

The dialogue will be truly fruitful insofar as all of us in common defense of man's basic values are rendered capable of integrating into ourselves the truth borne by our partner in dialogue.

JOHANNES METZ

The Future of Man

Naturally I can refer here to only a few points from M. Garaudy's lecture. I would like to choose those directly related to a central theological way of posing the question. None of us can take what was said in his paper lightly. Least of all we theologians. Thus, if what I say has a markedly critical character, it is not intended to deny, in blind self-righteousness, that here we have not only to contradict and defend, but also to listen reflectively and to learn with a willingness to correct ourselves. Finally, I hope that my sketch of the way of posing the question theologically, will itself betray something of theology's critical willingness to listen to its Marxist discussion partners. This willingness does not lead to unimaginative appropriation or solipsistic rigidity, but to such kind of fruitful conflict at which our dialogue is aiming and in which theology seeks to remain true to the message it has been entrusted with, by resolutely sharing the world's problems and questions.

In this dialogue I will try to concern myself critically with what is essential to our opposing conceptions. I am very grateful to M. Garaudy for saying that what is essential and proper to each cannot be the object of a casual compromise. Our dialogue is no sentimental one. It is not intended to hush up objections, but to provoke them critically. Only thus may it lead to a situation in which the discussion partners themselves change, rather than persist in an outdated neo-liberalistic position, which settles for anything and seeks an

From *Journal of Ecumenical Studies*, IV (Summer 1967), 224–34. Reprinted with permission of the publisher.

agreement with everything because it no longer possesses a productive imagination or power to change.

Mythologizing through Christianity?

M. Garaudy sincerely recognizes the decisive contribution which Christianity has made toward the humanizing of mankind. Yet, he likewise penetratingly accuses Christianity of having contributed, in no small degree, to a dangerous mythologizing of human existence. He sees in Christianity—at first entirely in the style of the classical Marxist criticism of religion—an expression of the fact that man does not withstand the infinite question which he himself is, and the endless need which drives him on, but surreptitiously seeks answers and satisfactions in an unhistorical way, namely by hypostasizing his infinite questioning into a deity, by objectifying his wishes into a transcendental heaven. But today Christianity itself has learned to look at religion and myth critically. It knows that myth (its negative sense is here intended) can spring from a propensity to answer, where, from our point of view, there is nothing to be answered; it knows that myth can hide the task of historical realization of existence, the task of finding an answer in history. Christianity itself has not seldom been in danger of drawing upon itself the suspicion attached to mythology because of a pretended superfluity of answers and the lack of true and painful questions. But has not this danger within Christianity always been recognized? Has not Christianity always had within itself a sort of "negative theology"?

Let us look more closely at the accusation that biblical religion in its understanding of God hypostasizes the unfulfilled expectations of man. How is God witnessed to in the Bible? Here I can consider only one line of biblical thought, one which is directly related to our question. It is expressed, I believe, very clearly in the central Old Testament account of God's revelation of himself in Exodus 3:14. Certainly God is here expressed as our future, but only as *our* future, insofar as it belongs *to itself*, is founded in itself, and is not merely a correlative of our own wishes and strivings: "I am who I am" runs the central phrase of this passage.[1] It defines the divinity of God as free "power of our future" belonging to itself, and not

---

[1] Translator's note: The German "Ich werde sein der ich sein werde" expresses an idea of futurity usually lacking in the English versions. The Hebrew tense system does not distinguish between present and future.

primarily as "being-over-us" in the sense of a transcendence that can be experienced unhistorically. The God so understood appears here not as a product of our impatience with our own wishes, or a result of resignation to the insatiability of our own unlimited strivings; he does not appear as a damper on the historical initiative of man, but as the liberation for this initiative. For only a future which is *more* than the prolongation of our own open or latent possibilities can truly call us out beyond ourselves (as M. Garaudy demands of man, and by which he characterizes his destination).

But it can free us for something truly new, which does not throw us again into the "melancholy of satisfaction" (E. Bloch); it can free us for what has never been as yet. Such an understanding of God disarms the suspicion that God is only an alienated and constantly alienating concept of our own historical existence. In fact, only such an understanding of God makes possible historical existence, for it makes the world appear as a world in history, rising toward this "new," and our freedom is involved in this process. When this biblical faith in promise is related to the "new," it awakens a revolutionary attitude to the world, if by revolution we mean the consciousness of an absolute *novum* which cannot be understood merely as an evolutionary extension of our own possibilities. When one considers this admittedly somewhat neglected side of the biblical faith in promise, can it really mean that this faith makes man languish in the midst of his historical struggle, that it has merely a comforting and appeasing function? Is not our modern understanding of the world, with its constant desire for the "new," with its primacy of the future, rooted therein? And if M. Garaudy has frequently defined Marxism as a "theory of historical initiatives," does he not base this definition on an understanding of the world which appears before us in the biblical belief in promise? By this I do not mean to accept anything or anyone prematurely or to embrace Marxism, so to speak, from behind. The concrete historical relations and distinctions have still other dimensions, and the question of truth in our argument cannot be decided with proof of historical causalities.

Allow me nevertheless to develop and complete my considerations with a critical remark: Can every belief in promise truly be criticized as a dangerous alienation and concealment of the radicality of the human quest, as a dangerous myth which tries to formulate and fix, in the category of an answer, what has been given to us in the category of a question? Is there not a belief in promise which does not do away with the quest, but intensifies it? How can the human quest be transformed into a historical demand if it is not guided by a promise? How and by what means can this quest become historical initiative if it is not warmed by hope, by the "Gulfstream of hope" as E. Bloch would say? Why does this question not remain in the order of pure contemplation about the world, of the speculative broadening of knowledge? Why does it not remain purely philosophical? What drives it on to become revolutionary and world-changing, to seize historical initiative, to understand the world as a historical world, as a world arising from history, and oriented toward the future? Do we not find here a primacy of hope in the human quest itself? But hope possesses a surplus of confidence and historical imagination which no total critique of religion and myth can take away.

I believe that within theology, too, there is a desire for the total demythologizing of the Christian message of promise in which its contents of hope would be emptied to become a symbolic paraphrase of the human question as such. But in this way these contents of hope would lose any true character of conflict and contradiction over against present reality, and thus be robbed of their power to move history. For history, if moved at all, is not moved by the self-evident in the common quest of human existence, but by what is far from obvious, by the "impossible," by the object of our hope.

Promise and Demand

In continuation I would like to say something about Christian eschatology in order to show that the alternatives developed by M. Garaudy between promise and demand, between expectation and struggle, so to speak between Christian eschatology and revolutionary world-planning, do not or must not exist for the Christian. For Christian hope cannot realize itself in purely contemplative expectation, not even—especially not—hope based on the cross. For pure contemplation refers by definition always to what has been existing and to what will exist for all time. But the future of the world, grounded in the cross of Christ, which Christian hope seeks and aims for, is ever yet becoming, not yet realized. This hope, therefore, must be essentially creative and struggling; it must realize itself in a creative, so to speak productive eschatology. It is always hope as waiting *and* as struggle. For faith in the New Testament way of thinking is always a victory, a victory not only over ourselves, but, according to Paul, a world-conquering victory. The imperative of this faith, namely "not to liken oneself to this world" means "not only to change oneself but also, by resistance and creative expectation, to change the form of the world in which one does his believing, hoping, and loving" (J. Moltmann). The New Testament community was characterized by its immediate expectation of the end of the world *and* by its universal missionary task; it was a community of expectation *and* of mission, even of expectation *in* mission. The eschatological expectation mirrored in the attitude of the first community is a belligerent, world-changing expectation. The experience of the approaching kingdom has nothing paralyzing about it, but something liberating and challenging over against the existing world. And Jesus is for the consciousness of this community not the teacher of a *Weltanschauung*, he is for them not a sage, not an interpreter of the world, but in fact a revolutionary who acted and suffered in conflict with the existing social order, and who thus needs not admirers, but followers in the service of his world-changing mission. The kingdom he announces does not simply lie ready-made like a distant goal before us, already existing and only hidden, to the pure notion of which we direct our desires. Rather, this eschatological city of God is itself in process; when we go toward it in hope we help build it, as builders and not merely as theoretical interpreters of a future whose awakening power is God himself. The council's new Constitution on the Church says, "The renewal of the world... is in this period in history, in a certain way, truly anticipated." The Christian must understand himself as a "collaborator" in this new world of universal peace and justice. The orthodoxy of his faith must continually "prove true" in the orthopraxy of his eschatologically oriented actions in the world; for the promised truth is a truth which "must be done," as John (3:21) quite clearly emphasizes. The Christian must create in the world conditions under which the promised truth is valid, is with him, is present; he himself must help to change his world. The Christian concept of the end-time is thus no present-tense eschatology in which all passion for the future is transformed into an unworldly representation of eternity within the moment of individual existence; nor is it an eschatology of merely passive waiting for which the world and its time appear as a sort of prefabricated waiting-room in which man is to sit unengaged and bored—the more hoping the more bored—until God's office door opens. Christian eschatology must be understood rather as productive and struggling eschatology. Christian hope is a hope which—as Ernst Bloch once pointedly remarked —gives us "not only something to drink, but also something to cook." Eschatological faith and earthly engagement do not exclude each other but include each other. I know that sounds very "theoretical." Did the Church ever fight for her promise? Or more exactly, has she always made it visible and credible *which* promises she is fighting for? Has she ever made it believable that the promise she proclaims, that the hope she bears witness to, is not a hope for the Church but a hope for the kingdom of God as future of the world, a hope for the kingdom of universal peace and justice (cf. 2 Pet 3:13), in which tears are known no more and in which there will be no "mourning nor crying nor pain any more" (Rev 21:4)? Has she pledged herself in creative, struggling expectation for *this* promise? Or for the promise of the Sermon on the Mount which makes her forever the church of the poor and enslaved? Here we will be questioned down to the roots of our Christian existence. And without painful conversion we can go no farther. Of course, the promises that shine forth in Christ are a spur to all our struggling efforts for the future, but likewise a thorn that cannot permit these efforts for the future to proceed in a simple, militant world optimism, but must also chafe them, resist them critically, in the name of oppressed and injured mankind. In the light of the scandal of the cross, Christian faith in promises can never become merely an ideological paraphrase of the modern belligerent consciousness of progress; it can never simply canonize the technical, economical, social progress that we, rightfully, have advocated. It is and remains always the expression of a struggling hope—against all hope. Thus it is and remains essentially "untimely," but not as it might be to the ever conservative, the sulking, or those filled with resentment. It is untimely in a productive sense: In reference to our movement toward the future it has a critical, liberating task and power. Karl Rahner has formulated it thus!

> The Church cannot seek to fulfill this "critical" task merely by reminding man of this "criticism," so to speak, from outside, while he moves toward his own creative future; rather, she must show him how this criticism results from the experience of the way toward his own future within the world. She must tell him that the growth of what has been planned is also always an increase of what

has not been expected and not been predicted; that the sacrifice for the future of coming generations loses its meaning and its value, and thus, in the long run, its power, if the sacrifice of the now-living man is seen only as a means to the building of the future regardless of the absolute value, the rights and the dignity of man now living. ... The Church must warn against any utopia that is not the beginning of a real future, but the program for the future that is unrealistic and thus, in seeking to realize itself, is forced to correct slowly (so that such a false ideology does not lose face) what has been falsely planned through great sacrifice and loss.

Christianity must understand its faith in promises as that sort of a critical, liberating power which constantly deritualizes any forced consciousness of progress. Of course, this faith in promises must not itself become—as it so often does—an ideology of the future. The poverty of its knowledge about the future must be dear to it. What distinguishes it from all Eastern and Western concepts of the future is not the fact that it knows more about the future sought by mankind, but that it knows less, and is able to face the poverty of its knowledge. "By faith Abraham obeyed when he was called to go out to a place which he was to receive as an inheritance; and he went out, not knowing where he was to go" (Heb 11:8). This faith in promises must always carry with it a "negative theology" of the future. In this light I would like to criticize the idea of the "total man," by which M. Garaudy characterizes the Marxist concept of the future, as a problematic abstraction and at the same time as an exorbitant demand on the quest concerning the future. Does not every vision of the future of an autonomous and perfect humanity always run aground on man himself? Does not his disenchanted consciousness always avenge itself on such forced visions and plans? Do we not clearly experience that the technical hominization of the world that we have planned, the process of transforming its possibilities into realities, does not unequivocally create increased humanization (and does not the dangerous deceit of Marxism lie in this very attempt to parallel these two processes)? Do we not know too exactly that we even as men of an extremely hominized world will always continue our quest for the outstanding *humanum*, as in Isaiah: "Watchman, what of the night? ... The watchman says: 'Morning comes and also the night. If you will inquire, inquire; come back again'" (Is 21:11f.).

The Struggle about Man

In M. Garaudy's lecture the question keeps returning whether Christianity is not after all a form of dangerous self-alienation of man. Who would want to deny—not I—that in the name of Christianity and the Church such self-alienation was often at least sanctioned? Or that, for example, certain social constellations have been canonized in the name of Christianity, and that for the poor and enslaved a verbose consolation in the beyond was too quickly handed out? That the Church has spoken her criticism of the mighty of the world often too softly, and often far too late? Do not answer that this is a question of tactics or expediency. It is a question of responsibility within history, if there is only a grain of truth in Camus' remark that there have been times when every sin was a mortal sin, and every indifference a crime. To be sure, the Church quite clearly claims to be the protector of "natural law." But has she always equally clearly and decisively fulfilled the consequent obligation to defend the humanity of *every* threatened man with every means at her disposal? Is not the crisis of so-called "natural law," before every purely theoretical problematic—a credibility crisis regarding the universal humanitarian involvement of Christianity "without regard to person"? Here history accuses, and we must take seriously this accusation, especially since Christianity as a historical reality must always account for its own concrete historical development. The question remains, however, whether Christianity, at its roots, advocates such pernicious self-alienation or whether, actually, merely seeks to sanction such self-alienation which cannot be solved through social progress. Let us leave aside, for the moment, the question whether the expression "self-alienation," which cannot deny its connection with an individualistic, romantic humanism, properly indicates the state of affairs important to our discussion. Are there really only such forms of self-alienation which, as Marxism proposes, can be overcome through social efforts, and which we Christians canonize by a theology of the beyond and of original sin? Are there not rather forms of man's self-alienation which cannot be removed by a release from economic-social situations, however successful, and from which man will always draw the "sorrow of his finiteness"? Are there not forms of self-alienation that cannot simply be dissolved into social-utopian expectation? Suppose that the great social utopias of East and West could be realized and led to man's next to complete independence from economic changes in a future society. Would then man's questioning confrontation with himself come to an end? Or would it not rather appear in a more radical form, since many factors which also divert from this confrontation and constantly allay it, like work and economic care, would *ex supposito*, vanish? What about the problem of guilt, the problem of evil? Or what about the experience to which we theologians have given the curious name "concupiscence"? This theological term expresses the experience of a self-alienation which is clearly not susceptible of a purely economic solution. We experience within ourselves a constant discrepancy between what we plan for ourselves and the way we really live, between the idea of our lives and its execution. We experience, for instance, that what might have been for us a transforming fate—a great sorrow, for example—is in the long run levelled down into everyday experience which is always ready for compromise. We experience the fact that pain, too, does not change us, that we seek and find a bourgeois way of getting along with it, and succeed in lowering everything to the routine of our muffled everyday life. By this I mean what Camus had in mind when he said, "It seems as though great souls are sometimes less frightened by pain than by the fact that it doesn't last." In such and similar experiences we meet a form of man's self-alienation that cannot be overcome economically. And, to mention here a particular example, what about the experience of suffering and death? If we take M. Garaudy at his word when he speaks about death then the question arises in mind (with all respect for the idealism of his conception); Is not this understanding of death exposed to the suspicion of the mythologizing and mystification of mortal existence at least to the same extent as he accuses the Christian concept of death of doing? What is this dying into the whole of future mankind? The Christian sees in death an experience that threatens his existence, an experience of radical self-alienation which he hopes to withstand only in solidarity with Jesus, the crucified and resurrected, and which he understands only within that horizon which is set up for him by the message of Jesus. This seems to me to include that element of the understanding of death which M. Garaudy's concept rightfully wants to emphasize: the essential *Entprivatisierung* of this relationship to death, the essential relation of the experience of death to other men. For the Christian attitude toward death must not be narrowed down to the individualistic, unworldly outlook. It too takes place with an eye to the world, to the world of our brothers; it takes place in self-forgetful expression of love for others, for "the least of these"; it takes place in selfless vicarious responsibility for *their* hope. For the anticipatory overcoming of death takes place in this hoping love. "We know that we have passed out of death into life, because we love the brethren" (1 Jn 3:14). Christian hope, conquering, takes to itself the passion of death which threatens our promised fulfillment by engaging itself in the hazard of brotherly love for the least of these—in the discipleship of Jesus, whose being a Protestant theologian once impressively defined as "existence for others."

The ultimate quality of a humanism comes to light, I believe, in the hermeneutic and productive power which it unfolds for such borderline situations of human existence, for such self-alienation as cannot be overcome merely through social operations, for guilt, concupiscence, death. Is Marx's answer to this really a better guide than Jesus'? However, a basic point in M. Garaudy's explanation of this theme seems to me especially important and indispensable, particularly for a Christian anthropology: What I would here like to call *Entprivatisierung* (not merely the depersonalization!) of the central human attitude, that is, the development of the consciousness that I can realize my hope only when I try to make room for such hope in others; the development of the consciousness that I can realize my freedom only in concrete decision for the freedom of others, against any form of servitude of man.

M. Garaudy has clearly stressed that the Marxist alternative to religion is not a materialistic atheism—as Christian scholasticism has always tried to refute it—but a humanism totally and radically determined on "saving the honor of man." The Marxist attitude, therefore, according to him, does not really contain "direct unbelief" built upon the express negation of faith in its religious manifestation. Thus, Marxism does not appear primarily as a world-design for existence *against* God, but as the offer of a positive possibility of existence, a total humanity *without* God. Thematic atheism is thus not truly an object but a presupposition of Marxism. I would certainly not say that this *unbelief of a so to speak post-atheistic age* is less disturbing than an expressly atheistic unbelief. However, it is here, I believe, that the possibility of responsible conversation and exchange offers itself. Christianity must take this humanitarian claim at its word and let its own solidarity in the struggle for the humanity of man be recognized—and this more decisively than ever. The threatened man: He could be the place where the truth of belief and unbelief is today tested and manifested. Here the Church that describes herself explicitly in the Council as "the church of the poor and the oppressed" and with her all Christianity, must meet the challenge of a great claim. Nothing could be more insidious for the Church than to give the impression that for her nothing more is at stake here and that she has nothing more to lose in this dialogue about "saving the honor of man." There is no premature purely religious or theological escape from her historical responsibility which has been laid upon her by her faith in the promises. That would in the end only betray the fact that Christianity, in its struggle for man, does not give itself credit for anything new or creative, and only too readily takes off the edge in the struggle about man.

Promise and Society

In the struggle for man which has broken out today, Christianity can no longer (in the name of the "unworldliness" of belief) take possession of the private subjectivity of the individual in the private intimacy of the I-Thou experience between men. Does not Christianity, through its exclusive concentration on subjectivity and relations between men fall more and more into a dangerous privateness and arbitrariness over against a continuing world process? Is not faith in danger, because of its tendency to pure subjectivity and existentiality, of losing exactly that provocatory power of its responsibility for the world which loyalty to the message of Jesus ever again demands? The cross of Jesus, from which faith receives its orientation and promises does not stand ultimately in the *privatissimum* of the purely individual-personal realm; neither does it stand in the *sanctissimum* of the purely religious realm. It stands outside the threshold of protected privacy or of the screened-off religion sphere; it stands "out there," as the Epistle to the Hebrews says, in the *profanum* of the world, as a scandal to it, as foolishness, and as promise. Therefore, faith must take its part in the struggle for the one world; it must relate itself to the publicity, the sociality, and the concrete history of this world. It must not go on to turn what is socially provoking in the gospel of Jesus into something purely individualistic and private ("modern" as this tendency in presentday theology may be: Radical demythologizing finally made the Christian understanding of faith and salvation into something completely private). Christian faith is confronted again and again with the task, springing from its orientation toward the central biblical content of promise, of relating itself to the world as society, and to the world-changing, revolutionary powers in this society. It must critically concern itself with the great political-social utopias, with the promises which grow out of our modern society, of universal peace and universal justice. Stress on this has nothing to do with a suspicious neo-politicizing of Christianity and of the Church. On the contrary! Only in the consciousness of their public responsibility can faith and Church take seriously their task of criticizing society. Only thus can the Church avoid becoming merely an ideological superstructure built above a certain existing social order. Only thus can she avoid becoming a well-received travesty of purely political urges to power. Certainly only thus will she avoid becoming the final religion of our fully secularized society to which credit is given for certain functions of relief for the individual, but no power to criticize society.

KARL RAHNER

Christology and an
Evolutionary World View

Our present concern is the relationship of Christology to an
evolutionary view of the world. By this relationship we do not
imply that the doctrine of the Incarnation is necessarily included
in or excluded from an evolutionary outlook. We simply want to
indicate an inner affinity between two dimensions of human thought
and the possibility of a mutual relationship. The problem involves
both the central mystery of Christianity and that which is most
familiar to modern man, namely, the material world.

Matter and Spirit Related

Having presupposed the evolutionary world view, we will first
investigate the relation between matter and spirit and thus the unity
of the world, of natural history, and of the history of man. Second,
we will consider man, the being in which the basic tendency of
matter toward self-discovery in spirit comes to its definitive break-
through. Thus the being of man can be viewed within the basic
and total concept of the world. It is this being of man that awaits
as its own fulfillment and that of the world what we call grace and
glory through its complete self-transcendence in God and God's
self-communication to it. The first step and the abiding beginning
and absolute guarantee that this ultimate self-transcendence has already begun is what we call the hypostatic union. Thus the Incar-

From *Theology Digest*, XIII (Summer 1965), 83–88. Abridged version based on
a chapter in *Theological Investigations*, V, 157–92 (Baltimore: Helicon Press,
1966). Reprinted with permission of the publishers.

nation is seen as the beginning of the divinization of the world as a whole.

The Christian believes that everything, heaven and earth, matter and spirit, is the creation of the one God. Not only does everything as different stem from *one* cause which, because infinite and almighty, can create the most diverse, but this diversity manifests an inner similarity and community and cannot be considered simply as contradictory or even disparate. This multiplicity and diversity forms a unity in origin, actuation, and determination: the one world.

The clearest example of the unity of matter and spirit is man. The Christian does not view man as a provisional juxtaposition of matter and spirit but as a unity, prior logically and ontologically to the diversity of his moments. Matter and spirit find their true meaning only within the unity of man. They can be understood only in terms of man. Christian doctrine corroborates this point by teaching that man's final perfection will include the perfection of his body and the cosmos. We must therefore see matter and spirit as essentially related to one another.

This fact does not exclude a distinction of matter and spirit. Man's basic experience of himself tells him he is spirit inasmuch as he is conscious of existing in a continuous relationship to the absolute whole of reality and its one source, God. His consciousness and this relationship mutually condition each other. This relationship does not mean that man knows the object of his knowledge exhaustively but that he both possesses himself and is taken up into the divine Mystery. Only when he lovingly receives the Mystery as it touches him, does he really experience this event in freedom. Man knows himself as matter insofar as he discovers himself in an encounter with a spatio-temporal world that is concretely and inescapably given. He stands as a stranger before the "otherness" of the world and himself, and it is precisely here that he becomes conscious of himself as an individual distinct from the rest of reality.

Matter Develops toward Spirit

What happens when we combine the ideas of the unity of spirit and matter and their duality and keep in mind that both realities are moments in a dynamic history? In such a case we can say that matter of itself essentially develops toward spirit. Here we are presupposing the existence of evolution in general. A true evolutionary dynamism does not consist of a pure mutation from one form to another on the same level of reality. Rather it is an increase of reality, an actual reception of a greater fullness of being. The increase is not only the effect of the basic reality but is also it own cause. That is, true evolution is an *active* self-transcendence. However, if we are to preserve the principle of causality, we must consider the evolution as depending on the power of the absolute fullness of being and not on nothingness. The power must be so intrinsic to finite realities that they are capable of actively transcending themselves. It must not be a constitutive element of finite realities, since evolution is unthinkable where the fullness of being is already present. Theologians label this phenomenon the divine concursus.

Essential Differences Not Denied

We are not denying the essential differences between matter, life, and consciousness. But if evolution includes the idea of a self-transcendence, there is no reason why it should not be able to bridge the essential differences existing between matter, life, and consciousness. Presentday scientific studies confirm the view that the history of matter, life, and man is a history including the notion of an evolution to essentially new and higher forms. The essential changes do not disrupt the flow of history, because the lower forms so transcend themselves that they preserve their own essential characteristics in the new forms. Still, the latter are essentially new variations of the lower forms.

Since man is the self-transcendence of matter, the history of nature and the history of man are stages of one continuum in which the history of nature finds its goal in man and his history. Conversely, man in his development is conditioned by the structure of the material world. What is the goal or outcome of this movement? We do not know since it is hidden in the infinite fullness of God. Insofar as the history of the cosmos is caught up in man, the outcome will depend on how man uses his freedom. His freedom is conditioned by the structure of the cosmos and—the Christian knows —is permeated by God's grace so that the end and fulfillment of the cosmos will coincide.

At present, matter is at a stage where in man it is conscious of itself and of its relationship to reality as a whole and to the source of its own existence. In its individual experience and objectivization matter can now see itself as object and can possess itself by its direct relationship to man as a living and conscious being. If we grant that this self-transcendence of matter is the term of cosmic history, we can safely say that the objective world finds itself in man and can actually see its relationship to its source as a goal before itself rather than a *post factum* conclusion.

Although this stage is still initial and the individual man is only a part of the world, it can occur in him precisely as a definite partial moment, as a spatio-temporal reality of the world. It takes place in a human way and therefore not just once and for all but again and again in its own unique way in individual men. To a certain extent, the material world is the one body of a manifold self-consciousness which incorporates its body into the relationship to its infinite source. And if the cosmic consciousness has reached its first step in man, it must continue to develop. Through his body man is allied to the whole cosmos and communicates with it. In their role as the reference point of the spirit, the body and the cosmos together press on to ever greater consciousness.

Drive to Consciousness Opposed

The developing consciousness of the world has its own history which occurs in the thinking and acting of individual men. But time and again the drive toward consciousness seems to be stopped by a hostile force; a kind of will to unconsciousness always seems to break through. But if evolution in general is directed toward a goal, then the growth of the cosmos into consciousness must also have a definite result. We often think cosmic evolution has relapsed into the diversity of its initial state, because we now are caught in a spatio-temporal situation and cannot experience the monadic unity of the world or its full consciousness. The cosmos will attain its goal only after death, when it will become perfectly conscious of itself in the souls of individual men who retain their essential relationship to it.

God Gives Himself to the World

The self-transcendence of the cosmos has not reached its final fulfillment in man who has fulfilled himself as a creature. It will find fulfillment only when the source of reality communicates himself directly to the world through man, in a sharing which we call "grace" in its historical phase, "glory" in its fulfillment. God does not stop short at the creation of things different from himself but actually gives himself to these things. In fact, he gives himself so generously to the world that he becomes its inner life. When the individual person accepts God's call, the cosmos finds itself in him. This is the goal of creation. It is the fullness which gives meaning to the partial and direction to the incipient; which supports evolution and enables it to grow both outwardly and inwardly.

Since cosmic evolution is supported at its beginning and in all its subsequent phases by the movement toward greater fullness, self-awareness, and an ever more conscious relationship to its source, it must eventually arrive at a direct encounter with the source. We cannot clearly see the divine theology in all the phases of the movement, yet it is a kind of absolute goal of the movement, planted in it and giving it a focal point to aim at. If cosmic history is basically a history of the will to consciousness and its source, we must presume that God's direct gift of himself to man and the cosmos is the goal of evolution. As physical individuals in a particular situation we can experience only the beginning of this movement; yet in all the conscious human actions of our lives we, unlike animals, formally anticipate its consummation. And in the subjective experience of grace we even encounter God's absolute proximity which assures us that cosmic history will find its conscious fulfillment when God gives himself in a most real and unveiled manner.

God in his ineffable mystery does not fall under any system of concepts but is presupposed as prior to every relationship that scientists may work with. Here the scientist discovers his beginning and his end. He may try to disregard the Mystery in the depths of his being and look to the clarity of science to explain his existence. But even if he could control the surface of his consciousness, he could not ignore the mysterious call from the depths of his person. The divine Mystery envelops man, supports him, and strives to permeate his whole being; it is its own explanation and becomes understandable to man only when he lovingly acquiesces in it.

What is the real nature of the self-communication of God? It is a sharing in the freedom and intercommunication of multiple subjectivities and can occur only when free subjects who are part of a common history receive it freely; that is, it must come about in a way that is human and historical, calling to the freedom of all men and occurring in a definite spatio-temporal situation.

Savior's Presence Historical

In this context a savior would be an historical person in whom all could see that God began to communicate himself to all men in an irreversible way. His advent does not mark the *temporal* beginning of God's gift of himself to man which is co-extensive with the history of the world. The savior is that historical figure in whom the event of God's absolute communication of himself is present as completely irreversible, in whom it reaches its high point in the total history of mankind. But insofar as God's self-communication is an historical phenomenon directed to all men, it must encounter every man before it reaches its end. To be complete the concept of a savior necessarily signifies both that God has given himself irreversibly to man and that man has accepted the gift.

Word Becomes Part of Cosmos

Now we can see the real meaning of the doctrine of the Incarnation, the union of God and man in Christ, and how it fits into an evolutionary view of the world. The savior must be a true man. He may not simply be God acting in the world. He must himself be a part of the cosmos, in fact, its high point. Jesus was precisely this. He was born of a woman and experienced a biological development in the world. Like us, he received God's communication of himself in his spiritual, human, finite subjectivity. In the obedience of his life and death, this communication found its perfect reception. He was not the appearance of man but true flesh. God laid hold of the world precisely at the point of unity in which matter became conscious and the spirit knew itself through that which was not itself, in the unity of human nature. In Jesus the Logos sustained matter just as it sustained the soul, and this matter is a part of reality and of the history of the cosmos. This materiality, moreover, was a true expression of himself.

When the Logos enters into the material-spiritual structure of the world, the divine dynamism, which sustains the self-transcendence of the world as a whole, reaches its zenith. For creation becomes a partial moment of the evolution of the world in which God truly expresses himself in the Word-become-flesh. Creation and incarnation, even though intrinsically differentiated, are simply two phases of the one event of God's emptying of himself.

Finally we come to the core of our investigation. It is not difficult to envision the history of the world and the spirit as the history of a self-transcendence toward God which in the case of Christ is identical with God's absolute communication of himself. Man too of his nature is the realized possibility of transcendence; he is consciously related to the Absolute Being and therefore as an individual can hardly be denied the same self-communication of God if it is given to other similar spiritual subjects. Christian revelation confirms this point by teaching that self-transcendence is offered to every individual in grace and that grace and glory are man's supreme fulfillment.

Incarnation Means Graced Man

Now how does the doctrine of the hypostatic union of an *individual* human nature with the divine Logos fit into this historical picture? Must we see it as an essentially new and higher step of the reciprocal self-transcendence of man and self-communication of God, which occurs only in the one case of Christ? Or is it a particular individual moment in the gracing of mankind which, nevertheless, is essential to the whole history and is its goal?

It is difficult to see how anyone can affirm that the Incarnation is the peak of cosmic realities and the goal of evolution without positing that it is likewise an inner moment of and condition for God's gracing of man in general. The hypostatic union will always be the peak of cosmic realities, but this fact does not make it the *goal* of cosmic and human evolution. The Incarnation preserves its full reality and uniqueness as the goal of evolution when seen as a necessary inner moment of God's gracing of the whole world. Yet there is a difficulty in this position which needs to be cleared up. Precisely how does the fulfillment of the man Christ in the hypostatic union differ from the consummation which will belong to every man who is taken up in grace and glory? The intrinsic effect of the hypostatic union for the humanity of the Logos is precisely and properly that which is the goal and fulfillment of every man, namely, the immediate vision of God. The Incarnation was "for our salvation" and added nothing to the divinity of the Logos.

More precisely, our question is this: Is Christogenesis the necessary goal for cosmogenesis so that all of us are implicity orientated toward the hypostatic union? And, if so, why? What specific quality of the hypostatic union makes it necessary for human and cosmic perfection in grace and glory? Our thesis affirms that the hypostatic union is unique as God's greatest gift of himself and a necessary moment in the gracing of all other spiritual creatures.

We have already indicated that a savior in an evolutionary view of the world must be an historical person in whom we can see God's promise of himself as irreversibly given and already fulfilled. But where God effects the self-transcendence of man through an absolute gift of himself in which his promise to all men is irreversibly fulfilled, there we have the hypostatic union. We must not restrict the idea of the hypostatic union to some prototypal union or relationship. Nor do we go far enough if we say that the divine Logos can tell us the full truth about the union.

Human Sharing Demands Union

The hypostatic union is characterized by a self-communication in which God gives himself to that which is lifted up, primarily Christ and then mankind. Here the sharing in the divine life takes place through grace and glory and is intended for every man. But *human* sharing is impossible without the hypostatic union. Although it takes place in man, it depends on its prototype in the hypostatic union. God's free decision to save man encompassed the gift of himself (grace) and the hypostatic union. Christ is the event of God's basic gift of himself to man, and insofar as this event has a definitive and conscious historical existence, it is a hypostatic union.

Whenever God expresses himself outside of the beatific vision, he does so through a work or event that belongs to the realm of the finite and creaturely. But as long as a finite expression of the divinity is not, strictly speaking, God himself, it is provisional and can be replaced by another finite creation. Therefore, if the reality of Jesus, in whom God gives himself absolutely to mankind, is definitively and irreplaceably present for us as promise and response, then we must admit he is not only a divine instrument but God himself. The promise itself must be a human reality graced in an absolute way since a pure word can only speak about God's self-giving and cannot be the event itself. If so, and if the event is divine, then we have the perfect relationship of a human reality to God, i.e., the hypostatic union.

So the hypostatic union differs from our grace not because it is a promise of grace but because Jesus is our promise, whereas we ourselves are only the recipients of it. The promise and the one promising are one. In the man Jesus God's call and our response are indivisibly and therefore irrevocably present.

EUGENE H. MALY

The Sign of Celibacy

Recent discussions have brought out the myriad aspects of our subject. It is necessary, therefore, that I circumscribe my own approach and indicate what aspect I plan to treat. First of all, I am not concerned here with the history of celibacy in the Church. Nor will I treat the question whether celibacy should be optional or not for the diocesan priest, although I recognize this as the burning issue in today's discussions. Again, I am not here interested, at least primarily, in the psychological, social or cultural aspects of celibacy. My sole concern is to present what I consider to be the principal biblical basis for celibacy and to indicate its motivational character for the young man of the twentieth century.

Before proceeding further I would like to remark briefly on an article by Monsignor Ivan Illich that appeared in a recent issue of *The Critic*,[1] principally because of the persuasive value it will no doubt have for many readers. In discussing celibacy he lists the various "reasons" that have been traditionally proposed for celibacy and finds them wanting. He then concludes, "Today, the Christian who renounces marriage and children for the kingdom's sake seeks no abstract or concrete *reason* for his decision. His choice is pure risk in faith. . . ."

That his choice can be ultimately and fully explained only in faith is not questioned. And it may well be that we have not stressed this

From *Bible Today*, XXXIV (February 1968), 2392–2400. Reprinted with permission of the author.
    [1] "The Vanishing Clergyman," *The Critic*, XXV, No. 6 (June–July 1967), 18–27.

sufficiently in the past. But that modern man seeks no reason whatsoever for his decision is denied by the very intensity and extent of the contemporary discussions. To say that the choice is a *pure risk* in faith smacks of that fideism that was a reaction to an extreme rationalism. But this is contrary to the best Christian tradition. Already Peter had encouraged his readers to "always be prepared to make a defense to anyone who calls you to account for the hope that is in you..." (1 Pet 3:15). Moreover, the major thrusts of Christian theology have begun with the principle that, while faith cannot be fully grasped by the reason, it is a reasonable faith. Similarly, while we may never fully explain the celibate's commitment, we are justified in seeking the reasons for celibacy. The Scriptures offer some basis for the search.

The Logion in Matthew 19:12

The logion of Jesus in Matthew's Gospel is well known to all. In it he distinguishes the various kinds of "eunuchs," or celibates, among whom are those who have made themselves such "for the sake of the kingdom of heaven" (19:12). There is no difficulty with the general interpretation: celibacy is not only a possible way of life in the Christian community; it is even implicitly recommended for some. Let us consider it in somewhat greater detail.

The phrase "for the sake of the kingdom of heaven" has a twofold application, ecclesiological and eschatological. In other words, it refers both to the building up of the kingdom in this world and to its final fulfillment at the end-time. It is my conviction that, once the eschatological meaning has been properly understood, the ecclesiological meaning will stand out in clearer relief. This eschatological orientation not only makes celibacy meaningful in a secular world but also affords an answer to the radically existentialistic standpoint that a permanent commitment is not possible for the developing human person.

Eschatology is the forgotten science of our traditional theology textbooks. Etymologically concerned with the "last things," it has been considered by theology almost exclusively in a chronological and individual sense. The "last things" are death, judgment, heaven and hell as they affect the individual human soul. If the kingdom of God is involved here, it is only indirectly. As a result, eschatology has become a kind of appendix to theology, not influencing in any notable manner the consideration of other Christian realities. An excellent illustration is had in the general reaction of celibates to the statement that they are eschatological signs; their rejection of the designation usually betrays an ignorance of what is meant.

Today the study of the *eschaton* is becoming one of the central concerns of the theologians. One of the most articulate of the Catholic theologians in this regard is Fr. Johann B. Metz, professor of theology at the University of Münster. On the Protestant side, the young theologian at the University of Mainz, Wolfhart Pannenberg, has stirred the imagination and the scholarly interest of other theologians around the world.

Eschatology and History

Basic to the centrality of eschatology is a conception of history that is peculiar to the biblical writer. It is a conception that modern studies in comparative religion have emphasized sharply. We will only briefly state the position here.

The pagan peoples of the ancient Near East saw history generally as a cyclic movement of events in time. There was no goal that had not already been achieved, no purpose of the gods that remained to be unfolded. The conception of history was rooted in the conception of the pantheon and that, in turn, was determined by those phenomena of nature that recurred with awesome regularity. Since these phenomena were cyclically patterned, so were the acts of the gods conceived to be cyclically patterned. And on those acts, because of their arche-typical nature, was the direction of history determined.

The Hebrews broke in on this world with a radically different conviction. The one God, Yahweh, an omni-competent and moral God who always acted for a purpose, had intervened in history and made his saving presence known, not primarily in the phenomena of nature but in the once-for-all events of history. The escape from Egypt, the crossing of the sea, the victory over the Amalecites, the conquest of the land—these were the unique acts of a unique God, and they revealed his will, his saving purpose, to Israel.

Since they did reveal a saving purpose and since those particular acts obviously did not exhaust his saving will, they pointed for Israel to a goal that would one day be achieved through a climactic divine intervention, to a "day of the Lord" when the divine purpose would be achieved. With this conception of history there was born within Israel a hope for an *eschaton*, a hope that would decisively color every expression of her religious aspirations, a hope that would not die despite the most serious threats to which it was exposed and despite the many false turnings that it took. Eschatology was a profoundly pervasive theme of biblical religion.

So pervasive was it that the description of God's actions in the past frequently took on the character of the future, climactic event. Von Rad has expressed it well in these words: "The later story-tellers are so zealous for Jahweh and his saving work that they over-step the limits of exact historiography and depict the event in a magnificence far transcending what it was in reality. These are texts which contain an implicit eschatological element, since they antici-pate a *Gloria* of God's saving action not yet granted to men." [2] In this view, then, the end or *eschaton* is not a chronological appendix to history but is the very warp and woof of all history; the end is really the beginning.

It should be easy to appreciate the dynamism with which history is invested in such an understanding. It has a forward thrust inher-ent in it by reason of the divine potential. Man's free response is seen by the sacred writers as an essential component of this move-ment. His yes or no to the divine imperative will condition the rapidity with which the *eschaton* is achieved; faith assures us of its ultimate achievement. God tells us through his prophet: "For just as from the heavens the rain and snow come down and do not re-turn there till they have watered the earth, making it fertile and fruitful, giving seed to him who sows and bread to him who eats, so shall my word be that goes forth from my mouth; it shall not return to me void, but shall do my will, achieving the end for which I sent it" (Is 55:10–11).

Eschatology's Influence

Western civilization has been heir, consciously or unconsciously, to this concept of history. The many messianic movements of our own day are expressions of it. The Marxist understanding of history is itself a messianic concept, even if it has deprived the concept of its personal messiah. Its dynamic presentation of the sweep of his-tory towards a goal has caught the imagination of dedicated men

[2] G. von Rad, *Old Testament Theology* (New York, 1902), I, 111.

and women throughout the world. To the extent that Judeo-Christianity has failed to arouse a similar or even greater enthusiasm, to that extent has it lost sight of a creedal conviction to which it first gave birth.

It is interesting to observe how the youth of today show a strong eschatological sense in their orientation to the new. Their rejection of the "good old days" is in a real sense a valid rejection; hankering after them can be a pagan temptation. Kierkegaard's "passion for the possible" can be rightly interpreted as a passion for future fulfillment.[3] Biblical eschatology is completely at home in this atmosphere.

It should also be evident that in this eschatological view of history there is a unity of past, present and future that would otherwise be in jeopardy. In fact, that unity is at least indirectly challenged today by many who, influenced by the strongly existentialistic philosophy of Heidegger as filtered down through the exegesis of Bultmann, deny or question the relevance of the historical past or future for the decision of the present moment. As Carl Braaten has expressed it, "In dependence on Heidegger's idea of time and history, they see the category of the future as an attribute of human existence, therefore designating primarily possibilities of existential decision, but not as an attribute of the historical reality of the world in purposeful forward movement under God's directing control toward an ultimate telos."[4]

It is no wonder, then, that the notion should be common today that man is incapable of a *permanent* decision, of one that will not be subject to change by reason of the purely existential character of its present and future forms. If the static world view is, rightly, abandoned now and the evolutionary world view accepted, then only an eschatological approach to history can safeguard that degree of permanence that we have always insisted is an essential part of the Christian tradition, safeguard, too, the concept of a permanent commitment to Christ realized in a special form.

Another philosophical emphasis that has had a great influence on contemporary society and that is relevant to our discussion is that of personalism. We must be prepared to accept its many insights into religious issues but at the same time recognize its dangers. Again we quote from Fr. Metz:

[3] Cf. J. B. Metz, "The Church and the World," in *The Word in History* (New York: Paulist Press-Newman Press, 1966), p. 71.
[4] *History and Hermeneutics* (New Directions in Theology Today, Vol. II) (Philadelphia: Westminster Press, 1966), p. 170.

This transcendental, personalistic, and existential theology has correctly emphasized the role of the human person in contrast to the mere objectivistic viewpoint of scholastic theology. It has brought the Christian faith into a proper relationship to human existence and subjectivity. However, this theology faces two dangers. On the one hand, this anthropological theology tends to limit the faith by concentrating on the *actual* moment of the believer's personal decision. The *future* is then all but lost. It becomes only another name for the intractable factors of the present decision. On the other hand, this anthropological theology tends to become private and individualistic. It fails to bring into sufficient prominence the social and political dimensions of the believer's faith and responsibility.[5]

Jesus and Eschatology

Let us return now to the biblical development of eschatology. The *eschaton* found concrete expression, for reasons that need not concern us here, in the concept of the kingdom of God, the absolute reign of God in the minds and hearts of men. This *eschaton*, in the conviction of the New Testament, was proleptically realized in the person of Jesus of Nazareth. "The time is fulfilled, and the kingdom of God is at hand..." (Mk 1:15). This was the good news with which Jesus began his public ministry. The validity of his claim was established in the expulsion of the evil spirits who represented the domain of sin operating in the world.

But while Jesus was aware of this fulfillment of the Father's plan in himself and in his ministry, he was also aware that that fulfillment had yet to be realized in the rest of mankind. This gives rise to that tension that is found throughout the New Testament, the tension between the "already" and the "not yet," between realized eschatology and nonrealized (*parousiac*) eschatology. It is because of the latter that history remains open and its forward thrust undiminished. In fact, it has been given greater urgency by the reality of its proleptic fulfillment in Jesus of Nazareth.

Albert Schweitzer is the theologian generally credited with restoring to the ministry of Jesus its strongly eschatological character. Before that, the liberal theologians of Europe had attempted to create an historical Jesus after their own image and likeness, one who preached a highly ethical religion divorced from historical tension

---

[5] *Op. cit.*, pp. 70f.

and amenable to a society that had attained a degree of cultural sophistication. Despite the extreme interpretation that Schweitzer gave to Jesus' eschatological preoccupation, his insights provided the basis for a new approach to the historical Jesus.

To put it simply, Jesus was a man in a hurry. Caught up wholly in the saving plan of the Father, he worked to achieve that plan in others that was realized fully in himself. "My Father is working still, and I am working," Jesus told the Jews who reprimanded him for healing on the Sabbath (Jn 5:17). The work of the Sabbath is precisely the work of making holy (Gn 2:3) and thereby making whole and bringing to perfection. Thus, in his own person Jesus can be compared with those texts of the Old Testament as explained by von Rad: He is God's word who contains within himself "an implicit eschatological element," an anticipation of the "*gloria* of God's saving action not yet granted to men."

To put it in another way, Jesus is the eschatological sign par excellence. But the word "sign" is, unfortunately, often misunderstood in this context. It is seen in the purely logical sense of a reality altogether separated from that other reality to which it points. It is the sign on the road whose reason for being lies solely in its ability to suggest a reality in which it does not itself participate. But the biblical sign is already the anticipation in itself of that reality of which it is a sign. The first of Jesus' miracles, John tells us, was the first of his "signs" (Jn 2:11a). It not only pointed to the work of salvation that he would accomplish in his hour of glorification, but it also anticipated by initiating that work of salvation, for John goes on to say that Jesus "manifested his glory, and his disciples believed in him" (2:11b). When we say, therefore, that Jesus in his own person is the eschatological sign par excellence, we mean to attribute to him not some kind of logical intentionality but a fullness of reality which it is his mission to communicate to others and which others see in him as a good to be shared ultimately by all.

Eschatology, Vertical and Horizontal

One more observation along these same lines will be extremely helpful in driving home our point. We have already spoken briefly of the treatment generally given eschatology in our theology textbooks. It might be described as a vertical eschatology in which heaven is seen as a superimposed layer into which man is sucked by some magic force at the end-time. Fr. Metz refers to this concept in these words:

> The Christian concept of the end-time is thus no present-tense (or vertical) eschatology in which all passion for the future is transformed into an un-worldly representation of eternity within the moment of individual existence; or is it an eschatology of merely passive waiting for which the world and its time appear as a sort of prefabricated waiting room in which man is to sit unengaged and bored—the more hoping the more bored—until God's office door opens.[6]

If eschatology is seen in this way, then we can understand why a dedicated Christian would strongly react to being considered an eschatological sign.

But if we can argue, as hopefully we have, for a horizontal eschatology in which the *eschaton* is the *fulfillment of all history*, in which the past, present and future all take on deeper meaning by reason of the one goal to which they are oriented and in which they proleptically share in Christ, then the eschatological sign should and must be terribly relevant to a concerned Christian. Then, the eschatological hope doesn't send him off into some dream world which might turn out to be a bad trip. Rather, it engages him all the more radically in the work of the moment, in the work of renewal and reformation in the deepest progressive sense.

Once more we may be permitted to quote from Fr. Metz because of his trenchant presentation.

> The kingdom he (Jesus) announces does not simply lie ready-made like a distant goal before us, already existing and only hidden, to the pure notion of which we direct our desires. Rather, this eschatological city of God is itself in process; when we go toward it in hope we help build it, as builders and not merely as theoretical interpreters of a future whose awakening power is God himself. ... The Christian must understand himself as a "collaborator" in this new world of universal peace and justice. The orthodoxy of his faith must continually "prove true" in the orthopraxy of his eschatologically oriented actions in the world; for the promised truth is a truth which "must be done," as John (3:21) quite clearly emphasizes. The Christian must create in the world conditions under which the promised truth is valid, is with him, is present; he himself must help to change his world. ... Christian eschatology must be understood ... as productive and struggling eschatology.[7]

[6] "The Controversy about the Future of Man: An Answer to Roger Garaudy," *Journal of Ecumenical Studies*, IV (1967), 228.
[7] *Ibid*.

We have said very little about celibacy as yet. But it is my conviction that any discussion of celibacy in a Christian sense can only be meaningful within this eschatological context. And the more profoundly eschatology is seen to influence our Judeo-Christian convictions, the greater value, it seems to me, can celibacy be seen to have as a relevant charism in the Church.

Celibacy and Eschatology

Celibacy in the Bible is always presented in an implicitly or explicitly eschatological context. In the Old Testament permanent voluntary celibacy was simply unheard of. Paradigmatic is the story of Jephthah's daughter who, before she was to die, spent two months mourning her virginity (Jgs 12:37). A man's purpose in life was to have sons who would carry on his name and, thereby, his life. It was a vicarious immortality that was achieved, for there was no conviction of an individual after-life until late in the Jewish period. Only during the holy wars did the fighting men refrain from sexual intercourse (cf. the story of Uriah in 2 Sm 11:6–13). But these, because of the conviction of Yahweh's saving power breaking in on Israel, were seen as sharing in the eschatological fulfillment.

There is evidence that at least some of the Essenes, of Dead Sea Scrolls fame, practiced a form of celibacy, which is an anomaly in the Jewish tradition. But if we keep in mind the strongly eschatological atmosphere of the period and especially the eschatological interpretation that they gave to their own community,[8] we can understand what is behind the practice: They were preparing for and, in a way, already engaged in the holy war of Yahweh, the final climactic battle between the sons of light and the sons of darkness.

Jesus moved within this same atmosphere and, as we have already seen, saw himself as the personal fulfillment of the eschatological inbreak of God's saving power. The end-time had, in a real sense, begun: "The time is fulfilled, and the kingdom of God is at hand..." (Mk 1:15). The biblical evidence leads us to the conclusion that he saw his own celibacy in this light. Certainly the logion about celibacy in Matthew 19:12 is directly associated with the "kingdom of heaven," which is an eschatological expression.

What meaning celibacy would have in this eschatological context

[8] Cf. T. H. Gaster, *The Dead Sea Scriptures* (Garden City, N.Y.: Doubleday & Company, Inc., 1956), pp. 275–321.

can only be deduced from its relationship to marriage. (We might insist here that, if our remarks about a horizontal eschatology have any validity, then celibacy must have a *positive* meaning, not simply a negative one of deprivation or abstinence.) The saying of Jesus in Mark 12:25 (and parallels) informs us that in heaven there will be neither marrying nor giving in marriage. If all that Christian theology has been saying about marriage is true, then this saying must not be understood in the sense that an imperfect state will be replaced by a perfect state. Rather, it can only mean that the purpose of marriage will have been achieved. That purpose is the establishment of community, both among man and woman and among all their descendants. The two stories of creation in Genesis are in implicit accord on this (cf. 1:27f., 2:24), and the story of Babel's tower, climaxing in the dissipation of all community, is the lesson of sin's awesome effect.

But if the story of man begins with the act of creation of male and female, it can only end with the achievement of that purpose which originally motivated it, the perfect unity of man and woman and of all mankind, perfect community with God. When that is achieved, then there will be no marrying and giving in marriage.

An interesting interpretation of Genesis 1:27 has been proposed that corroborates what we have just said. We read there: "So God created man in his own image, in the image of God he created him; male and female he created them." There is an apparently intended correspondence between man as the image of God and man as male and female. Could that correspondence not consist in this that the perfect community that already exists in the unity of the Godhead is expressed in man through the male and female relationship? Through the latter union would the former unity be expressed and, ultimately, perfectly achieved.

That the goal of God's saving action is the ultimate unity of man in God could be argued from many passages of the Scriptures. We will content ourselves here with a reference to Jesus' priestly prayer in John's Gospel where a strong insistence on the unity of man in God is provided by a comparison of that unity with the unity of Father and Son: "That they may all be one; even as thou, Father, art in me, and I in thee, that they also may be one in us..." (Jn 17:21). The passage could almost be seen as complementary to the interpretation of Genesis 1:27 suggested above.

The celibate expresses in his person the goal of God's saving action. But if our contention is correct that horizontal eschatology demands engagement in rather than disengagement from the daily struggle that leads to the *eschaton*, then, the celibate, while and because he is a celibate, a living sign of the goal, must strive to achieve the perfect community of all mankind which is that goal. The celibate is dedicated, by reason of the very sign that he is, to the establishment of community among men. To this extent do the eschatological and ecclesiological aspects of Jesus' word on the celibate and the kingdom of heaven merge into one.

The celibate, like Jesus, is a man in a hurry. Seeing in his own celibate commitment to God through Christ an anticipation of that perfect community in the Father, he is eager to bring about that community in every way that is compatible with his own commitment. In fact, he must be eager about this or he will not be true to the commitment. His celibacy cannot be separated from his ministry, of reconciling man to man and man to God, the work of atonement.

Obviously, not all men are called to the celebate state. Otherwise there would be no human family to bring to community in God. But it seems worthy of credence that, once that human family is supposed, there be those chosen by God to live in a way that both points to the goal of all human existence and, in pointing, works towards it.

> The New Testament community was characterized by its immediate expectation of the end of the world *and* by its universal missionary task; it was a community of expectation *and* of mission, even of expectation *in* mission. The eschatological expectation mirrored in the attitude of the first community is a belligerent, world-changing expectation. The experience of the approaching kingdom has nothing paralyzing about it, but something liberating and challenging over against the existing world. And Jesus is for the consciousness of this community not the teacher of a *Weltanschauung;* he is for them not a sage, not an interpreter of the world, but in fact a revolutionary who acted and suffered in conflict with the existing social order, and who thus needs not admirers, but followers in the service of his world-changing mission.[9]

We today no longer share the early Christian community's sense of the imminence of the *eschaton*, but we do share the sense of its certainty. It is this certainty that alone provides the thrust to history and makes celibacy as meaningful for the twentieth-century youth as it was for Jesus of Nazareth.

[9] Metz, *op. cit.*, pp. 227f.

ROBERT O. JOHANN

The Pragmatic
Meaning of God

What contemporary man wants to know is precisely those variables that affect his situation here and now, and which can be so modified as to bring about a general improvement of the human condition. Hence, his fascination with science. For science is concerned, not with the fixed, but with the variable. It is interested in corollating change with change, changes going on here with changes going on elsewhere, so that man may be provided with a measure of control and direction over what happens in his world. Thus we are beginning to hear, even from Catholic writers, that we must temper our passion for ultimate meanings, let go our preoccupation with philosophy and theology, even our efforts to construct new philosophies and new theologies, and busy ourselves with the physical and social sciences if we are going to catch up with our world.

The integral "this-worldliness" of the contemporary mind also lies behind the contemporary rejection of religion. As one writer expresses it: "The epoch whose ethos is quickly spreading into every corner of the globe is an age of 'no religion at all.' It no longer looks to religious rules and rituals for its morality or its meanings." [1] In other words, contemporary man finds that being in the world makes sense without God. This was not the case so long as the world could not provide scope for personal creativity, but called instead for conformity. As long as it was considered necessary simply to accept

From *The Pragmatic Meaning of God* (Milwaukee: Marquette University Press, 1966), pp. 14–20, 40–66. Reprinted with permission of the publisher. For full footnote documentation, see original publication.
[1] Harvey Cox, *The Secular City* (New York: The Macmillan Company, 1965), p. 3.

things the way they were, God provided a motive for doing so. Conforming to the *status quo*, however contingent it was recognized to be, was viewed as conforming to God's will. Since there was no place for creative intervention on the part of the individual with regard to the given patterns and structures of this world, it was *in his relationship to God*, not in his relationship to the world, that the individual person found his final meaning and fulfillment.

But a world conceived as beckoning to be transformed, and transformed by man's own intelligence, is one which does not need God for man's place in it to make sense. Such a world, by the very fact that it provides an outlet equal to man's powers, offers itself as the place of his fulfillment. God may still be necessary to account for the world's and man's existence. He is not, however, a factor in their mutual and harmonious fit. Indeed, He is not even needed as a motive for personal dedication. One man realizes that his vocation is to intervene creatively in his environment for the achievement of a more truly human life, he finds the goods already present in experience sufficiently attractive to inspire his efforts to secure and extend them. Is not this the chief source of embarrassment for religious people today? They find those who profess no religion at all even more energetic than themselves in working for social justice and the achievement of a better life for mankind.

But God and religion are more than irrelevant to man's vocation; preoccupation with them also prevents its achievement. To situate man's goal beyond and outside this world reduces the present scene to a passing phase and encourages passivity regarding its shortcomings rather than active concern. One cannot serve two Masters. If the point of life lies outside life itself, how work wholeheartedly for life's enhancement? Moreover, the idea that eternal salvation is to be reached only through certain institutional channels, by discouraging individual and critical discernment, retards the development of the very skills needed for coping with this world. Religion is thus felt to be prolonging man's childhood instead of helping him to come of age. Indeed, the particularism of its institutional forms reduces mankind to quarreling children, divided from one another in their deepest concerns and unable to work together.

It will be noted that, as we have presented them, these criticisms all form a piece, a logical whole. The logic, however, is not speculative and abstract, but concrete. In other words, Godlessness today is not the conclusion of a syllogism which starts out from the Sartrean premise: There is no God. Nor do I think it the case that the Godless man arises primarily from a decision to ignore God. The whole point of our remarks so far is that contemporary man's negative attitude toward God and religion has its roots in a new and positive awareness of himself. Contemporary man is not so much anti-theistic as he is pro-human. His present experience has provided him with a new sense and feel for the human, with which the notion of God embodied in traditional religions seems at loggerheads.

What we are dealing with, therefore, is not primarily a philosophy. It is really a new way of life—one whose implications and exigencies are only beginning to be grasped reflectively. The unifying focus of this new style is the challenge to intelligence inherent in the experiential process itself. The resultant sense of creative responsibility gives contemporary experience its distinctive and integrating quality, which is felt to be sufficient without God. Today's Godlessness, then, springs neither from theory nor choice, but from the felt discrepancy between our theological images and the concrete quality of our lives. Since this notion of "equality of life" is central to our thesis, a more detailed analysis of it is called for.

.   .   .

As already suggested, the incoherence of theological images with the concrete shape of life today is what lies behind much of the contemporary rejection of religion. When people say today that talk of God is meaningless and irrelevant, what they mean is that traditional religious beliefs and practices are no longer determining the actual quality of contemporary life. Not only are they not felt to enhance that quality; they really have nothing to do with it. In the measure, therefore, they are still entertained, they cannot but be experienced as so much excess baggage. The honest and practical thing to do is to cut loose from them.

Pragmatic considerations of this sort are characteristic of the contemporary mind. The difficulty, however, is that they manifest small regard for method. There has been little or no attempt to spell out, even tentatively, a contemporary ideal of humanness. The ultimacy of contemporary man's general orientation, his this-worldliness, with which traditional beliefs are in conflict, is taken for granted. And these beliefs, instead of being subjected to any kind of searching and discriminating criticism, are simply being rejected because of that conflict. Because the cultivation of God has not succeeded in humanizing man completely, indeed because it has had obvious negative consequences on this process of humanization—separating man from his world, dividing him from his fellows, introducing a kind of split between the human and the spiritual within man himself—it should be dropped altogether.

According to Dewey, a piety towards man's inventive intelligence should *replace* the traditional and historic piety towards a transcendent God. A kind of religious humanism, i.e., a whole-hearted devotion to human values conceived in exclusive terms, can do the job of traditional religion without its drawbacks. Implicit and presupposed in all this is a kind of essential opposition between the human and the divine. Because God is Other, He must be alien. Because the human is self-sufficient, God must be an intruder.

It is this presupposition that I want to question. The purpose of what follows is to show not only how God is intrinsically constitutive of the human, but how explicit and thematic attention to Him alone makes possible the full realization of the human. In other words, granting the failures and shortcomings of traditional religious orientations, one can still maintain that these are accidental rather than essential. The task confronting us today, then, is not one of building a world from which God is deliberately excluded. It is rather a work of criticism, of rethinking and purifying our notions of both God and religion, so that their influence on our lives, far from being distorting, can be seen as wholly constructive.

In order to show this, I propose to proceed in three steps. The first step will consist in sketching out a conception of the ideal. I shall try to point out what that wholeness is to which we aspire in all our actions. The second step will indicate the positive bearing of belief in God on the realization of this ideal. For, not only is an idea of God implicit in the ideal; the ideal itself cannot be realized without explicit attention being paid to Him. Thirdly, since the ideal embraces every dimension of our lives, I shall try to spell out some possible effects of religious belief on these various dimensions. My purpose will be to clarify how belief in God, instead of being a force for alienation, is actually what restores us to our neighbor, to ourselves, and to our world.

To constuct an ideal of human action is to indicate what is required for a person's life, we have said, is the continuous interaction between himself and the whole range of the other. The quality of this life, the quality of personal experience, will consist in the sort of relations that prevail between the self and the other.

Now, the first prerequisite, if this quality is to be characterized as one of wholeness or coherence, is that these relationships be basically interpersonal. The reason is clear. For the impersonal is by definition that which leaves the person out of account, that which is indifferent to and exclusive of the person. If, then, the other to which the self is related, were wholly impersonal in being and behavior, the self would be radically isolated, shut off from union and wholeness. Indeed, apart from another who awaits the self's response, the very capacity to give such a response, i.e., one's very selfhood, becomes meaningless.

More, however, is needed if the interaction between self and other is to be qualified by wholeness. The merely personal nature of the other is not yet sufficient. For example, were self and other related only in terms of cooperation in the pursuit of some particular objective which each one desires on the basis of self-interest and yet cannot secure without the other's help, then the relationship prevailing between them would still be more functional than personal. They would be related to one another in terms of their respective contributions to the common enterprise, not in terms of themselves. Hence, the selfhood of each would be left on the margin of the unity established. Only when I am responsive to a personal other who is turned toward me and gives me access to his very life and reality as a person, that is to say, only when the relationship between us is one of mutual responsiveness to one another as persons, is wholeness achieved. This, of course, is the exciting and satisfying thing about personal love and friendship. It gives us an experiential taste of that wholeness to which as persons we are called.

However, a friendship between myself and one or other person does not yet constitute my life as wholly satisfactory. For the personal other within whose love I seek inclusion is not made up of one or other person; it breaks down into an indefinite multitude of persons. Unless, therefore, you and I are lovingly related to these other persons who are actively part of our lives and determinants of its shape, our own friendship, instead of being a kind of final fulfillment, will be experienced as a minor mutuality constantly threatened and on the defensive against a potentially hostile environment. Instead of wholeness and harmony, it will be the divisions and antagonisms born of fear that will characterize our lives. The kind of wholeness, therefore, to which we as persons aspire, the ideal towards which our actions as rational are implicitly directed, is a wholeness of universal fellowship. It is a universal community of persons each of whom is lovingly disposed towards every other. Only the achievement of such a community can make our lives fully whole.

Such an ideal, admittedly, sounds utopian. Lest we be put off at the outset by this, a word of explanation is called for. In the first place, it should be remarked that this ideal is not, as it were, cut from whole cloth. Universal community is not an imaginatively constructed ideal that is unrelated to goods and values we actually experience. On the contrary, it is simply the extension of something we not only enjoy, but know to be that without which we could not even begin to function as persons. Indeed, it is precisely because we find this essential value threatened by its partial realization, by the fact that it does not actually function universally, that we are pushed to extend its range.

Secondly, to proclaim universal community as the ideal is not to imply that it can be realized overnight, or even within the confines of historical time. Having a goal is not useless simply because it can never be fully realized. As we pointed out above, the whole work of evaluating specific beliefs and practices presupposes that we have at least tentatively determined an ideal of comprehensive satisfactoriness. Moreover, to reject the ideal merely because it is an ideal, not to take steps to extend fellowship because the fruit of all our efforts will always be limited in scope, would be to undermine that degree of community which has already been achieved. For community is not a settled fact. It is a matter of intention. It depends on the abiding intention of each of the members to behave reasonably and responsibly, i.e., lovingly, towards the others, to work continuously for a coherent order of harmonious relations. In other words, it requires on the part of each an unselfish concern for others, a will to promote wholeness. But to will wholeness in a limited way is not to will it at all. It is to settle for an overall orientation of opposition and conflict which makes self-interest primary and so corrupts all personal community at its root.

If we accept the idea of universal community as a required extension of that which makes life human and personal in the first place, our next step must be to explore the conditions presupposed for its effective pursuit. We have already indicated our conviction that explicit belief in God is such a condition. Why is this so?

Any unity of persons as persons involves *personal response* to an intention of unity. This notion of response is important. I can decide to love another (in the sense of being devoted to his welfare) regardless of his attitude towards me. I cannot, however, simply decide on my own to be friends with him. Friendship, as a mutual relationship, must be mutually intended. If the other is uninterested or for any reason does not intend the union, no efforts on my part will be enough to constitute it. Our friendship can become a reality only in the measure each of us is *responsive to an intention of unity on the part of the other.*

What is true here of friendship is true of any personal community. Participation in such a union is achieved only through an individual's responsiveness to the will of another intending that relationship. But there is this difference. When the relationship of personal community is not restricted to pairs of individuals but extends to an indefinite plurality of persons, there must be one to whom all are responsive. I do not become a member of a community by entering into a personal union with one or other of its members, nor even with all of them taken separately. I become a member only by responding to that other who by being in reciprocal relation with every member of the group, is the source of their unity. He is one who comprehends each of them (and me too), not in isolation nor in relation only to himself, but precisely as related to the others, and his intention of unity, as already responsively recognized by the plurality, is precisely what makes it a community instead of a mere collection.

In other words, personal community among many individuals implies a personal head, through responsiveness to whom each of the individuals enters into responsive relationship with all the others. Without a personal head, whose intention of unity for the many is commonly—and in common—recognized by them, there is no personal community. Hence, just as the achievement of friendship requires initiative on the side of the other, so also here. One can no more achieve personal community by going around loving everybody than one can achieve friendship simply on one's own. However, whereas the other, whose initiative is required in the case of friendship, is one among the many and on equal footing with them, the other needed for community is a principle (of unity) for the many, a kind of universal focus. Thus, if community implies headship (authority), headship always involves a measure of transcendence.

What this means for the problem confronting us is clear. If man's personal nature orients him towards the ideal of universal personal community, a universal fellowship of persons, it must at the same time situate him in a relation of responsibility towards a transcendent ground and universal focus of the whole interpersonal order. The very idea of universal community involves the idea of an already existing Other who is in a position of headship (authority) over all persons, such that actual responsiveness to Him actually unites them to one another as persons. Indeed, it implies that even prior to the achievement of personal community, men are already in an ontological relationship of common responsibility, that to be a person is to be in *moral solidarity* with other persons, called to answer the same Transcendent Initiative.

Now, such a Universal Initiative, constitutively present and correlative to every self, the unifying ground or "head" of the whole order of persons, the Person of persons (in Scheler's phrase), whose intention is the unity of all our intentions, i.e., the realization of genuine and universal community, is, I suggest, God. God and the community of persons go together. Not only can I not think universal community without thinking God; I cannot effectively intend such community without intending responsiveness to Him. For, as we have seen, membership in community demands conscious conjunction with others in common recognition of, and response to, the authoritative intention of community. Unless members of a community are jointly aware of their unity with one another through their allegiance to a common head, they simply are not members and there is no community. To aim at a universal community of persons, therefore, is to aim at a universal responsiveness to God.

God, then, is not to be conceived the way Dewey maintains He is traditionally, i.e., as the antecedent realization of the ideal. Dewey sees the traditional concept of God as a kind of imaginative projection of the ideal into the order of actuality. It is as if people were constrained to think of the ideal as actual in order to give it solidity and the ability to mobilize their energies. But the ideal is neither actual nor is it God. The ideal is the unification of men as persons. God is not that unification, but the Transcendent Initiative whose intention makes it possible. It is because each person is constituted a person by being in a relationship of responsibility towards God that the plurality of persons is able to share the exercise of that responsibility and form itself into a community of persons.

The bearing of religion and belief in God on the social dimension of our lives, on our relationship with one another, is therefore clear. Cultivation of the divine is not a force of alienation but a source of unification. If this has not always worked out historically, if religion in practice has all too often turned out to be a divisive factor among men, the fault does not lie in the fact that men have believed in God. It is because they have confused the Transcendent with their own limited and particular representations of Him. Men need to represent God if they are, deliberately and socially, to relate themselves to Him and in that relationship establish themselves as a community of persons. But they must also constantly move beyond their representations if their relationship to God and to one another is not to be falsified. All too often this further move has not been made. The objective signs and symbols pointing to that Presence which exceeds the possibilities of direct conceptual representation, begin to be taken as adequate representations of God Himself. Man's attention, then, instead of being directed to the hidden One who is the correlative constituent of selfhood and the unifying principle of community, becomes focused on idols. What was present, but hidden, becomes absent as well. God becomes a particular being to be served in particular ways, and it is this particularism which then divides men from one another.

If this is the case, however, the problem of achieving community cannot be solved by eliminating God or such acknowledgment as there is of Him. In particular, the community of persons will not be realized by following an ideal of this-worldly humanism. So long as humanistic aspirations are conceived as the product of an individual's own mind and heart, adherence to them, while it may engender a true service of others and contribute to the improvement of man's lot (which is no small thing), will not establish the individual in an actual relationship of community with others. He will remain an individual following his own bent, however noble. Through lack of shared responsiveness to a universal Other, he will never feel himself caught up in an all-encompassing love nor have the redeeming awareness of actual fellowship. If, as Macmurray remarks, the function peculiar to religion is "to create, maintain and deepen the community of persons and to extend it without limit," [2] the suppression of religion does more than wipe out its past shortcomings; it makes genuine human community impossible.

Since the human reaches fulfillment in the community of persons, the considerations we have so far developed indicate, I think, the primary bearing of God on human affairs. Since, on the other hand, God is able to unify the human community only because He is the universal Other for each of us taken singly, attention to Him or the lack of it has also a profound bearing on the quality of our individual lives. Let me indicate briefly, therefore, three ways in which I think this is so. My contention will be that only an individual's awareness of and responsiveness to God allows him to achieve in his own life a sense of wholeness, identity and of final import.

For my life to have the quality of wholeness and coherence, there must be a way of binding together all the various responsibilities that define me at a given moment, as well as all the various episodes in which I am successively an actor. Since the self is correlative to the other, the self can be one only if the other is one. But the other in its immediacy is anything but one. It breaks down into a plurality of individuals, institutions, and systems each of which is continually making demands upon me. I have public responsibilities and private responsibilities, personal responsibilities and professional responsibilities. What is it that ties all these together? So long as they remain irreducibly many, my life is inevitably fragmented, compartmentalized. But suppose, as we have supposed, that my selfhood is constituted by a relation of responsibility towards a Transcendent Other whose intention must be met in all the situations of my life. If that is the case, everything is transformed. "... I am one within myself as I encounter the One in all that acts upon me." [3] When my world is divided, I am divided. But when everything is viewed in its bearing on the accomplishment of Your will, the achievement of community, then the world has a focus and I am one. My response to every particular action takes the form of a response to You. And since no matter where I go I am never out of Your presence, the successive phases of my life likewise cease to be disconnected episodes. Instead,

---

[2] John Macmurray, *Persons in Relation* (New York: Humanities Press, 1961), p. 163.
[3] H. Richard Niebuhr, *The Responsible Self* (New York: Harper & Row, Publishers, 1963), p. 122.

they take on the structure of a continuing and developing encounter. It is thus my relation to God that enables me, as nothing else can, to conceive my life simultaneously and successively as constituting a single whole.

By the same token, it is also God Who gives me identity as a person. One of the troubling features of our times is that people in general seem to have lost the sense of any defining and constitutive relationships. Whereas in the past, the institutions to which they belonged and in which they participated gave them a sense of identity, the general questioning of institutions prevalent today has left them without this support. They literally do not know who they are or what they are called upon to do. Nor can they ever know so long as God is forgotten. If beyond the structures and patterns which are today called into question there is nothing at all, then the self is inevitably uprooted and lost. But if beyond the changing patterns it is You who call to me, then I have a defining vocation and identity no matter how fluid and transitory my surroundings. I am Your agent and servant, called with all men to promote Your reign in all that I do. Thus just as You make my life whole, You also give me back to myself.

Moreover, it is as an answer to You that each of my actions has an import it would otherwise lack. Arising from contemporary man's grasp of the tremendous sweep of time and from his new sense of himself as involved in a creative process that opens out endlessly into the future, there is a gnawing feeling abroad that the individual and his actions are without any final significance. If everything is in transition, are not all my efforts doomed to be swept aside in the creative advance of life? If any particular deed is but an infinitesimal dot on the endless line of becoming, a process whose goal I shall never know, then what real difference does it make? Without God, the answer is clear: not very much. But if in the present deed I stand before the Transcendent and say Yes or No to Him, then however slight the mark of my deeds on the course of History, they each bear the absolute weight of acceptance or rejection of God. If they are deeds of love, so that He has a part in them, then this gives them a substance which outweighs their effects. As responsive to His presence, they are more than merely contributory to the on-rushing course of events. They also have in themselves a kind of final and ultimate worth.

Finally, what about God and progress? What is the bearing of belief in God on man's vocation to share in the world's making? For religion has often been charged with being, and historically has often been, a rigidly conservative force bent on maintaining the *status quo*. Does not the centering of a person's life on a focus outside of time inevitaby distract him from the work at hand and lead him to minimize temporal concerns? The answer, of course, depends on how our relationship to God is understood. If our relationship to God were something distinct from and independent of our relationship to the things and people who surround us, then the objection would have force. But if this relationship is one with our vocation to community, then a love for God cannot be realized as something in itself but only as qualifying all our particular relationships. The reality of our responsiveness to God will be the humanity of our dealings with one another. It is only as working always for a fuller realization of the ideal of community that we are truly responsive to Him. Far, then, from restricting us to the actual shape of things, God's presence in our life is what continually calls us to move beyond where we are. We cannot rest until we have done all that we can to make love prevail in our world.

God, then, is not irrelevant, however much our images of Him may be. Nor is belief in Him, properly conceived, without positive bearing on the quality of our lives. In this last section, we have tried to sketch the kind of humanness belief alone makes possible. We might sum it up this way. Eliminating the idea of God does not diminish His constitutive presence nor efface the effect of that presence in us, our native humanity. It simply precludes human wholeness and compels us to settle for less. But why settle for less?

JÜRGEN MOLTMANN

Theology of Hope

What Is the "Logos" of Christian Eschatology?

Eschatology was long called the "doctrine of the last things" or the "doctrine of the end." By these last things were meant events which will one day break upon man, history and the world at the end of time. They included the return of Christ in universal glory, the judgment of the world and the consummation of the kingdom, the general resurrection of the dead and the new creation of all things. These end events were to break into this world from somewhere beyond history, and to put an end to the history in which all things here live and move. But the relegating of these events to the "last day" robbed them of their directive, uplifting and critical significance for all the days which are spent here, this side of the end, in history. Thus these teachings about the end led a peculiarly barren existence at the end of Christian dogmatics. They were like a loosely attached appendix that wandered off into obscure irrelevancies. They bore no relation to the doctrines of the cross and resurrection, the exaltation and sovereignty of Christ, and did not derive from these by any logical necessity. They were as far removed from them as All Souls' Day sermons are from Easter. The more Christianity became an organization for discipleship under the auspices of the Roman state religion and persistently upheld the claims of that religion, the more eschatology and its mobilizing,

From *Theology of Hope* (New York: Harper & Row, Publishers, 1967; and London: SCM Press, 1967), pp. 15-36. Reprinted with permission of the publishers.

revolutionizing, and critical effects upon history as it has now to be lived were left to fanatical sects and revolutionary groups. Owing to the fact that Christian faith banished from its life the future hope by which it is upheld, and relegated the future to a beyond, or to eternity, whereas the biblical testimonies which it handed on are yet full to the brim with future hope of a messianic kind for the world—owing to this, hope emigrated as it were from the Church and turned in one distorted form or another against the Church.

In actual fact, however, eschatology means the doctrine of the Christian hope, which embraces both the object hoped for and also the hope inspired by it. From first to last, and not merely in the epilogue, Christianity is eschatology, is hope, forward looking and forward moving, and therefore also revolutionizing and transforming the present. The eschatological is not one element *of* Christianity, but it is the medium of Christian faith as such, the key in which everything in it is set, the glow that suffuses everything here in the dawn of an expected new day. For Christian faith lives from the raising of the crucified Christ, and strains after the promises of the universal future of Christ. Eschatology is the passionate suffering and passionate longing kindled by the Messiah. Hence eschatology cannot really be only a part of Christian doctrine. Rather, the eschatological outlook is characteristic of all Christian proclamation, of every Christian existence and of the whole Church. There is therefore only one real problem in Christian theology, which its own object forces upon it and which it in turn forces on mankind and on human thought: the problem of the future. For the element of otherness that encounters us in the hope of the Old and New Testaments—the thing we cannot already think out and picture for ourselves on the basis of the given world and of the experiences we already have of that world—is one that confronts us with a promise of something new and with the hope of a future given by God. The God spoken of here is no intraworldly or extraworldly God, but the "God of hope" (Rom 15:13), a God with "future as his essential nature" (as E. Bloch puts it), as made known in Exodus and in Israelite prophecy, the God whom we therefore cannot really have in us or over us but always only before us, who encounters us in his promises for the future, and whom we therefore cannot "have" either, but can only await in active hope. A proper theology would therefore have to be constructed in the light of its future goal. Eschatology should not be its end, but its beginning.

But how can anyone speak of the future, which is not yet here, and of coming events in which he has not as yet had any part? Are these not dreams, speculations, longings and fears, which must all remain vague and indefinite because no one can verify them? The term "eschato-*logy*" is wrong. There can be no "doctrine" of the last things, if by "doctrine" we mean a collection of theses which can be understood on the basis of experiences that constantly recur and are open to anyone. The Greek term *logos* refers to a reality which is there, now and always, and is given true expression in the word appropriate to it. In this sense there can be no *logos* of the future, unless the future is the continuation or regular recurrence of the present. If, however, the future were to bring something startlingly new, we have nothing to say of that, and nothing meaningful can be said of it either, for it is not in what is new and accidental, but only in things of an abiding and regularly recurring character that there can be log-ical truth. Aristotle, it is true, can call hope a "waking dream," but for the Greeks it is nevertheless an evil out of Pandora's box.

But how, then, can Christian eschatology give expression to the future? Christian eschatology does not speak of the future as such. It sets out from a definite reality in history and announces the future of that reality, its future possibilities and its power over the future. Christian eschatology speaks of Jesus Christ and *his* future. It recognizes the reality of the raising of Jesus and proclaims the future of the risen Lord. Hence the question whether all statements about the future are grounded in the person and history of Jesus Christ provides it with the touchstone by which to distinguish the spirit of eschatology from that of utopia.

If, however, the crucified Christ has a future because of his resurrection, then that means on the other hand that all statements and judgments about him must at once imply something about the future which is to be expected from him. Hence the form in which Christian theology speaks of Christ cannot be the form of the Greek *logos* or of doctrinal statements based on experience, but only the form of statements of hope and of promises for the future. All predicates of Christ not only say who he was and is, but imply statements as to who he will be and what is to be expected from him. They all say: "He is our hope" (Col 1:27). In thus announcing his future in the world in terms of promise, they point believers in him towards the hope of his still outstanding future. Hope's statements of promise anticipate the future. In the promises, the hidden future already announces itself and exerts its influence on the present through the hope it awakens.

The truth of doctrinal statements is found in the fact that they can be shown to agree with the existing reality which we can all experience. Hope's statements of promise, however, must stand in contradiction to the reality which can at present be experienced. They do not result from experiences, but are the condition for the possibility of new experiences. They do not seek to illuminate the reality which exists, but the reality which is coming. They do not seek to make a mental picture of existing reality, but to lead existing reality towards the promised and hoped-for transformation. They do not seek to bear the train of reality, but to carry the torch before it. In so doing they give reality a historic character. But if reality is perceived in terms of history, then we have to ask with J. G. Hamann: "Who would form proper concepts of the present without knowing the future?"

Present and future, experience and hope, stand in contradiction to each other in Christian eschatology, with the result that man is not brought into harmony and agreement with the given situation, but is drawn into the conflict between hope and experience. "We are saved by hope. But hope that is seen is not hope; for what a man seeth, why doth he yet hope for? But if we hope for that we see not, then do we with patience wait for it" (Rom 8:24f.). Everywhere in the New Testament the Christian hope is directed towards what is not yet visible; it is consequently a "hoping against hope" and thereby brands the visible realm of present experience as a godforsaken, transient reality that is to be left behind. The contradiction to the existing reality of himself and his world in which man is placed by hope is the very contradiction out of which this hope itself is born—it is the contradiction between the resurrection and the cross. Christian hope is resurrection hope, and it proves its truth in the contradiction of the future prospects thereby offered and guaranteed for righteousness as opposed to sin, life as opposed to death, glory as opposed to suffering, peace as opposed to dissension. Calvin perceived very plainly the discrepancy involved in the resurrection hope: "To us is given the promise of eternal life—but to us, the dead. A blessed resurrection is proclaimed to us—meantime we are surrounded by decay. We are called righteous—and yet sin lives in us. We hear of ineffable blessedness—but meantime we are here oppressed by infinite misery. We are promised abundance of all good things—yet we are rich only in hunger and thirst. What would become of us if we did not take our stand on hope, and if our heart did not hasten beyond this world through the midst of the darkness upon the path illumined by the word and Spirit of God!" (on Heb 11:1).

It is in this contradiction that hope must prove its power. Hence eschatology, too, is forbidden to ramble, and must formulate its statements of hope in contradiction to our present experience of suffering, evil and death. For that reason it will hardly ever be possible to develop an eschatology on its own. It is much more important to present hope as the foundation and the mainspring of theological thinking as such, and to introduce the eschatological perspective into our statements on divine revelation, on the resurrection of Christ, on the mission of faith and on history.

The Believing Hope

In the contradiction between the word of promise and the experiential reality of suffering and death, faith takes its stand on hope and "hastens beyond this world," said Calvin. He did not mean by this that Christian faith flees the world, but he did mean that it strains after the future. To believe does in fact mean to cross and transcend bounds, to be engaged in an exodus. Yet this happens in a way that does not suppress or skip the unpleasant realities. Death is real death, and decay is putrefying decay. Guilt remains guilt and suffering remains, even for the believer, a cry to which there is no ready-made answer. Faith does not overstep these realities into a heavenly utopia, does not dream itself into a reality of a different kind. It can overstep the bounds of life, with their closed wall of suffering, guilt and death, only at the point where they have in actual fact been broken through. It is only in following the Christ who was raised from suffering, from a god-forsaken death and from the grave that it gains an open prospect in which there is nothing more to oppress us, a view of the realm of freedom and of joy. Where the bounds that mark the end of all human hopes are broken through in the raising of the crucified one, there faith can and must expand into hope. There it becomes παρρησία and μακροθυμία. There its hope becomes a "passion for what is possible" (Kierkegaard), because it can be a passion for what has been made possible. There the *extensio animi ad magna*, as it was called in the Middle Ages, takes place in hope. Faith recognizes the dawning of this future of openness and freedom in the Christ event. The hope thereby kindled spans the horizons which then open over a closed existence. Faith binds man to Christ. Hope sets this faith open to the comprehensive future of Christ. Hope is therefore the "inseparable companion" of faith.

> When this hope is taken away, however eloquently or elegantly we discourse concerning faith, we are convicted of having none. ... Hope is nothing else than the expectation of those things which faith has believed to have been truly promised by God. Thus, faith believes God to be true, hope awaits the time when this truth shall be manifested; faith believes that he is our Father, hope anticipates that he will ever show himself to be a Father toward us; faith believes that eternal life has been given to us, hope anticipates that it will some time be revealed; faith is the foundation upon which hope rests, hope nourishes and sustains faith. For as no one except him who already believes His promises can look for anything from God, so again the weakness of our faith must be sustained and nourished by patient hope and expectation, lest it fail and grow faint.... By unremitting renewing and restoring, it [hope] invigorates faith again and again with perseverance.[1]

Thus in the Christian life faith has the priority, but hope the primacy. Without faith's knowledge of Christ, hope becomes a utopia and remains hanging in the air. But without hope, faith falls to pieces, becomes a fainthearted and ultimately a dead faith. It is through faith that man finds the path of true life, but it is only hope that keeps him on that path. Thus it is that faith in Christ gives hope its assurance. Thus it is that hope gives faith in Christ its breadth and leads it into life.

To believe means to cross in hope and anticipation the bounds that have been penetrated by the raising of the crucified. If we bear that in mind, then this faith can have nothing to do with fleeing the world, with resignation and with escapism. In this hope the soul does not soar above our vale of tears to some imagined heavenly bliss, nor does it sever itself from the earth. For, in the words of Ludwig Feuerbach, it puts "in place of the beyond that lies above our grave in heaven the beyond that lies above our grave on earth,

---

[1] Calvin, *Institutio* III.242. ET: *Institutes of the Christian Religion* (Library of Christian Classics, Vols. XX and XXI), ed. John T. McNeill, trans. Ford Lewis (London: Battles, 1961), p. 590.

the historic *future*, the future of mankind." [2] It sees in the resurrection of Christ not the eternity of heaven, but the future of the very earth on which his cross stands. It sees in him the future of the very humanity for which he died. That is why it finds the cross the hope of the earth. This hope struggles for the obedience of the body, because it awaits the quickening of the body. It espouses in all meekness the cause of the devastated earth and of harassed humanity, because it is promised possession of the earth. *Ave crux— unica spes!*

But on the other hand, all this must inevitably mean that the man who thus hopes will never be able to reconcile himself with the laws and constraints of this earth, neither with the inevitability of death nor with the evil that constantly bears further evil. The raising of Christ is not merely a consolation to him in a life that is full of distress and doomed to die, but it is also God's contradiction of suffering and death, of humiliation and offence, and of the wickedness of evil. Hope finds in Christ not only a consolation *in* suffering, but also the protest of the divine promise *against* suffering. If Paul calls death the "last enemy" (1 Cor 15:26), then the opposite is also true: that the risen Christ, and with him the resurrection hope, must be declared to be the enemy of death and of a world that puts up with death. Faith takes up this contradiction and thus becomes itself a contradiction to the world of death. That is why faith, wherever it develops into hope, causes not rest but unrest, not patience but impatience. It does not calm the unquiet heart, but is itself this unquiet heart in man. Those who hope in Christ can no longer put up with reality as it is, but begin to suffer under it, to contradict it. Peace with God means conflict with the world, for the goad of the promised future stabs inexorably into the flesh of every unfulfilled present. If we had before our eyes only what we see, then we should cheerfully or reluctantly reconcile ourselves with things as they happen to be. That we do not reconcile ourselves, that there is no pleasant harmony between us and reality, is due to our unquenchable hope. This hope keeps man unreconciled, until the great day of the fulfillment of all the promises of God. It keeps him *in statu viatoris*, in that unresolved openness to world questions which has its origin in the promise of God in the resurrection of Christ and can therefore be resolved only when the same God fulfills his promise. This hope makes the Christian Church a constant disturbance in

[2] *Das Wesen der Religion* (1848).

human society, seeking as the latter does to stabilize itself into a "continuing city." It makes the Church the source of continual new impulses towards the realization of righteousness, freedom and humanity here in the light of the promised future that is to come. This Church is committed to "answer for the hope" that is in it (1 Pet 3:15). It is called in question "on account of the hope and resurrection of the dead" (Ac 23:6). Wherever that happens, Christianity embraces its true nature and becomes a witness of the future of Christ.

The Sin of Despair

If faith thus depends on hope for its life, then the sin of unbelief is manifestly grounded in hopelessness. To be sure, it is usually said that sin in its original form is man's wanting to be as God. But that is only the one side of sin. The other side of such pride is hopelessness, resignation, inertia and melancholy. From this arise the *tristesse* and frustration which fill all living things with the seeds of a sweet decay. Among the sinners whose future is eternal death in Revelations 21:8, the "fearful" are mentioned before unbelievers, idolaters, murderers and the rest. For the Epistle to the Hebrews, falling away from the living hope, in the sense of being disobedient to the promise in time of oppression, or of being carried away from God's pilgrim people as by a flood, is the great sin which threatens the hopeful on their way. Temptation then consists not so much in the titanic desire to be as God, but in weakness, timidity, weariness, not wanting to be what God requires of us.

God has exalted man and given him the prospect of a life that is wide and free, but man hangs back and lets himself down. God promises a new creation of all things in righteousness and peace, but man acts as if everything were as before and remained as before. God honors him with his promises, but man does not believe himself capable of what is required of him. That is the sin which most profoundly threatens the believer. It is not the evil he does, but the good he does not do, not his misdeeds but his omissions, that accuse him. They accuse him of lack of hope. For these so-called sins of omission all have their ground in hopelessness and weakness of faith. "It is not so much sin that plunges us into disaster, as rather despair," said Chrysostom. That is why the Middle Ages reckoned *acedia* or *tristitia* among the sins against the Holy Spirit which lead to death.

Joseph Pieper in his treatise *Über die Hoffnung* (1949) has very neatly shown how this hopelessness can assume two forms: It can be presumption, *praesumptio,* and it can be despair, *desperatio.* Both are forms of the sin against hope. Presumption is a premature, self-willed anticipation of the fulfillment of what we hope for from God. Despair is the premature, arbitrary anticipation of the non-fulfillment of what we hope for from God. Both forms of hopeless-ness, by anticipating the fulfillment or by giving up hope, cancel the wayfaring character of hope. They rebel against the patience in which hope trusts in the God of the promise. They demand im-patiently either fulfillment "now already" or "absolutely no" hope. "In despair and presumption alike we have the rigidifying and freez-ing of the truly human element, which hope alone can keep flowing and free" (p. 51).

Thus despair, too, presupposes hope. "What we do not long for, can be the object neither of our hope nor of our despair" (Augus-tine). The pain of despair surely lies in the fact that a hope is there, but no way opens up towards its fulfillment. Thus the kindled hope turns against the one who hopes and consumes him. "Living means burying hopes," says Fontane in one of his novels, and it is these "dead hopes" that he portrays in it. Our hopes are bereft of faith and confidence. Hence despair would seek to preserve the soul from disappointments. "Hope as a rule makes many a fool." Hence we try to remain on the solid ground of reality, "to think clearly and not hope any more" (Camus), and yet in adopting this so-called realism dictated by the facts we fall victim to the worst of all utopias—the utopia of the *status quo,* as R. Musil has called this kind of realism.

The despairing surrender of hope does not even need to have a desperate appearance. It can also be the mere tacit absence of mean-ing, prospects, future and purpose. It can wear the face of smiling resignation: *bonjour tristesse!* All that remains is a certain smile on the part of those who have tried out the full range of their possi-bilities and found nothing in them that could give cause for hope. All that remains is a *taedium vitae,* a life that has little further in-terest in itself. Of all the attitudes produced by the decay of a non-eschatological, bourgeois Christianity, and then consequently found in a no longer Christian world, there is hardly any which is so general as *acedia, tristesse,* the cultivation and dandling manipulation of faded hopes. But where hope does not find its way to the source of new, unknown possibilities, there the trifling, ironic play with the existing possibilities ends in boredom, or in outbreaks of absurdity.

At the beginning of the nineteenth century the figure of presumption is found at many points in German idealism. For Goethe, Schiller, Ranke, Karl Marx and many others, Prometheus became the great saint of the modern age. Prometheus, who stole fire from the gods, stood in contrast to the figure of the obedient servant of God. It was possible to transform even Christ into a Promethean figure. Along with that there frequently went a philosophical, revolutionary millenarianism which set itself to build at last that realm of freedom and human dignity which had been hoped for in vain from the God of the divine servant.

In the middle of the twentieth century we find in the literary writings of the existentialists the other form of apostasy from hope. Thus the patron saint that was Prometheus now assumes the form of Sisyphus, who certainly knows the pilgrim way, and is fully acquainted with struggle and decision and with patient toil, yet without any prospect of fulfillment. Here the obedient servant of God can be transformed into the figure of the honest failure. There is no hope and no God any more. There is only Camus' "thinking clearly and hoping no more," and the honest love and fellow-feeling exemplified in Jesus. As if thinking could gain clarity without hope! As if there could be love without hope for the beloved!

Neither in presumption nor in despair does there lie the power to renew life, but only in the hope that is enduring and sure. Presumption and despair live off this hope and regale themselves at its expense. "He who does not hope for the unexpected, will not find it," runs a saying of Heraclitus. "The uniform of the day is patience and its only decoration the pale star of hope over its heart" (I. Bachmann).

Hope alone is to be called "realistic," because it alone takes seriously the possibilities with which all reality is fraught. It does not take things as they happen to stand or to lie, but as progressing, moving things with possibilities of change. Only as long as the world and the people in it are in a fragmented and experimental state which is not yet resolved, is there any sense in earthly hopes. The latter anticipate what is possible to reality, historic and moving as it is, and use their influence to decide the processes of history. Thus hopes and anticipations of the future are not a transfiguring glow superimposed upon a darkened existence, but are realistic ways of perceiving the scope of our real possibilities, and as such they set everything in motion and keep it in a state of change. Hope and the kind of thinking that goes with it consequently cannot submit to the reproach of being utopian, for they do not strive after things that have "no place," but after things that have "no place *as yet*" but can acquire one. On the other hand, the celebrated realism of the stark facts, of established objects and laws, the attitude that despairs of its possibilities and clings to reality as it is, is inevitably much more open to the charge of being utopian, for in its eyes there is "no place" for possibilities, for future novelty, and consequently for the historic character of reality. Thus the despair which imagines it has reached the end of its tether proves to be illusory, as long as nothing has yet come to an end but everything is still full of possibilities. Thus positivistic realism also proves to be illusory, so long as the world is not a fixed body of facts but a network of paths and processes, so long as the world does not only run according to laws but these laws themselves are also flexible, so long as it is a realm in which necessity means the possible, but not the unalterable.

Statements of hope in Christian eschatology must also assert themselves against the rigidified utopia of realism, if they would keep faith alive and would guide obedience in love on to the path towards earthly, corporeal, social reality. In its eyes the world is full of all kinds of possibilities, namely all the possibilities of the God of hope. It sees reality and mankind in the hand of him whose voice calls into history from its end, saying, "Behold, I make all things new," and from hearing this word of promise it acquires the freedom to renew life here and to change the face of the world.

Does Hope Cheat Man of the Happiness of the Present?

The most serious objection to a theology of hope springs not from presumption or despair, for these two basic attitudes of human existence presuppose hope, but the objection to hope arises from the religion of humble acquiescence in the present. Is it not always in the present alone that man is truly existent, real, contemporary with himself, acquiescent and certain? Memory binds him to the past that no longer is. Hope casts him upon the future that is not yet.

He remembers having lived, but he does not live. He remembers having loved, but he does not love. He remembers the thoughts of others, but he does not think. It seems to be much the same with him in hope. He hopes to live, but he does not live. He expects to be happy one day, and this expectation causes him to pass over the happiness of the present. He is never, in memory and hope, wholly himself and wholly in his present. Always he either limps behind it or hastens ahead of it. Memories and hopes appear to cheat him of the happiness of being undividedly present. They rob him of his present and drag him into times that no longer exist or do not yet exist. They surrender him to the nonexistent and abandon him to vanity. For these times subject him to the stream of transience—the stream that sweeps him to annihilation.

Pascal lamented this deceitful aspect of hope:

> We do not rest satified with the present. We anticipate the future as too slow in coming, as if in order to hasten its course; or we recall the past, to stop its too rapid flight. So imprudent are we that we wander in times which are not ours, and do not think of the only one which belongs to us; and so idle are we that we dream of those times which are no more, and thoughtlessly overlook that which alone exists.... We scarcely ever think of the present; and if we think of it, it is only to take light from it to arrange the future. The present is never our end. The past and the present are our means; the future alone is our end. So we never live, but we hope to live; and, as we are always preparing to be happy, it is inevitable we should never be so.[3]

Always the protest against the Christian hope and against the transcendent consciousness resulting from it has stubbornly insisted on the rights of the present, on the good that surely lies always to hand, and on the eternal truth in every moment. Is the "present" not the only time in which man wholly exists, which belongs wholly to him and to which he wholly belongs? Is the "present" not time and yet at once also more than time in the sense of coming and going— namely, a *nunc stans* and to that extent also a *nunc aeternum?* Only of the present can it be said that it "is," and only present being is constantly with us. If we are wholly present—*tota simul*—then in the midst of time we are snatched from the transient and annihilating workings of time.

Thus Goethe, too, could say: "All these passing things we put up

[3] Blaise Pascal, *Pensées*, No. 172, ed., trans. W. F. Trotter (Everyman ed.) (1943), pp. 49f.

with; if only the eternal remains present to us every moment, then we do not suffer from the transience of time." He had found this eternally resting present in "nature" itself, because he understood "nature" as the *physis* that exists out of itself: "All is always present in it. Past and future it does not know. The present is its eternity." Should not man, too, therefore become present like nature?

> Why go chasing distant fancies?
> Lo, the good is ever near!
> Only learn to grasp your chances!
> Happiness is always here.

Thus the true present is nothing else but the eternity that is immanent in time, and what matters is to perceive in the outward form of temporality and transience the substance that is immanent and the eternal that is present—so said the early Hegel. Likewise Nietzsche endeavored to get rid of the burden and deceit of the Christian hope by seeking "the eternal Yea of existence" in the present and finding the love of eternity in "loyalty to the earth." It is always only in the present, the moment, the *kairos*, the "now," that being itself is present in time. It is like noon, when the sun stands high and nothing casts a shadow any more, nor does anything stand in the shadow.

But now, it is not merely the *happiness of the present*, but it is more, it is the *God of the present*, the eternally present God, and it is not merely the present being of man, but still more the eternal presence of being, that the Christian hope appears to cheat us of. Not merely man is cheated, but still more God himself is cheated, where hope does not allow man to discover an eternal present. It is only here that the objection to our future hopes on the ground of the "present" attains to its full magnitude. Not merely does life protest against the torture of the hope that is imposed upon it, but we are also accused of godlessness in the name of the God whose essential attribute is the *numen praesentiae*. Yet what God is this in whose name the "present" is insisted upon as against the hope of what is not yet?

It is at bottom ever and again the god of Parmenides, of whom it is said in Fragment 8 (Diels): "The unity that is being never was, never will be, for now it Is all at once as a whole" νῦν εστιν ὁμοῦ πᾶν. This "being" does not exist "always," as it was still said to do in Homer and Hesiod, but it "is," and is "now." It has no extension in time, its truth stands on the "now," its eternity is present, it "is" all at once and in one (*tota simul*). In face of the epiphany of the eternal presence of being, the times in which life rises and passes fade away to mere phenomena in which we have a mixture of being and non-being, day and night, abiding and passing away. In the contemplation of the eternal present, however, "origin is obliterated and decay is vanished." In the present of being, in the eternal Today, man is immortal, invulnerable and inviolable (G. Picht). If, as Plutarch reports, the divine name over the portal of the Delphic temple of Apollo was given as *EI*, then this, too, could mean "Thou art" in the sense of the eternal present. It is in the eternal nearness and presence of the god that we come to knowledge of man's nature and to joy in it.

The god of Parmenides is "thinkable," because he is the eternal, single fullness of being. The nonexistent, the past and the future, however, are not "thinkable." In the contemplation of the present eternity of this god, nonexistence, movement and change, history and future become unthinkable, because they "are" not. The contemplation of this god does not make a meaningful experience of history possible, but only the meaningful negation of history. The *logos* of this being liberates and raises us out of the power of history into the eternal present.

In the struggle against the seeming deceit of the Christian hope, Parmenides' concept of God has thrust its way deeply indeed into Christian theology. When in the celebrated third chapter of Kierkegaard's treatise on *The Concept of Dread* the promised "fullness of time" is taken out of the realm of expectation that attaches to promise and history, and the "fullness of time" is called the "moment" in the sense of the eternal, then we find ourselves in the field of Greek thinking rather than of the Christian knowledge of God. It is true that Kierkegaard modified the Greek understanding of temporality in the light of the Christian insight into our radical sinfulness, and that he intensifies the Greek difference between *logos* and *doxa* into a paradox, but does that really imply any more than a modification of the "epiphany of the eternal present"? "The present is not a concept of time. The eternal conceived as the present is arrested temporal succession. The moment characterizes the present as a thing that has no past and no future. The moment is an atom of eternity. It is the first reflection of eternity in time, its first attempt as it were to halt time." It is understandable that then the believer, too, must

be described in parallel terms to the Parmenidean and Platonic con-
templator. The believer is the man who is entirely present. He is in
the supreme sense contemporaneous with himself and one with himself. "And to be with the eternal's help utterly and completely contemporaneous with oneself today, is to gain eternity. The believer
turns his back on the eternal so to speak, precisely in order to have
it by him in the one day that is today. The Christian believes, and
thus he is quit of tomorrow."

Much the same is to be found in Ferdinand Ebner, whose person-
alist thinking and pneumatology of language has had such an influence on modern theology: "Eternal life is so to speak life in the
absolute present and is in actual fact the life of man in his consciousness of the presence of God." For it is of the essence of God to be
absolute spiritual presence. Hence man's "present" is nothing else
but the presence of God. He steps out of time and lives in the
present. Thus it is that he lives "in God." Faith and love are timeless
acts which remove us out of time, because they make us wholly
present."

Christian faith then means tuning in to the nearness of God in
which Jesus lived and worked, for living amid the simple, everyday
things of today is of course living in the fullness of time and living
in the nearness of God. To grasp the never-returning moment, to be
wholly one with oneself, wholly self-possessed and on the mark, is
what is meant by "God." The concepts of God which are constructed in remoteness from God and in his absence fall to pieces
in his nearness, so that to be wholly present means that "God" happens, for the "happening" of the uncurtailed present is the happening of God.

This mysticism of being, with its emphasis on the living of the
present moment, presupposes an immediacy to God which the faith
that believes in God on the ground of Christ cannot adopt without
putting an end to the historic mediation and reconciliation of God
and man in the Christ event, and so also, as a result of this, putting
an end to the observation of history under the category of hope.
This is not the "God of hope," for the latter is present in promising
the future—his own and man's and the world's future—and in sending men into the history that is not yet. The God of the exodus and
of the resurrection "is" not eternal presence, but he promises his
presence and nearness to him who follows the path on which he is
sent into the future. YHWH, as the name of the God who first of

all promises his presence and his kingdom and makes them prospects for the future, is a God "with future as his essential nature," a God of promise and of leaving the present to face the future, a God whose freedom is the source of new things that are to come. His name is not a cipher for the "eternal present," nor can it be rendered by the word *EI*, "thou art." His name is a wayfaring name, a name of promise that discloses a new future, a name whose truth is experienced in history inasmuch as his promise discloses its future possibilities. He is therefore, as Paul says, the God who raises the dead and calls into being the things that are not (Rom 4:17). This God is present where we wait upon his promises in hope and transformation. When we have a God who calls into being the things that are not, then the things that are not yet, that are future, also become "thinkable" because they can be hoped for.

The "now" and "today" of the New Testament is a different thing from the "now" of the eternal presence of being in Parmenides, for it is a "now" and an "all of a sudden" in which the newness of the promised future is lit up and seen in a flash. Only in this sense is it to be called an "eschatological" today. "Parousia" for the Greeks was the epitome of the presence of God, the epitome of the presence of being. The parousia of Christ, however, is conceived in the New Testament only in categories of expectation, so that it means not *praesentia Christi* but *adventus Christi*, and is not his eternal presence bringing time to a standstill, but his "coming," as our Advent hymns say, opening the road to life in time, for the life of time is hope. The believer is not set at the high noon of life, but at the dawn of a new day at the point where night and day, things passing and things to come, grapple with each other. Hence the believer does not simply take the day as it comes, but looks beyond the day to the things which according to the promise of him who is the *creator ex nihilo* and raiser of the dead are still to come. The present of the coming parousia of God and of Christ in the promises of the gospel of the crucified does not translate us out of time, nor does it bring time to a standstill, but it opens the way for time and sets history in motion, for it does not tone down the pain caused us by the non-existent, but means the adoption and acceptance of the nonexistent in memory and hope. Can there be any such thing as an "eternal Yea of being" without a Yea to what no longer is and to what is not yet? Can there be such a thing as harmony and contemporaneity on man's part in the moment of today, unless hope reconciles him with what is noncontemporaneous and disharmonious? Love does not snatch us from the pain of time, but takes the pain of the temporal upon itself. Hope makes us ready to bear the "cross of the present." It can hold to what is dead, and hope for the unexpected. It can approve of movement and be glad of history. For its God is not he who "never was nor will be, because he now Is all at once as a whole," but God is he "who maketh the dead alive and calleth into being the things that are not." The spell of the dogma of hopelessness—*ex nihilo nihil fit*—is broken where he who raises the dead is recognized to be God. Where in faith and hope we begin to live in the light of the possibilities and promises of this God, the whole fullness of life discloses itself as a life of history and therefore a life to be loved. Only in the perspective of this God can there possibly be a love that is more than *philia*, love to the existent and the like—namely, *agape*, love to the nonexistent, love to the unlike, the unworthy, the worthless, to the lost, the transient and the dead; a love that can take upon it the annihilating effects of pain and renunciation because it receives its power from hope of a *creatio ex nihilo*. Love does not shut its eyes to the nonexistent and say it is nothing, but becomes itself the magic power that brings it into being. In its hope, love surveys the open possibilities of history. In love, hope brings all things into the light of the promises of God.

Does this hope cheat man of the happiness of the present? How could it do so! For it is itself the happiness of the present. It pronounces the poor blessed, receives the weary and heavy laden, the humbled and wronged, the hungry and the dying, because it perceives the parousia of the kingdom for them. Expectation makes life good, for in expectation man can accept his whole present and find joy not only in its joy but also in its sorrow, happiness not only in its happiness but also in its pain. Thus hope goes on its way through the midst of happiness and pain, because in the promises of God it can see a future also for the transient, the dying and the dead. That is why it can be said that living without hope is like no longer living. Hell is hopelessness, and it is not for nothing that at the entrance to Dante's hell there stand the words: "Abandon hope, all ye who enter here."

An acceptance of the present which cannot and will not see the dying of the present is an illusion and a frivolity—and one which cannot be grounded on eternity either. The hope that is staked on the *creator ex nihilo* becomes the happiness of the present when it loyally embraces all things in love, abandoning nothing to annihilation but bringing to light how open all things are to the possibilities in which they can live and shall live. Presumption and despair have a paralyzing effect on this, while the dream of the eternal present ignores it.

Hoping and Thinking

But now, all that we have so far said of hope might be no more than a hymn in praise of a noble quality of the heart. And Christian eschatology could regain its leading role in theology as a whole, yet still remain a piece of sterile theologizing if we fail to attain to the new thought and action that are consequently necessary in our dealings with the things and conditions of this world. As long as hope does not embrace and transform the thought and action of men, it remains topsy-turvy and ineffective. Hence Christian eschatology must make the attempt to introduce hope into worldly thinking, and thought into the believing hope.

In the Middle Ages, Anselm of Canterbury set up what has since been the standard basic principle of theology: *fides quaerens intellectum—credo, ut intelligam.* This principle holds also for eschatology, and it could well be that it is of decisive importance for Christian theology today to follow the basic principles: *spes quaerens intellectum—spero, ut intelligam.* If it is hope that maintains and upholds faith and keeps it moving on, if it is hope that draws the believer into the life of love, then it will also be hope that is the mobilizing and driving force of faith's thinking, of its knowledge of, and reflections on, human nature, history and society. Faith hopes in order to know what it believes. Hence all its knowledge will be an anticipatory, fragmentary knowledge forming a prelude to the promised future, and as such is committed to hope. Hence also *vice versa* the hope which arises from faith in God's promise will become the ferment in our thinking, its mainspring, the source of its restlessness and torment. The hope that is continually led on further by the promise of God reveals all thinking in history to be eschatologically oriented and eschatologically stamped as provisional. If hope draws faith into the realm of thought and of life, then it can no longer consider itself to be an eschatological hope as distinct from the minor hopes that are directed towards attainable goals and visible changes in human life, neither can it as a result dissociate itself from

such hopes by relegating them to a different sphere while considering its own future to be supraworldly and purely spiritual in character. The Christian hope is directed towards a *novum ultimum*,
towards a new creation of all things by the God of the resurrection
of Jesus Christ. It thereby opens a future outlook that embraces all
things, including also death, and into this it can and must also take
the limited hopes of a renewal of life, stimulating them, relativizing
them, giving them direction. It will destroy the *presumption* in these
hopes of better human freedom, of successful life, of justice and
dignity for our fellow men, of control of the possibilities of nature,
because it does not find in these movements the salvation it awaits,
because it refuses to let the entertaining and realizing of utopian
ideas of this kind reconcile it with existence. It will thus outstrip
these future visions of a better, more humane, more peaceable world
—because of its own "better promises" (Heb 8:6), because it knows
that nothing can be "very good" until "all things are become new."
But it will not be in the name of "calm despair" that it seeks to
destroy the presumption in these movements of hope, for such kinds
of presumption still contain more of true hope than does sceptical
realism, and more truth as well. There is no hope against presumption to be found in the despair that says, "It will always be the same
in the end," but only in a persevering, rectifying hope that finds
articulated expression in thought and action. Realism, still less cyni-
cism, was never a good ally of Christian faith. But if the Christian
hope destroys the presumption in futuristic movements, then it does
so not for its own sake, but in order to destroy in these hopes the
seeds of resignation, which emerge at the latest with the ideological
reign of terror in the utopias in which the hoped-for reconciliation
with existence becomes an enforced reconciliation. This, however,
brings the movements of historic change within the range of the
novum ultimum of hope. They are taken up into the Christian hope
and carried further. They become precursory, and therewith provisional, movements. Their goals lose the utopian fixity and become
provisional, penultimate, and hence flexible goals. Over against impulses of this kind that seek to give direction to the history of mankind, Christian hope cannot cling rigidly to the past and the given
and ally itself with the utopia of the *status quo*. Rather, it is itself
summoned and empowered to creative transformation of reality, for
it has hope for the whole of reality. Finally, the believing hope will
itself provide *inexhaustible resources* for the creative, inventive imag-

ination of love. It constantly provokes and produces thinking of an anticipatory kind in love to man and the world, in order to give shape to the newly dawning possibilities in the light of the promised future, in order as far as possible to create here the best that is possible, because what is promised is within the bounds of possibility. Thus it will constantly arouse the "passion for the possible," inventiveness and elasticity in self-transformation, in breaking with the old and coming to terms with the new. Always the Christian hope has had a revolutionary effect in this sense on the intellectual history of the society affected by it. Only it was often not in church Christianity that its impulses were at work, but in the Christianity of the fanatics. This has had a detrimental result for both.

But how can knowledge of reality and reflection upon it be pursued from the standpoint of eschatological hope? Luther once had a flash of inspiration on this point, although it was not realized either by himself or by Protestant philosophy. In 1516 he writes of the "earnest expectation of the creature" of which Paul speaks in Romans 8:19:

> The apostle philosophizes and thinks about things in a different way from the philosophers and metaphysicians. For the philosophers fix their eyes on the presence of things and reflect only on their qualities and quiddities. But the apostle drags our gaze away from contemplating the present state of things, away from their essence and attributes, and directs it towards their future. He does not speak of the essence or the workings of the creature, of *actio*, *passio* or movement, but employs a new, strange, theological term and speaks of the expectation of the creature (*exspectatio creaturae*).

The important thing in our present context is, that on the basis of a theological view of the "expectation of the creature" and its anticipation he demands a new kind of thinking about the world, an expectation-thinking that corresponds to the Christian hope. Hence in the light of the prospects for the whole creation that are promised in the raising of Christ, theology will have to attain to its own, new way of reflecting on the history of men and things. In the field of the world, of history and of reality as a whole, Christian eschatology cannot renounce the *intellectus fidei et spei*. Creative action springing from faith is impossible without new thinking and planning that springs from hope.

For our knowledge and comprehension of reality, and our reflections on it, that means at least this: that in the medium of hope our theological concepts become not judgments which nail reality down to what it is, but anticipations which show reality its prospects and its future possibilities. Theological concepts do not give a fixed form to reality, but they are expanded by hope and anticipate future being. They do not limp after reality and gaze on it with the night eyes of Minerva's owl, but they illuminate reality by displaying its future. Their knowledge is grounded not in the will do dominate, but in love to the future of things. *Tantum cognoscitur, quantum diligitur* (Augustine). They are thus concepts which are engaged in a process of movement, and which call forth practical movement and change.

"*Spes quaerens intellectum* is the first step towards eschatology, and where it is successful it becomes *docta spes*.